D0611304

Additional Praise for
Where the Jobs Are

"Ultimately U.S. growth and welfare rest on entrepreneurship. Dearie and Geduldig vividly analyze what has ailed us recently. They also provide concrete and practical proposals for what needs to be done to promote new U.S. firms. This book should be required reading for all policymakers interested in revitalizing the economy."

—Robert Z. Lawrence,
Albert L. Williams Professor of International Trade and Investment,
John F. Kennedy School of Government, Harvard University

"A broad, comprehensive look at what drives the U.S. economy; John Dearie and Courtney Geduldig outline specific policy initiatives to jump-start job creation. Their work is inspired by their first-hand experience in financial and economic policy. They present thoroughly-researched findings from a cross-section of those in the know—employers, academics, investors, developmental organizations, lending institutions, and local government leaders. Dearie and Geduldig's thought-provoking book provides plenty of real-life examples to further the conversation of what could be done to inspire and support a new generation of successful American entrepreneurs."

—Congressman Pat Tiberi (R-OH)

"I started my own construction company when I was 25 years old and have spent my life in business, so I can certainly relate to many of the issues raised in this book. I appreciate Courtney and John sharing their research, analysis, and recommendations, and hope it helps unleash the tremendous, entrepreneurial potential that exists throughout our country."

—Senator Bob Corker (R-TN)

"A thorough and enlightening survey of the state of American entrepreneurship, and a must-read for policy makers (or anyone) interested in restarting the American jobs engine. Dearie and Geduldig have pulled together a solid set of recommendations—ones I hope will be taken seriously and acted upon."

—David A. Owens, PhD,
director of the Executive Development Institute,
Owen Graduate School of Management, Vanderbilt University

"John Dearie and Courtney Geduldig have written an original, provocative, and persuasive book. It is filled with the wisdom of scores of real entrepreneurs whose experiences since the Great Crash of 2008 explain why our recovery has been so feeble. And they offer a menu of common-sense reforms that just might revive America's entrepreneurial spirit."

—Robert G. Kaiser,
author of "Act of Congress: How America's
Essential Institution Works, and How it Doesn't"

"Dearie and Geduldig address head-on the most significant driver of economic growth: new business formation. In the 1840's the United States and Britain passed laws that for the first time allowed corporate formation without legislative action. This launched the industrial revolution, a 25-fold increase in per capita income, a doubling of human life expectancy, and the creation of the modern world. *Where the Jobs Are* is a passionate call for action to once again ignite the animal spirits that drive job creation and economic growth. Feeble economic growth and millions of unemployed Americans are proof positive that Dearie and Geduldig's call must be answered."

—Chris Wright, founder and CEO of
Liberty Resources and Liberty Oilfield Services

Where
the Jobs Are

Where the Jobs Are

Entrepreneurship and the Soul of the American Economy

John Dearie
Courtney Geduldig

WILEY

Cover image: Getty Images
Cover design: Paul McCarthy

Copyright © 2013 by John R. Dearie and Courtney C. Geduldig. All rights reserved.

Published by John Wiley & Sons, Inc., Hoboken, New Jersey.
Published simultaneously in Canada.

No part of this publication may be reproduced, stored in a retrieval system, or transmitted in any form or by any means, electronic, mechanical, photocopying, recording, scanning, or otherwise, except as permitted under Section 107 or 108 of the 1976 United States Copyright Act, without either the prior written permission of the Publisher, or authorization through payment of the appropriate per-copy fee to the Copyright Clearance Center, Inc., 222 Rosewood Drive, Danvers, MA 01923, (978) 750-8400, fax (978) 646-8600, or on the Web at www.copyright.com. Requests to the Publisher for permission should be addressed to the Permissions Department, John Wiley & Sons, Inc., 111 River Street, Hoboken, NJ 07030, (201) 748-6011, fax (201) 748-6008, or online at http://www.wiley.com/go/permissions.

Limit of Liability/Disclaimer of Warranty: While the publisher and author have used their best efforts in preparing this book, they make no representations or warranties with respect to the accuracy or completeness of the contents of this book and specifically disclaim any implied warranties of merchantability or fitness for a particular purpose. No warranty may be created or extended by sales representatives or written sales materials. The advice and strategies contained herein may not be suitable for your situation. You should consult with a professional where appropriate. Neither the publisher nor author shall be liable for any loss of profit or any other commercial damages, including but not limited to special, incidental, consequential, or other damages.

For general information on our other products and services or for technical support, please contact our Customer Care Department within the United States at (800) 762-2974, outside the United States at (317) 572-3993 or fax (317) 572-4002.

The opinions and proposals expressed in this book are the authors' alone and should not be interpreted as representing the views of the Financial Services Forum or its members, or Standard & Poor's or McGraw Hill Financial.

Wiley publishes in a variety of print and electronic formats and by print-on-demand. Some material included with standard print versions of this book may not be included in e-books or in print-on-demand. If this book refers to media such as a CD or DVD that is not included in the version you purchased, you may download this material at http://booksupport.wiley.com. For more information about Wiley products, visit www.wiley.com.

ISBN 978-1-118-57324-2 (Hardcover); ISBN 978-1-118-74572-4 (ebk);
ISBN 978-1-118-74553-3 (ebk)

Printed in the United States of America
10 9 8 7 6 5 4 3 2 1

. . . there is the dream and the will to found a private kingdom . . . there is the will to conquer: the impulse to fight, to prove oneself superior to others, to succeed for the sake, not of the fruits of success, but of success itself. . . Finally there is the joy of creating, of getting things done, or simply of exercising one's energy and ingenuity.

JOSEPH SCHUMPETER, ON THE NATURE AND ESSENTIAL
CHARACTER OF THE ENTREPRENEUR,
THE THEORY OF ECONOMIC DEVELOPMENT

Contents

Foreword

Before any candidates for Congress are permitted to have their names placed on the ballot, they should have to certify that they have read John Dearie and Courtney Geduldig's book *Where the Jobs Are*.

The reason for this is that once elected they will suddenly be confronted with such challenges as assuring the supply of clean, affordable energy, providing health care to the nation's citizens, preserving the natural environment of our planet, assuring national security, and more—yet *none* of these can be accomplished without first building a strong economy. And no nation can have a strong economy without producing jobs for its citizens—jobs that both underpin the quality of life of individuals and families, and generate the tax revenues that permit government to fulfill its obligations to its citizenry. Furthermore, an important but often overlooked point is that one can't be *for* jobs and be *against* employers.

But this is just one of the conundrums and misunderstandings that plague those who seek to find—or, better yet, create—jobs. It is occasionally announced by deans at medical school graduations that "half of what we taught you is wrong—the problem is that we don't know which half." This caveat has relevance to the beliefs held by many concerning the jobs dilemma. Consider the following beliefs:

- Permitting foreign scientists and engineers to immigrate to the United States takes jobs away from Americans.
- Start-up companies, which usually fail anyway, are simply too small to make much difference in the overall job market.
- The government doesn't need to invest in research, because corporations will; they realize that if they don't invest they can't survive over the long term.
- The sole reason unemployment is as high as it is today is that there aren't enough jobs to go around.
- The true unemployment rate today is only a few percentage points above the norm.
- The country doesn't need more engineers; it already has too many.
- The problem with U.S. public schools is a lack of funding.
- Americans place greater emphasis on engineering and innovation than the citizens of most industrialized nations.
- When corporations are taxed, no one gets hurt.

If our nation's score in judging these beliefs concerning jobs were as good as the alleged 50 percent achieved by professors in our medical schools, we would indeed be fortunate. But, as it happens, *all* of these statements are *wrong*.

First of all, scientists and engineers represent less than 5 percent of the U.S. workforce, but they disproportionately create jobs for the other 95 percent. Encouraging talented scientists and engineers, especially those with an entrepreneurial bent, to immigrate to the United States actually creates jobs, not destroys them. The *Journal of International Commerce and Economics* notes that a few years ago the 700 engineers working on Apple's iPod were accompanied by 14,000 other workers in the United States alone. In fact, numerous studies have shown that 50 to 85 percent of the growth in the country's Gross Domestic Product (read jobs) can be attributed to the work of scientists and engineers. Foreign-born scientists and engineers have disproportionately created new companies and won Nobel Prizes for the United States.

Furthermore, the constructive destruction that takes place in a free market is such that most new jobs are created and sustained by relatively new companies that once were very small. Large public companies respond to the pressures of the marketplace—which means that they must seek short-term gains, even at the expense of the long-term survival that frequently comes from investing in delayed-payoff endeavors such as research. A few decades ago stockholders held their shares an average of eight years; today the figure is 18 months and declining.

And while there is indeed a shortage of jobs, as attested to by the 12 million Americans who are currently unemployed, there are also three million job *openings* waiting to be filled by individuals with suitable skills. Thus, not only is there a jobs shortage, but there is also a skills gap.

Although today one hears a great deal about unemployment being in the 7 or 8 percent range, that figure does not include individuals who have given up searching for a job, are only able to find part-time employment, or are underemployed relative to their qualifications. Taking a more realistic view of the unemployment picture indicates a problem nearly double that about which we read in the newspapers and see on television.

Then there is the perennial argument that there are already too many scientists and engineers in the United States—witness the proverbial engineer taxicab driver. It is certainly true that if the nation does not adequately invest in research there will be too many scientists. If it lets its infrastructure crumble, there will be too many engineers. If we do not plant seeds, we will not need farmers. Microsoft recently opened a new software engineering facility across the border in Canada because U.S. regulations made it too difficult to hire engineers in the United States.

Correspondingly, there will be no *shortage* of engineers and innovators in the United States because companies will simply move their research and development (R&D) abroad—and follow it with their factories, administrative offices, and logistics hubs. What there *will* be in the United States is a lack of jobs for nonengineers, nonscientists, and nonentrepreneurs who otherwise would have been the beneficiaries of the work of those job creators who will now be found elsewhere.

Turning to the question of funding the nation's K–12 public schools, these institutions are already the most highly funded per student in the world, with the exception of Switzerland. The problem is not *how* we fund our schools; it is *how we spend* the funds.

Then there is the emphasis American society places on careers in engineering (and innovation). A National Science Foundation study of 93 nations ranked the United States in 79th place in terms of the fraction of all baccalaureate degrees that are awarded in engineering. The nation that we most closely resemble in this regard, in both science and engineering, is Mozambique.

And, finally, when corporations are excessively taxed, *everyone* gets hurt. The reason is straightforward: firms simply move to where conditions, including taxes, are more conducive to business success.

All of which brings us to the question: Where *are* the jobs going to be? In this book one finds a highly documented discussion of where the jobs are, and why. This is an issue that will drive the prosperity of individual Americans and the nation as a whole as they are forced to compete in a global economy, the growth of which will increasingly reside outside the United States. Isolationism is not an option; we cannot, as the title of the Broadway show suggested, stop the world and get off.

The authors of this book have traveled far and wide to listen to the experiences of hundreds of entrepreneurs, some successful, some not. The result is a book worthy of reading by anyone who knows someone who has, or would like to have, a job. The reward of doing so is to gain hard-earned experience—without accumulating one's own scar tissue.

Norman R. Augustine*

---

*Norman R. Augustine chaired the "Gathering Storm" committee that was established on a bipartisan basis by both the U.S. House of Representatives and Senate to assess the nation's future competitiveness demands. He is also the retired chairman and CEO of Lockheed Martin Corporation and has attended over 500 board meetings of Fortune 100 companies, as well as serving on the boards of start-ups.

Preface

Persistently high unemployment in the wake of the Great Recession is one of the great economic challenges of our time. Twenty-four million Americans remain unemployed or underemployed, or have left the workforce discouraged. Fewer things are harder on families than the inability to find a job. Unemployment not only threatens the financial security of jobless Americans and their families, but also robs the broader economy of production and wealth creation and produces a wide range of painful and damaging social problems.

In March of 2011, John Dearie, the Financial Services Forum's Executive Vice President for Policy, and Courtney Geduldig, the Forum's General Counsel and Managing Director for Government Affairs, came to me and proposed a major initiative on job creation. At that time, unemployment remained above 9 percent, despite the unprecedented fiscal and monetary policy measures taken by Congress, the White House, and the Federal Reserve. Policymakers needed new ideas, my colleagues argued, and the Forum should try to help.

For those not aware of our organization, the Financial Services Forum is a financial and economic policy group comprised of the chief executives of 19 of the largest financial institutions operating in the United States. The group was organized by its founding members to deliberate on the major financial and economic challenges facing Washington policymakers and to offer well-considered potential policy solutions. The Forum is strictly nonpartisan; we do not operate a political action committee, nor do we organize or host fund-raisers for office holders.

I agreed with my colleagues and proposed the initiative to our member CEOs the following month at the Forum's spring meeting. The members approved the project.

For reasons they explain in the pages that follow, John and Courtney focused their examination of job creation on entrepreneurs and the new companies they launch, and spent the summer of 2011 traveling the nation—meeting, talking with, and listening to the nation's innovators and job creators.

I don't think it's an exaggeration to say that the summer was a revelation to my colleagues. I vividly recall them returning from the various roundtables they had organized around the country tremendously excited about the entrepreneurs they had met, what they had heard, particular anecdotes and insights, and the implications for economic policy.

By September of 2011, having conducted roundtables in 12 cities across the country, and recognizing the importance and power of what they had heard and learned—and realizing that too few policymakers back in Washington fully appreciated the unique nature, contribution, vulnerabilities, and needs of start-ups—John and Courtney wanted to do more than simply produce a white paper report to the Forum's members. So they decided to write a book.

The book you're holding is the result of that remarkable summer on the road, and amounts to a first-of-its-kind and critically important contribution to addressing the policy challenge of persistently high unemployment. To my knowledge, no one else has invested the time, energy, and resources to travel the nation and methodically assess the challenges and needs of the country's job creators. Having done so, John and Courtney have produced a book that deserves a great deal of attention from policymakers, the media, businesspeople, and any American interested in how to get, keep, and create jobs.

My sincere hope is that policymakers in Washington and in state-houses and legislatures around the country will read and absorb the major themes and recommendations of the book, and give serious consideration to implementing many of the insightful and thoughtful policy recommendations that John and Courtney propose. While policymakers are a principal audience for this book, the true beneficiaries will ultimately be those Americans—hopefully millions of them—who are more able either to create jobs or to find jobs as a result of this book.

Finally, I think it's important to note that John and Courtney voluntarily declined any compensation for writing this book. With the intention of supporting American entrepreneurship, all proceeds from this book will be donated to one or more of the start-up incubators and accelerators that John and Courtney encountered during their summer on the road.

This project was the result of John and Courtney's initiative and passion for public policy that makes a difference in people's lives. I am fortunate to have both as friends.

Rob Nichols
President and CEO
The Financial Services Forum
Washington, DC

Introduction

We know some of their names—Samuel Morse, Eli Whitney, Thomas Edison, Henry Ford, Andrew Carnegie, Walt Disney, Ray Croc, Mary Kay Ash, Bill Hewlett, Sam Walton, Fred Smith, Ted Turner, Oprah Winfrey, Bill Gates, Steve Jobs, Martha Stewart, Jeff Bezos, Larry Page and Sergey Brin, Mark Zuckerberg. Such people are not notable merely because they amassed great wealth, or because they led corporations of enormous consequence, or because they achieved a kind of celebrity status. Rather, they are illustrious members of the pantheon of American capitalism because they launched iconic companies like Ford, Disney, Hewlett-Packard, Mary Kay, Walmart, Federal Express, CNN, Microsoft, Apple, Amazon, Google, and Facebook from scratch—in the basement, on the dining room table, in college dorm rooms, in their parents' garage—forever altering the nation's economic landscape and creating jobs, careers, and wealth for millions of Americans. They, and countless others like them, are the visionaries, the innovators, the risk-takers—the entrepreneurs.

As people who have spent our careers in various positions within economic and financial policymaking, we certainly knew that entrepreneurship is a marvelous and critically important aspect of our nation's economy. We understood that new businesses are an important source of the remarkable dynamism and innovation that defines the American economy. We understood that new businesses bring new ideas, new technologies, and new products and services to the marketplace. We knew that new businesses, if they succeed, create new value and new wealth that drives living standards higher and benefits broader society tremendously. We even knew that new businesses—by definition—can create new jobs.

We now know that we didn't understand the half of it.

■ ■ ■

Like all Americans, we witnessed with horror the Great Recession of 2008–2009 and its devastating impact on the nation's labor markets. Between February of 2008 and February of 2010, almost 9 million jobs were eliminated. Just as alarming, in a break from the historical pattern of deep recessions being followed by sharp rebounds, the U.S. economy's recovery from the Great Recession has been frustratingly sluggish. By early 2011—18 months following the resumption of economic growth—only about a million jobs had been created, less than an eighth of those eliminated during the downturn, and more than 25 million Americans remained unemployed or underemployed. To survive the worst economic contraction in 80 years, American businesses had learned to do more with fewer people.

Then, in the spring of 2011, circumstances worsened. After growing by nearly 2.5 percent in 2010, the U.S. economy seemed to stall. Despite an $800 billion fiscal stimulus signed into law by President Barack Obama two years before, and despite 28 months of short-term interest rates near zero thanks to the Federal Reserve, economic growth dwindled to a barely detectable 0.1 percent in the first quarter of 2011.

Progress in the labor market also stalled. After creating an average of 195,000 jobs in each of the first four months of 2011, job creation fell to just 115,000 in May—and then to 78,000 in July. Over that summer, the economy created a monthly average of only 140,000 jobs. Economists generally agree that sustained monthly job creation of 150,000 to 200,000 is necessary just to keep up with population growth, with much faster growth required to meaningfully reduce unemployment. The unemployment rate, which had fallen a full percentage point from its peak of 10 percent in October of 2009, leveled off in early 2011 and seemed stuck at 9 percent—double the rate in 2007.[1]

Something was wrong. Despite unprecedented efforts to stimulate growth and job creation, the economy was not responding as expected. Having done what history had taught must be done, policymakers in Washington seemed out of ideas—at a loss for what to do next.

With the hope of generating new policy alternatives, and within the context of our responsibilities at the Financial Services Forum—a Washington, DC–based financial and economic policy group—we launched an effort in April of 2011 to better understand the crippled labor markets in the wake of the Great Recession, what had happened during the recent recession that might explain the halting pace of hiring, and any structural obstacles to growth and job creation that might not have been part of previous post-recession recoveries.

Shortly after we began our investigation, we learned of research that had been conducted within the last few years—first by economists at the U.S. Census Bureau, then at the Ewing Marion Kauffman Foundation in Kansas City, MO—which had apparently demonstrated that virtually all net new job creation in the United States over the past 30 years has come from businesses less than a year old—true "start-ups." Moreover, existing businesses, of any size or age, according to the research, shed a net average of about a million jobs each year. Intrigued, we flew out to Kansas City, met with the economists who had done the work, examined the evidence, and were convinced.

Stunned, we realized that policymakers in Washington, focused as they are, and for very good reasons, on the needs and priorities of either large corporations or the small business community, tend to overlook the economy's true engine of job creation—new businesses. Moreover, because start-up businesses are new, and have leaders who are naturally and intently focused on launching and growing their fragile new firms, America's entrepreneurial economy has little organized representation in Washington to educate policymakers and advocate on behalf of its needs and priorities. And those needs and priorities, as we came to understand, are unique.

As we continued to investigate new businesses—their role in the economy and recent trends—we also learned that, alarmingly, America's job creation engine is breaking down. After remaining remarkably consistent for decades, the number of new firms launched each year—and the number of new jobs created by those new firms—has declined precipitously in recent years.

But why?

If America's entrepreneurs have historically served as the engine of virtually all net new job creation, as the research had demonstrated, what was suddenly in their way? What was causing the drop-off in new business formation and the decline in the number of new jobs those businesses create? We realized that unless these key questions can be answered—and unless those answers can be converted into compelling solutions—the U.S. economy stands little chance of creating the jobs necessary to put millions of unemployed Americans back to work.

After considering a number of alternatives, we decided there was only one way to really get to the bottom of what was happening and find the answers we were looking for—get out of Washington, DC, and talk to America's job creators face to face.

In April of 2011, we launched an ambitious summer road trip, conducting in-person roundtables with entrepreneurs in 12 cities across the nation. Specific cities were chosen in order to cover both the broad geographic territory of the country, as well as the industrial diversity of the U.S. economy. More than 200 entrepreneurs participated in our roundtables, explaining in specific and vividly personal terms the obstacles that are undermining their efforts to launch new businesses, expand existing young firms, and create jobs. Many more shared their thoughts and ideas by e-mail.

In addition to our roundtables with entrepreneurs, we also convened a fascinating yet sobering discussion among eight noted economists regarding the nature and depth of the recent recession, the extent of the damage to labor markets, changes to the labor markets either caused by or accelerated by the severe downturn, structural obstacles to recovery, and policy alternatives.

Along the way, we also conducted numerous interviews with representatives from every aspect of the entrepreneurship ecosystem—business and entrepreneurship academics; leaders of start-up incubators, accelerators, and facilitators; venture capitalists; angel investors; community development organizations; officials from mayors' and governors' offices; and lending institutions. Working with the Kauffman Foundation and Adam Geller of the polling firm National Research, Inc., we also conducted a first-of-its-kind nationwide poll of more than 800 entrepreneurs, which generated results that confirmed and added additional texture to what we learned at our in-person roundtables.

We came away from our summer on the road struck most of all by our nation's stunning entrepreneurial dynamism. Despite the downward trend in the rate of new business formation in recent years, and despite very challenging economic circumstances, entrepreneurs all across America—driven by a desire to create and build, and enabled by the development of new technologies—continue to launch new companies, build those businesses, and pursue their dreams of independence and wealth. Having witnessed such dynamism and commitment first hand, we are more optimistic about the future of the U.S. economy than ever.

But for that tremendous potential to be fully unleashed, America's entrepreneurs need help. Given the critical role they play in our nation's economy as the principal source of innovation, dynamism, growth, and job creation, America's young businesses need and deserve a comprehensive and *preferential* policy framework designed to cultivate new business formation and dramatically enhance the prospects of new business survival and growth.

Fortunately, Washington is beginning to listen. On December 8, 2011, Senator Jerry Moran (R-KS) and Senator Mark Warner (D-VA)—himself a successful telecommunications entrepreneur—introduced legislation called the Start-Up Act, which aims to help new businesses by reducing regulatory burdens, attracting business investment, accelerating the commercialization of university research, and attracting and retaining the world's best entrepreneurial talent. On February 14, 2013, Senators Moran and Warner introduced an updated version of the plan, Start-Up Act 3.0, along with co-sponsors Senator Chris Coons (D-DE) and Senator Roy Blunt (R-MO). Similarly, the Jumpstart Our Business Startups ("JOBS") Act, enacted in April of 2012, is intended to improve new businesses' access to financing. Both pieces of legislation are important steps in the right direction. But more progress is urgently needed on many other fronts—and help is needed from both the public and private sectors.

In the chapters that follow, we first document the extraordinary damage to U.S. labor markets caused by the Great Recession and its immediate aftermath. We then explain how and why new businesses account for virtually *all* net new job creation in America. Most significantly, we recount the findings of the remarkable summer we spent traveling from city to city to meet the nation's entrepreneurs—listening to them explain in their own words the issues, frustrations, and obstacles that are undermining their efforts to launch new businesses, expand existing young firms, and create jobs. We also present a detailed, innovative, and uniquely credible policy agenda based on what America's job creators told us they need.

It's important to emphasize that in highlighting the critical role of new businesses and focusing on their unique policy needs, our intent is neither to glamorize entrepreneurs nor to exaggerate the job-creating capacity of the businesses they launch. Not all new companies create jobs, or even survive. On the contrary, half of all new businesses fail within the first five years and only a few companies among the survivors go on to create hundreds or thousands of new jobs. Indeed, most new businesses launched in America each year are sole proprietorship "Main Street" businesses like restaurants, fitness clubs, construction firms, hair salons, tax preparers, and financial advisors businesses started by people looking for professional independence, but not intending to hire hundreds of people and never expecting to make millions of dollars. In fact, as Scott Shane, professor of entrepreneurial studies, has pointed out, most entrepreneurs work more hours and earn less money than they would if they worked for someone else.[2] Moreover, public policy shouldn't promote or protect poor business ideas simply because they are new, nor should government pick winners and losers.

But if new businesses account for virtually all net new job creation, and if some fraction of the new firms launched each year go on to create hundreds or even thousands of new jobs, then America needs to get serious about enhancing the circumstances for new business formation, survival, and growth—particularly given the alarming reality that the number of new firms launched each year, and the number of new jobs created by those firms, has declined significantly in recent years.

In August of 2011, a few days after an ailing Steve Jobs resigned as chief executive of Apple, the *Wall Street Journal* wrote: "When the history of the past 40 years is written, who will be seen as the more consequential figure—the average American President, or a college drop-out who built the first personal computer in a garage and went on to lead the most important company of the 21st century? We'll put our history money on Steve Jobs. . . There's a large lesson here about economic growth and its sources. . . Another lesson is that the future belongs to the risk-takers, who sense opportunities when others see only folly or danger."[3]

The grim economic circumstances that gave rise to this project have only persisted. Economic growth remains anemic and 24 million Americans—of all ages, backgrounds, education levels, and skills sets—remain either unemployed, underemployed, or have left the workforce discouraged. Without decisive action soon, entire generations of Americans might be left behind in the wake of the Great Recession. The strength and stability of our economy, and the health, vitality, and social cohesion of our nation are at stake.

The job creators have told us what they need. There's no time to waste.

Let's get to work.

Chapter 1

America's Jobs Emergency

According to the Bureau of Labor Statistics (BLS), nearly 12 million Americans remain unemployed—more than four years *after* the official end of the Great Recession. To put that figure in perspective, 12.8 million Americans were unemployed in 1933, the worst year of the Great Depression, and 11.9 million Americans were unemployed in November of 1982, the deepest point of the severe 1981–1982 recession. Another eight million Americans currently work part-time involuntarily, while an estimated 4 million have simply given up looking for work. More than four years into the current economic recovery, 15 percent of the American workforce is either without work, underemployed, or has left the workforce discouraged. At the current pace of job creation—a monthly average of just 180,000 new jobs since the beginning of 2012—America will likely not return to pre-recession levels of employment until 2023.[1]

■ ■ ■

The economic downturn that began in December of 2007 certainly earned the grim and, by now, familiar moniker "The Great Recession." According to the National Bureau of Economic Research (NBER), the unofficial arbiter of recession start and end dates, the recent recession stretched 18 months—until June of 2009—making it the longest period of economic contraction since World War II. The longest post-war recessions had been those of 1973–1975 and 1981–1982, both of which lasted 16 months.

The recent recession was also the most severe post-war downturn, with the nation's gross domestic product (GDP) contracting by more than 5 percent. The next most severe downturn was the 1957–1958 recession, during which GDP contracted by 3.7 percent. At the depth of the recent recession—the fourth quarter of 2008—the economy contracted at a frightening annualized rate of nearly 9 percent.

Perhaps most alarming, the recent recession destroyed 7.5 million American jobs, or more than 5 percent of the pre-recession total. By comparison, the 1973–1975 recession eliminated 2 million jobs or about 2.5 percent of the pre-recession total, while the 1981–1982 downturn destroyed 2.8 million jobs or 3 percent of the pre-recession total.

As Figure 1.1 shows, the damage to U.S. labor markets continued until February of 2010, with an additional 1.3 million jobs eliminated in the eight months following the official end of the recession, bringing the total number of jobs lost since the beginning of the recession to a staggering 8.8 million—wiping out all employment growth achieved over the previous decade.

As Figure 1.2 shows, every other decade since World War II produced employment base growth of at least 20 percent.[2]

After fluctuating between 4 and 6 percent for most of the previous 15 years, the unemployment rate began a steep climb from 5 percent in April of 2008, doubling in just 18 months to 10 percent by October of 2009—breaching double-digit territory for only the second time since World War II.

Policymakers responded to the severe recession and the damage to U.S. labor markets with unprecedented measures. On February 17, 2009, newly inaugurated President Barack Obama signed into law the

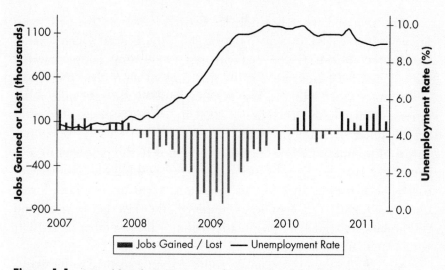

Figure 1.1 Monthly Job Gain/Loss and Unemployment Rate
SOURCE: Bureau of Labor Statistics.

American Recovery and Reinvestment Act, the principal purpose of which was to save or create jobs. The $800 billion fiscal stimulus provided unemployment relief, subsidies to states, and investments in infrastructure, education, health, and "green" energy. A number of temporary, more targeted programs followed, including "cash-for-clunkers," "cash-for-caulkers," tax credits for home buyers, and 99 weeks of jobless benefits.

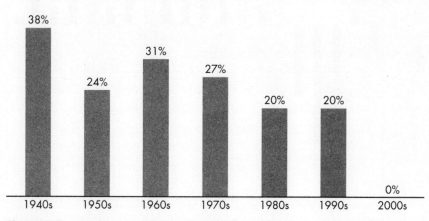

Figure 1.2 Employment Base Growth by Decade
SOURCE: Bureau of Labor Statistics.

On the monetary policy side, the Federal Reserve ("the Fed") also aggressively engaged. In September of 2007, the Federal Open Market Committee (FOMC)—the Fed's interest rate setting body—lowered the targeted fed funds rate[3] for the first time in more than four years. Over the next 15 months, the FOMC lowered the rate nine more times—ultimately, in December of 2008, to 0-to-0.25 percent, where it has remained for nearly five years.

In November of 2008, the Fed also turned to the power of its balance sheet, launching a program to purchase $600 billion in mortgage-backed securities in an effort to force long-term interest rates lower. Unsatisfied with the economy's response, the Fed began a second $600 billion program of "quantitative easing" in November of 2010. It would later launch a third.[4]

For a while, the extraordinary policy response seemed to be working. As Figure 1.3 shows, the economy emerged from recession in the third quarter of 2009, expanding by a weak yet welcome 1.4 percent. Growth continued through 2010, accelerating to 2.4 percent. And as the economy expanded, the nation's unemployment rate improved,

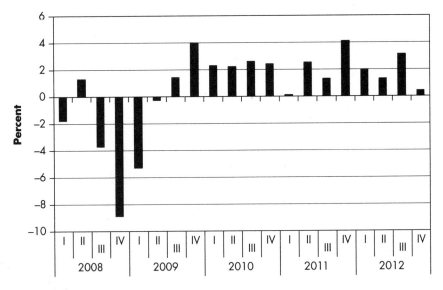

Figure 1.3 Quarterly GDP Growth
Source: Bureau of Economic Analysis.

dropping from its peak of 10 percent in October of 2009 to 9 percent by February of 2011.

By early 2011, however, the economy seemed to stall. Growth slowed to a barely detectable 0.1 percent in the first quarter, followed by better but still sluggish performances of 2.5 and 1.3 percent in the second and third quarters—making the nine-quarter recovery the weakest in post-war history. Growth accelerated again in the fourth quarter, but for the year the economy expanded by a meager 1.8 percent. After its initial improvement, the unemployment rate leveled off, hovering at or near 9 percent for most of 2011.

On January 25, 2012, the Federal Reserve, citing slowing business investment and a "depressed" housing sector, announced its intention to keep short-term interest rates near zero "at least through late 2014." A week later, the nonpartisan Congressional Budget Office (CBO) lowered its forecast for economic growth to just 2 percent in 2012 and only 1 percent in 2013.[5] And, indeed, the economy expanded by just 2.2 percent in 2012. Sustained growth in excess of 3 percent is generally regarded as necessary to meaningfully reduce unemployment.

■ ■ ■

More than four years after the end of the Great Recession, the U.S. economy is only scarcely larger than it was in 2007 and economic output is more than 10 percent lower than it would have been had the economy continued on its pre-2008 trend.[6] Even worse, only 6.5 million jobs have been created—about 70 percent of the jobs lost between February of 2008 and February of 2010. Moreover, a disproportionate share of the jobs created since economic growth resumed in mid-2009 has been in low-wage and temporary categories such as retail, "leisure and hospitality" (wait staff and bartenders), and "health care and social assistance."[7] Federal Reserve Board Governor Sarah Bloom Raskin lamented this reality in a speech in March of 2013:

> [R]ecent job gains have been largely concentrated in lower-wage occupations such as retail sales, food preparation, manual labor, home health care, and customer service . . . There is no simple cure to these conditions, but government policymakers

need to focus seriously on the problems, not simply because of notions of fairness and justice, but because the economy's ability to produce a stable quality of living for millions of people is at stake.[8]

Moody's Analytics has projected that 42 percent of the jobs created between 2011 and 2015 will be low-wage, while only 19 percent will be high-wage.

As Figures 1.4 and 1.5 show, the economy's weak performance since emerging from recession represents a stark break from the historical pattern. Since World War II, U.S. recessions have tended to be brief and recoveries sharp—with the strength of the recovery generally correlated

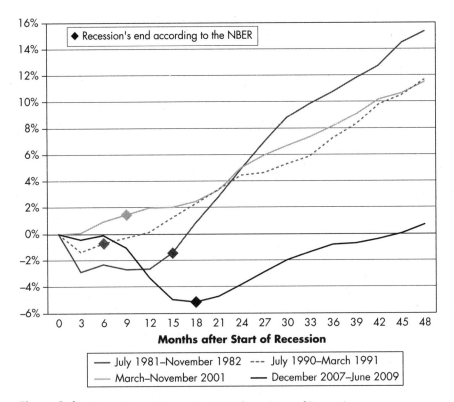

Figure 1.4 Cumulative Change in GDP from Start of Recession
SOURCE: Commerce Department; National Bureau of Economic Research.

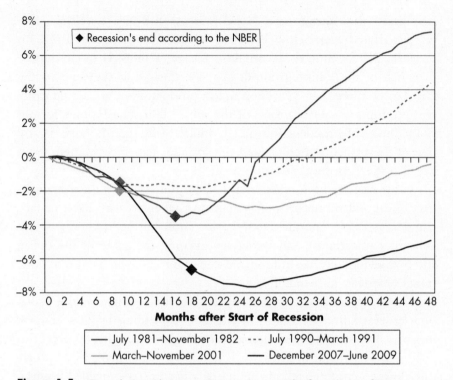

Figure 1.5 Cumulative Change in Private Sector Jobs from Start of Recession
SOURCE: Bureau of Labor Statistics; National Bureau of Economic Research.

with the depth of the downturn. Given the severity of the Great Recession, the historical pattern would predict a roaring recovery. But over the three years following the recession, the economy expanded by just 6.8 percent. Over the eight other post-war recoveries that lasted three years, the economy expanded an average of 15.5 percent.[9]

Had the current recovery followed typical patterns of post-recession growth and job creation, growth would have been more than double what it has been and, according to some estimates, as many as 14 million more Americans would be working.[10]

Identifying likely reasons for the economy's stunted recovery has preoccupied economists and other observers. Some have argued that the government's fiscal response, while unprecedented in magnitude, was nevertheless too small given the severity of the recession.

Economist Paul Krugman, a Nobel laureate and *New York Times* columnist, argued even before President Obama was inaugurated that his proposed $775 billion fiscal stimulus package "is unlikely to close more than half of the looming output gap"—estimated at the time by the CBO to be more than $2 trillion in lost production—"and could easily end up doing less than a third of the job."[11] Christina Romer, former chairwoman of President Obama's Council of Economic Advisers and one of the principal architects of the stimulus has since written about the plan: "[O]bviously, it was too small."[12]

Conservatives have countered that, on the contrary, the extraordinary fiscal and monetary policy measures taken to date have, in fact, hamstrung the economic recovery by contributing to business and consumer uncertainty and anxiety, weakening the value of the dollar, and by fueling increases in food and energy prices, which cut into consumers' capacity to spend.[13]

Other explanations have been offered. For example, as the economy emerged from recession in late 2009, spending by U.S. companies on equipment and technology surged, growing nearly 9 percent in 2010 and 11 percent in 2011. Such purchases—encouraged by historically low costs of capital and temporary tax breaks—enabled companies struggling to maintain profitability to enhance productivity while putting off more expensive hiring.[14]

Technology may also be causing some companies actually looking to hire to become overly picky—passing over applicants who just a few years ago would likely have been hired to fill the same or a similar job, according to Peter Capelli, director of the Center for Human Resources at the University of Pennsylvania's Wharton School and author of the recent book *Why Good People Can't Get Jobs*. Overwhelmed by the number of job applicants and under pressure to cut costs, many companies have replaced recruiters and other human resources personnel with on-line applications. In addition, eager to reduce or eliminate the costs of training new employees, companies are increasingly using screening software to sift through submitted applications, looking for candidates with *precisely* the right mix of skills.[15] The software incorporates what Cappelli calls employers' often "ridiculous hiring requirements," then weeds out as unacceptable any candidate who doesn't meet the overly specific parameters.[16] The practice, contends Cappelli, is contributing to a growing disconnect between employers who claim to have open positions but can't find suitable candidates, and a bounty of available candidates who could successfully fill those positions with a modest amount of on-the-job training.[17]

Also undermining the recovery is the inability of millions of would-be borrowers and spenders to take advantage of historically low interest rates engineered by the Federal Reserve because their credit scores have been significantly damaged by plunging home prices, foreclosures, lost jobs, reduced wages, late bill payments, or bankruptcy. African-American households have been particularly hard hit, losing on average half their wealth due to the recession,[18] with some reportedly experiencing what has been called a kind of "financial segregation."[19] Many banks, having survived a financial crisis stemming largely from poor underwriting standards, remain reluctant to lend to households with blemished credit histories.[20] According to Moody's Analytics and the credit monitoring service Equifax Inc., nearly 90 percent of all new mortgages in 2011 went to borrowers with high credit scores. Before the recent crisis, mortgages were evenly divided between high-score borrowers and those with lower scores.[21]

The unusually weak recovery may also have much to do with the nature of the recent recession. Rather than a contraction caused by high interest rates or sharp increases in supply prices, as is more typical, the recent recession was the result of a severe financial crisis sparked by the bursting of a historic housing bubble.

In their 2009 book *This Time Is Different*, economists Kenneth Rogoff and Carmen Reinhart point out that deleveraging and other balance sheet adjustments made by consumers and businesses—painful adjustments that follow debt-driven financial crises—take time and, therefore, delay and subdue subsequent economic recovery.[22] Following financial crises, economies have historically required more than four years to re-achieve pre-crisis levels of output.[23] Ms. Reinhart and her husband, economist Vincent Reinhart, have further demonstrated that economic growth rates tend to be lower for as much as a decade following financial crises.[24] In half of the 15 most severe post–World War II financial crises they studied, unemployment had not returned to pre-crisis levels within a decade following the crisis.

Whatever the nature of, or reasons for, the subpar recovery—and while the net effects of the extraordinary fiscal and monetary responses to the recent downturn continue to be debated—statistics make two realities undeniably clear: The economic recovery remains weak and fragile, and labor market conditions remain poor. Prior to dipping below 8 percent in September of 2012, the unemployment rate had remained above 8 percent for 43 consecutive months. Over the 60 years prior to the Great Recession, the unemployment rate topped 8 percent only 39 times *in total.*

■ ■ ■

The extraordinary jobs crisis has affected Americans of all categories and age groups. As of May of 2013, 6.7 percent of white Americans were unemployed, with Hispanic and African-American unemployment at 9.1 and 13.5 percent, respectively.[25]

Unemployment among young Americans 16 to 19 years of age, at 25 percent, remains near post-war highs,[26] with 22 percent of white youth, 29 percent of Hispanic youth, and an astounding 43 percent of African-American youth out of work.[27] A recent study estimates the aggregate economic cost to society of "disconnected youth"—the nearly 7 million young people who are neither in school nor working—to be $4.75 trillion.[28] High youth unemployment has led to a "dramatic increase" in the rate of homelessness among those 18 to 24 years old, according to the U.S. Interagency Council on Homelessness.[29]

Half of recent college graduates cannot find jobs or are under-employed,[30] and half of those who are employed report that their jobs don't require the degrees they earned.[31] A growing number of college graduates are resorting to unpaid internships to acquire experience and build relationships that might eventually lead to gainful employment.[32] Because unused skills atrophy, and because reduced salaries lower earnings trajectories, the damage to underemployed graduates' careers and lifetime earnings could be permanent.[33]

Older Americans have not been spared. As of May of 2013, unemployment among those 25 to 34 years of age was 7.2 percent, 6.2 percent for those between 35 and 44, and 5.3 percent for those 55 and older. The proportion of Americans in their prime working years, between 25 and 54, who currently have jobs remains at or near the lowest level in 30 years, with 6.5 million Americans in the age group still unemployed.[34] The drop has been particularly severe for men, with the percentage of prime-age men with jobs falling to a 60-year low in the spring of 2012, and recovering only slightly since.[35] In addition, 3.5 million Americans in their prime *earning* years, between 45 and 65, during which people build careers and wealth in preparation for retirement, are out of work. Many of these Americans, their skills eroded or outdated, may never work again.[36] As Figure 1.6 shows, while rates of unemployment are lower for older age groups, government statistics show that, once unemployed, older workers have greater difficulty finding new jobs and endure unemployment for much longer periods.[37]

Long-term unemployment is an especially pernicious aspect of the nation's current job crisis. As Figure 1.7 shows, more than 4 million Americans, almost 40 percent of those unemployed—more than twice the rate during the severe 1981–1982 recession—have been out of work for more than six months, a third for more than a year. As of May of 2013, the average unemployed American had been out of work for 37 weeks, up from 17 weeks in 2007.

Long-term unemployment entails severe and far-reaching implications for the economy, and for society. For example, the skills and knowledge base of idle workers deteriorate over time, making finding work even less likely. Extended unemployment also reduces the

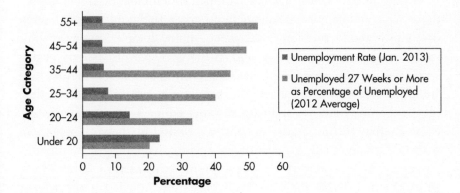

Figure 1.6 Unemployment Rate and Long-Term Unemployment by Age Group
SOURCE: Bureau of Labor Statistics.

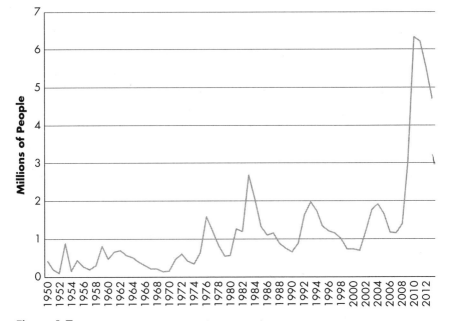

Figure 1.7   Civilians Unemployed for 27 Weeks or More
SOURCE: Bureau of Labor Statistics.

economy's long-term growth potential as the extra production, con-
sumption, and wealth creation that unemployed workers would have
contributed is lost.[38]

Even more serious, from a national and sociological standpoint,
those who endure long-term unemployment suffer from higher rates
of anxiety and depression,[39] substance abuse, divorce, domestic vio-
lence,[40] and even premature death.[41] A Rutgers University study of the
long-term unemployed found that 60 percent said their economic situation has had a "major impact" on their family, and half reported that
they had avoided friends and former associates—a kind of self-imposed
isolation that further undermines their ability to network and find
work.[42] Cruelly, many Americans struggling with long-term unemployment cannot afford to seek professional counseling or other kinds
of treatment because they lost their employer-provided health insurance with their jobs.[43] Federal Reserve Chairman Ben Bernanke has
called current levels of long-term unemployment "a national crisis."[44]

In addition to the unemployed, nearly eight million *employed* Americans are "underemployed"—working less than full-time involuntarily because their hours have been cut back or because they could only find temporary work. Together, those without work and the underemployed account for 11 percent of white Americans, 15 percent of Hispanics, and 20 percent of African-Americans.[45] Though fortunate enough to have jobs, the underemployed suffer hardships and anxieties similar to those endured by the unemployed, as earnings are often insufficient to meet expenses. According to the Census Bureau, one-third of adults living in poverty work but do not earn enough to support themselves and their families.[46] The frustration and pain of underemployment is worsened by the fact that median hourly wages were lower in 2011 than a decade earlier,[47] and because most temporary jobs offer no benefits.[48]

Perhaps most alarming, since the onset of the recent recession an estimated 4 million unemployed Americans have simply left the labor force.[49] Were these discouraged workers included in the government's calculation, the unemployment rate would be nearly 10 percent.[50] As Figure 1.8 shows, in March of 2013 the labor force participation rate—the share of Americans who are working or actively looking for jobs—declined to a 35-year low.[51]

More than four years into the recovery from the Great Recession, America's total jobs deficit—jobs lost but not yet recovered, plus

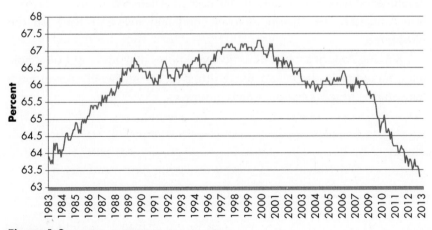

Figure 1.8 Labor Force Participation Rate
SOURCE: Bureau of Labor Statistics.

the jobs that should have been created to keep up with population growth—has been estimated to be more than 11 million jobs.[52] Private sector payrolls, currently about 135 million working Americans, are only slightly higher than the 132.5 million employed in late 2000, despite population growth over the period of more than 30 million.

Alarmingly, if not entirely surprisingly, given the surplus of idle workers, a recent study shows that American incomes declined by nearly 5 percent over the first three years of the recovery that began in June of 2009—more than they fell during the Great Recession itself.[53] Gordon Green, co-author of the study and former director of the Census Bureau's income and poverty statistics program, told *Bloomberg News*: "Almost every group is worse off than it was three years ago, and some groups had very large declines in income. We're in an unprecedented period of economic stagnation."[54]

Meanwhile, a record 11 million Americans are on federal disability insurance,[55] a record 48 million—up 70 percent since 2008—currently rely on food stamps,[56] and the Census Bureau has reported that the U.S. poverty rate has surged to the highest levels since the administration of Lyndon B. Johnson, with nearly 50 million Americans, one in six, living below the poverty line.[57]

America's jobs crisis remains a national emergency. The Great Recession was atypical in nature and historic in duration and severity. Conventional policy remedies, despite being applied in historic magnitudes, have not achieved the desired results. As many as 24 million Americans remain unemployed, underemployed, or have left the workforce.

Solving America's jobs emergency requires new ideas and new policies, including a sharp and unrelenting focus on the U.S. economy's true engine of job creation—new businesses.

Chapter 2

Not Just Small
Businesses ... *New*

An often-repeated truism of the U.S. economy is that small businesses—generally defined as those with fewer than 500 employees—account for about two-thirds of job creation. This claim is easy to accept, given that businesses with fewer than 500 employees account for 99 percent of the nation's businesses and employ about half of working Americans. Indeed, firms with fewer than 20 employees account for 89 percent of all firms and 18 percent of total employment.[1] The sheer number of small businesses across the nation, the significant proportion of total employment they account for, and the independence and self-sufficiency they represent help make small businesses a favorite constituency of elected officials of both parties.

But the reputation of small business as the engine of job creation is inaccurate—or, perhaps better stated, imprecise.

15

A breakthrough 2009 study of U.S. Census Bureau statistics—new data called Business Dynamics Statistics (BDS) that allow for unprecedented analysis of the creation and development of U.S. businesses—reveals that America's true engine of job creation is not small businesses broadly defined, but rather *new* businesses. According to the study, over the period 1980 to 2005 businesses less than five years old accounted for *all* net new job creation in the United States.[2]

Even more remarkable, subsequent analysis of the BDS data by Tim Kane, a former research scholar at the Ewing Marion Kauffman Foundation and currently chief economist at the Hudson Institute, demonstrates that in 22 of the 29 years between 1977 and 2005, all net new job creation was due to businesses less than one year old—true "start-ups."[3] In the seven other years over the period, older firms also contributed to job creation. But start-ups contributed an average of 3 million new jobs *every* year. In other words, without new businesses and the jobs they create, net job creation in all but seven years between 1977 and 2005 would have been *negative*.

Can this be true? Are start-ups really the source of virtually *all* job creation in America? What about every other kind of business—small and large, older and younger—don't they create jobs too?

To grasp the critical importance of start-ups to job creation, it's important to first understand how tremendously dynamic the U.S. labor market is. Most of the activity in the labor market each year reflects "churn"—the continuous process of hiring and separation that occurs as new businesses form and others close, as existing businesses create new jobs and eliminate others, and as workers leave old jobs for new opportunities. When the Labor Department reports that 200,000 jobs were created in a particular month, it's because there were 4.8 million separations—people either losing or leaving their jobs—and 5 million new hires, or some similar differential. In 2011, for example, 47.5 million separations occurred while 49.6 million Americans took new jobs, for a net gain of about 2.1 million new jobs. Assuming a 40-hour work-week, monthly hire and separation figures imply that approximately 25,000 jobs are destroyed, and slightly more are created, every hour America is open for business. Indeed, about a third of the U.S. labor force turns over in a typical year.

Before the recent recession—in 2006 and 2007—the economy produced an average of 5.4 million hires and 5.2 million separations each month. As Figure 2.1 shows, *both* figures dropped sharply during the Great Recession. In other words, a healthy labor market is a dynamic labor market, characterized by high levels of both hiring and separation.[4]

In March of 2009, for example, at the deepest point in the recent recession, 830,000 jobs were eliminated in a single month. Separations that month totaled 4.6 million—down from the monthly average of 5.2 million in 2006–2007. But monthly hires, at just 3.8 million, were down substantially more.[5]

Monthly separations continued to fall through 2009 and most of 2010, reaching a low of 3.8 million in October of 2010. Since then, separations have risen to a monthly average of about 4.1 million. Meanwhile, monthly hires have been stuck at an average of about 4.2 million for more than three years. The modest improvement in U.S. labor markets since the end of the recession, therefore, is mostly due to a reduction in separations, not to a significant increase in hiring.[6]

So what do monthly hires and separations have to do with new businesses being the engine of job creation?

The 2009 Census Bureau study and economist Tim Kane's subsequent work show that existing firms, of any age or size, in aggregate, nearly always produce more separations than hires. Indeed, existing businesses shed on a net basis—total separations subtracted from total new hires—a combined average of about 1 million jobs each year as some businesses fail, as others become more efficient and reduce headcount, and as separations simply outpace new hires. By stark contrast, new firms in their first year of existence create an average of 3 million new jobs every year.

But how many of those new jobs survive? New businesses are inherently risky and fragile. Roughly a third close by their second year, half within the first five years, suggesting that many of the jobs initially created are eventually lost. It's wonderful that new businesses create millions of jobs, but how many of those new jobs actually stick?

Robert Litan[7] and Michael Horrell,[8] colleagues of Tim Kane at the Kauffman Foundation, answered this critical question in the summer of 2010. Using the Census Bureau's BDS series, they

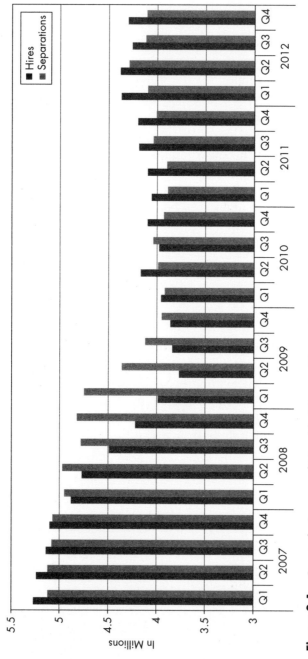

Figure 2.1 Quarterly Average of Monthly Hires and Separations

SOURCE: Bureau of Labor Statistics.

constructed start-up "classes"—that is, new businesses grouped by the year of their formation. By tracking the total employment of the various classes year after year, Litan and Horrell showed that, after five years, the surviving firms of each class retain about 80 percent of the total initial employment created by that class.[9]

In 2000, for example, new businesses created 3,099,639 jobs. By 2005, the surviving firms of that class—while only half the number that had launched in 2000—employed 2,412,410 people, or about 78 percent of the jobs initially created by the year-2000 class, as job growth at surviving firms offset job losses at shrinking or failed firms.

Helping to further explain this reality is a 2010 Census Bureau study, which determined that new firms that survive tend to grow at much faster rates than older businesses. The study's authors found what they described as a "rich 'up-or-out' dynamic for start-ups and young firms," meaning that while there is a high failure rate among new businesses, those that survive tend to grow and hire at very rapid rates.[10] A recent example of this pattern is Groupon, which had 37 employees in 2009 and grew to 10,000 employees by 2011—a two-year growth rate of 27,000 percent.

In 1994, economist David Birch referred to rapidly growing new businesses as "gazelles." Defining such enterprises as those whose sales grow by 20 percent per year, or double every four years, Birch estimated that such firms account for only 4 percent of all U.S. companies, yet are responsible for 70 percent of all new jobs. The growth pace of gazelle companies, he noted, far outpaced that of the Fortune 500 "elephants" and Main Street "mice."

To be sure, companies that grow and create jobs at such exponential rates are rare. Even so, the research makes clear that new businesses are America's true engine of job creation, adding an average of 3 million net new jobs each year, while ongoing churn at existing firms eliminates a net average of about 1 million jobs annually.

The survival and growth of as many new firms as possible is the critical factor. Without substantial growth among surviving firms, the new jobs created by start-ups would disappear within a few years, with no meaningful impact on the employment base or the broader economy. Fortunately, new firms that do survive tend to grow and hire at rapid rates.

This is not to argue that existing small businesses or larger firms are unimportant. Older small businesses account for 99 percent of U.S. businesses and more than half of total employment. U.S. multinational companies employ tens of millions of Americans, account for outsized proportions of U.S. exports, R&D spending, and productivity growth, and provide much of the demand for the goods and services produced by smaller firms, including new firms.[11] Policies that enhance the circumstances for existing businesses also enhance prospects for economic growth and job creation.

But if the policy target is job creation, new business formation is the bull's-eye.

Start-ups are also a major source of innovation, which, as we will discuss in more detail in Chapter 9, is the principal force that drives economic progress. A recent study by the Small Business Administration found that, between 2002 and 2006, firms with fewer than 500 employees registered 15 times more patents per employee than large firms.[12] We strongly suspect that, as with job creation, start-ups are responsible for most of small business innovation and registered patents. As Robert Litan and Carl Schramm point out in their recent book *Better Capitalism*:

> [E]ntrepreneurs throughout modern economic history, in this country and others, have been disproportionately responsible for truly radical innovations—the airplane, the railroad, the automobile, electric service, the telegraph and telephone, the computer, air conditioning, and so on—that not only fundamentally transformed consumers' lives, but also became platforms for many other industries that, in combination, have fundamentally changed entire economies. . .Large companies, with their large fixed costs of plant, equipment, and to some extent personnel, have perfected the economic arts of economies of scale production and incremental innovation. But . . . most large companies are less eager to pursue radical innovations—those that disrupt current business models in which the firms are heavily invested.[13]

From the standpoint of job creation and innovation—arguably the two most critical metrics of economic progress—new businesses are the essential core of any healthy, vibrant, and growing economy.

■ ■ ■

Unfortunately, the vital signs for America's job-creating entrepreneurial economy are flashing red alert. As Figure 2.2 shows, after remaining remarkably consistent for decades,[14] the number of new businesses created annually peaked in 2006, and then began a precipitous decline—a decline accelerated by the recent recession. Though recovering somewhat over the past two years, the number of start-ups in the year ending March of 2012 remained down 15 percent from the 2006 peak.[15] As the Bureau of Labor Statistics has observed: "New establishments are not being formed at the same levels seen before the economic downturn began, and the number is much lower than it was during the 2001 recession."[16]

Even more alarming, in a trend that began in 2000—and also accelerated during the recent recession—the new businesses that are being formed each year are creating fewer new jobs. Historically, each new firm has created an average of more than seven new jobs in its

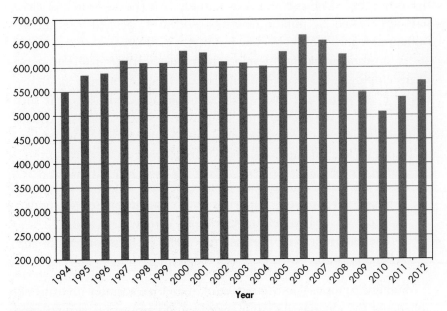

Figure 2.2 Number of Businesses Less Than One Year Old
Source: Bureau of Labor Statistics.

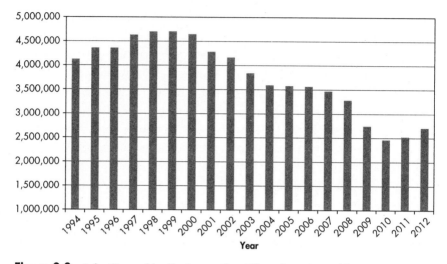

Figure 2.3   Jobs Created by Businesses Less Than One Year Old
SOURCE: Bureau of Labor Statistics.

first year. In recent years, however, that average has fallen to less than five new jobs.[17] As Figure 2.3 shows, in the year ending March of 2012, start-ups created 2.7 million new jobs—down 43 percent from the 4.7 million new jobs created by new businesses in 1999.[18]

A similar pattern has developed among existing small businesses. Firms employing 10 to 249 people hired 31 million people in 2012—nearly 8 million fewer than such businesses hired in 2006.[19] If such patterns persist, the jobs created by new and small businesses will be millions fewer than historical levels, virtually ensuring that America will face elevated unemployment for many years.[20]

America's jobs emergency, therefore, has two critical dimensions:

1. Some 24 million Americans remain unemployed, under-employed, or have left the labor force discouraged; and,
2. The nation's job creation engine—new business formation—has been breaking down in recent years.

Solving America's jobs emergency, therefore, requires dramatically enhancing the circumstances for new business formation, survival, and growth. And the first step toward improving the prospects for America's entrepreneurs is to identify and understand the issues, problems, and challenges that are currently in their way.

Chapter 3

On the Road with America's Job Creators

N ew businesses are clearly the engine of job creation in the United States, creating an average of about 3 million new jobs each year and accounting for virtually all net new job creation.

But in recent years, that job creation engine has begun to break down. The number of new businesses launched each year—and the number of new jobs created by those new firms—has suddenly and significantly declined.

But why?

If America's entrepreneurs have historically served as the engine of job creation, launching new businesses at a remarkably consistent rate for decades regardless of broader economic circumstances, as research has demonstrated, what is suddenly in their way? What explains the drop-off in new business formation and the decline in the number of new jobs those businesses create? Unless these key questions can be answered—and unless those answers help produce compelling policy solutions—the U.S. economy stands little chance of creating the jobs necessary to put millions of unemployed Americans back to work.

There are any number of ways to assess the condition, challenges, and prospects of America's new and young businesses. One might visit various start-up incubators and accelerators—facilities that provide support, technical assistance, and mentoring services to entrepreneurs as they perfect their product or service idea—or interview a number of entrepreneurship experts. One could construct a detailed survey of active entrepreneurs, review the academic research on entrepreneurship, or study start-up magazines, websites, and blogs. After considering the full range of procedural and analytic options, we decided on a multi-faceted approach that included several of these alternatives.

Most fundamentally, and importantly, we decided that the best and most reliable way to really hear and understand the aspirations, challenges, frustrations, and offered solutions of American entrepreneurs was to get out of Washington, DC, and talk to them face to face. And so, beginning in April of 2011, we hit the road—crisscrossing the country to conduct in-person roundtables with entrepreneurs in 12 cities.

Along the way, we conducted dozens of meetings with business and entrepreneurship academics, leaders of start-up incubators and accelerators, venture capitalists, angel investors, community development organizations, and lending institutions.

Working with the Kauffman Foundation and Adam Geller, founder and chief executive officer of the polling firm National Research, Inc., we also conducted a first-of-its-kind nationwide poll of more than 800 new and small business leaders during the week of September 19, 2011. While the poll asked entrepreneurs similar questions regarding the same topics and issues discussed at our 12 roundtables, polling produces data that allows for different kinds of analysis and interpretation as compared to the information derived from in-person group conversations. The results from our poll tended to confirm and add texture to what we heard at our roundtables.

In structuring our summer road trip, we selected the specific cities we visited with three objectives in mind. First, and most obviously, we wanted to cover the broad geographic territory of the country.

Second, because the U.S. economy is not a monolithic whole, but rather an amalgam of many regional economies, with certain cities or regions often closely associated with certain industries, we picked our locations with an eye for covering the industrial diversity of the country. For example, the Cambridge/Boston, Massachusetts, area is known for its robust biotech and life science start-up scene, whereas Herndon, Virginia, is known for defense-related and government-servicing companies.

Finally, we factored into our city selections the realization that implementing whatever policy proposals our project might generate would require champions on Capitol Hill. With this understanding in mind, we reviewed the membership of the relevant Congressional committees, in both the House and the Senate, and determined which states and which cities those members, Republican and Democrat, represent. Having identified the members whose states or districts matched the cities that met our other two criteria, we visited many of those members' offices to tell them about our project, methodology, and objectives, and to invite them or their staff, if interested, to participate as observers at our roundtables. Many did. Our hope is that this front-loading of Congressional awareness of, and interest in, the objectives and recommendations of our project will help accelerate implementation of many of our policy proposals.

■ ■ ■

Our first roundtable took place in York, Pennsylvania, on April 12, 2011. Over the course of the following summer we conducted additional roundtables in New York, New York; Columbus, Ohio; Richmond, Virginia; Herndon, Virginia; Kansas City, Missouri; Memphis, Tennessee; Austin, Texas; Los Angeles, California; Seattle, Washington; Orlando, Florida; wrapping up in Boston/Cambridge, Massachusetts, on September 8.

More than 200 diverse entrepreneurs took part in our roundtables— from a web-based software company in Seattle to an industrial construction firm in Orlando, from a developer of bioscience technologies in Boston to a distributor of glow-in-the-dark fluorescent fish in Austin.

We identified potential invitees in each city by reaching out to local start-up incubators, accelerators, and other facilities, entrepreneurship programs at local colleges and universities, and local Chambers of Commerce. Invitation lists were structured with an eye toward assembling a group of businesses reflective of the start-up scene in that particular city or region, but were not strictly limited to those concentrations. Occasionally, entrepreneurship facilitators—such as managers of local start-up incubators, mentoring facilities, or leaders of research commercialization offices at local universities—also participated in the roundtables. Many of these facilitators are themselves current or former entrepreneurs and all brought valuable experience and insights regarding local start-up activity to our roundtables.

To ensure impartiality and the methodological consistency of our roundtables from city to city, we retained an outside consultant—Greg Hitt of Hill+Knowlton Strategies—to moderate the discussions. Greg spent more than two decades covering Congress and the White House for the *Wall Street Journal* and Dow Jones Newswires, and brought his reporting skills to bear in facilitating our roundtables, making participants feel comfortable and asking the kinds of questions in the kinds of ways that served to draw out our guests and produce the comments and insights we were after. We attended all the roundtables, primarily in a listening capacity—asking only occasional questions to follow up on particular concepts or observations.

Each roundtable was scheduled for 90 minutes and typically consisted of 15 to 20 entrepreneurs, although occasionally we had more than 20 participants. We kept our discussions relatively small in order to promote an atmosphere of intimacy and engagement in which all our attendees would feel comfortable participating, and to ensure that we were able to hear, process, and understand the ideas, issues, and perspectives they shared.

■ ■ ■

As might be anticipated, our roundtables were lively events. Entrepreneurs are by nature highly motivated, high-energy people with lots of ideas and, though the discussions were facilitated by Greg, participants were generally eager to share their experiences, observations, and insights. Though scheduled for 90 minutes, the discussions frequently stretched to two hours and occasionally beyond.

Our discussions were conducted as interactive conversations that began with an assessment of both local and broader economic conditions, followed by an in-depth discussion of the issues, problems, and challenges that are undermining or obstructing new business formation, growth, and job creation. Most of the entrepreneurs—unrelenting optimists by nature—remained hopeful about the long-term prospects for their companies, despite difficult circumstances. Others were less sanguine, reporting that they had either been forced to trim payrolls to survive or had no plans to expand or hire additional workers anytime soon. Nearly all were deeply concerned about the pace of the economic recovery, and all came to the table with a list of specific concerns, problems, and frustrations.

Those concerns and frustrations notwithstanding, we came away from our series of roundtables struck most of all by the stunning degree of the nation's entrepreneurial dynamism. Despite the downward trend in the rate of new business formation in recent years, and despite the most difficult economic circumstances in decades, entrepreneurs all across America—driven by a desire to create and build, and enabled by the development of new technologies—continue to launch new companies, build those businesses, and pursue their dreams of independence and wealth.

Nancy Simmons, president of AERO Industries, a manufacturer and distributor of industrial materials in Orlando, Florida, articulated the kind of "damn the torpedoes" resolve we heard everywhere we went: "If we can survive this economy, God help us, what's going to knock us down? We've got to get past the point of despair. We have to think positively. We have to know that there's a way out of this. And there is no knight on a white horse coming to save us. We're going to save each other. We're going to innovate. We're going to team, we're going to work together. Nobody else is coming to bail us out."

In addition, incubators, accelerators, and other start-up facilitators are flourishing across the country, bringing to bear a wide variety of assistance and instruction in helping new companies form, perfect their product ideas, better organize, secure funding, and grow. Having witnessed such dynamism and commitment firsthand, we came away from our summer on the road enormously optimistic about the future of the U.S. economy.

The second major take-away from our series of roundtables—and enormously significant from the standpoint of potential policy solutions—is that the problems and obstacles encountered by entrepreneurs and other small business owners across the country are remarkably consistent. Notwithstanding differences in local economic conditions and regulatory environments from region to region—and acknowledging differences in emphasis from one city to the next—entrepreneurs from Austin to Boston and from Seattle to Orlando identified the same burdens, frustrations, and difficulties that are undermining their efforts to start new businesses, expand young firms, and hire.

■ ■ ■

Our summer on the road with American entrepreneurs made several critical realities vividly clear to us:

First, new businesses are extremely fragile—a third fail by their second year, half by their fifth. And yet, those new businesses that survive tend to grow and create jobs at very rapid rates.

Second, the policy needs and priorities of new businesses are unique. Start-ups are different from existing businesses. The challenges they confront are different and their ability to successfully navigate those challenges is more limited. Policies intended to enhance the circumstances of large corporations or even existing small businesses—however well intended or legitimate—often miss the needs of new businesses and can even undermine their prospects.

Third, policymakers in Washington do not sufficiently understand or appreciate the unique nature, importance, vulnerability, and needs of start-ups. Focused on the priorities of either large corporations or the small-business community, policymakers too often overlook and neglect the economy's true engine of job creation.

Finally, policy help for America's job creators is urgently needed. Twenty-four million Americans remain unemployed or under-employed, and the engine that has historically produced all net new jobs is breaking down. Given the critical role they play in our nation's economy as a principal source of innovation, growth, and job creation, America's young businesses need and deserve a comprehensive and *preferential* policy framework designed to cultivate and nurture start-ups.

Fortunately, we now know what needs to be done. Our remarkable summer on the road meeting and listening to America's entrepreneurs revealed with unprecedented clarity the major obstacles undermining their ability to launch new businesses, grow those businesses, and create jobs. Over the next six chapters, we report what they told us.

Our journey also provided a road map for success. The 30 specific policy proposals presented over the remainder of the book amount to an altogether new, uniquely credible, and vitally important game plan for unleashing the job-creating capacity of America's entrepreneurial economy, and putting a beleaguered nation back to work.

Chapter 4

"Not Enough People with the Skills We Need"

T he most startling message we heard from entrepreneurs at our roundtables was that the most serious obstacle to additional hiring by new businesses is a pronounced shortage of qualified talent. With 24 million Americans either unemployed or underemployed, we did not expect to hear about a labor shortage.

"We're in the fortunate situation where we're experiencing a lot of growth—the company's doubled in size in six months," said Chad Bockius, chief executive officer of Austin, Texas-based Socialware, which provides software and social media products to financial services firms. "The biggest concern I have from a hiring perspective is getting the talent in this town . . . I have the jobs, I just don't have the talent to fill them. We're really all fighting over the same talent."

Clay Banks, director of Economic Development at the Chamber of Commerce in Bartlett, Tennessee, outside Memphis agreed: "I just got off a two-week tour with 15 medical device manufacturers," he told us. "The jobs are available, [but] the skill sets out there don't meet the needs of these companies. . . They don't have a miracle pool to pull talent from. The technology and vocational schools aren't keeping up with the changes in advanced manufacturing and struggle to keep up with companies' demand for talented workers. It's not uncommon for companies to hire 5 to 10 in hopes of finding one qualified worker. Then they ask that employee if they know of anyone else or have siblings with a similar work ethic."

"It's very hard to find technically competent talent," said Paula Soileau, co-founder of Austin-based Affintus, LLC, which developed a system of cognitive and psychological testing that helps match job candidates with open positions. "Even people with great resumes can't do the work of modern businesses. This country needs a much better pipeline of qualified, highly skilled talent."

Entrepreneurs all across the country identified the same two culprits:

1. A U.S. education system that simply isn't producing enough graduates with the skills and training that twenty-first century companies need; and,
2. A scarcity of qualified foreign talent due to irrational and self-defeating immigration policies.

"There's a supply and demand problem," said Travis McCready, former Executive Director of the Kendall Square Association, an organization whose mission is to promote the vitality of the entrepreneurial enclave in Cambridge, Massachusetts. "On the supply side, there is increasing concern about education and preparedness for success in the workforce of today's economy. We're also concerned about increasingly rigid visa policies. We can't get enough home-grown talent, and we can't import enough foreign-born talent."

In this chapter we explore the reported skilled talent shortage, focusing on what we heard from our roundtable participants regarding the state of higher education in America, what it means for the nation's economic competitiveness, and how an under-trained and ill-equipped workforce is undermining entrepreneurs' capacity to launch new businesses and create jobs.

■ ■ ■

The indictment of American education—at all levels, but particularly at four-year colleges and universities—was sharp and stinging, and we heard it over and over again, in every city we visited:

New York, New York: "We don't have kids graduating with the skills to really make an impact at our companies. I'm a professor at Stern [School of Business at NYU] and most of my students had never heard of SEM (search engine marketing) or SEO (search engine optimization)—and they're marketing majors."

Columbus, Ohio: "There are problems in the education system, both delivering it and having the right people in place to deliver it."

Richmond, Virginia: "I'm just stunned how irrelevant our business schools are."

Kansas City, Missouri: "Quite frankly, the curriculum is just not there. Graduates are not qualified to do the work that I need them to do."

Memphis, Tennessee: "What's coming out of the tech schools is completely inadequate. . . They're completely underfunded and have outdated equipment. The teachers at the tech schools are outdated and can't teach the programs and skills that companies require."

Austin, Texas: "We are so focused on four-year programs that are basically worthless. . . There is a big gap between the talent that's available and the requirements of the jobs that exist. And it's not expected to go away anytime soon. There needs to be more energy put into training people so that we can close the gap."

Herndon, Virginia: "When you go to hire, what about English? Kids can't analyze, write, or communicate. We are creating a group of kids that are analytical and can focus on technology, but have no sense of the world, no sense of how to write, no sense of history."

Los Angeles, California: "The whole school system needs to change. What they're doing to our children is ridiculous. They are coming out completely incapable of running their own lives. If they could just write an invoice and print and spell, that would be very helpful."

Seattle, Washington: "We need to get back to reading, writing, and arithmetic. Why is German engineering the best in world? Because they focus on it, and with a sense of national pride. I think that needs to be instilled in our educational process."

Even students who graduate from the nation's elite universities often lack basic workplace skills, according to many of our participants. "They go to schools that we're all familiar with that are supposed to be producing great talent," said Mitch Jacobs, founder of On Deck Capital in New York City, and recipient of Ernst & Young's 2010 Entrepreneur of the Year Award. "But in terms of being useful on day one, they're just not. There's not enough focus on the fundamentals that ultimately make you useful and productive on day one."

Clay Banks from the Chamber of Commerce in Bartlett, Tennessee agreed: "Companies want real life, hands-on experience . . . but they're saying they'll get an engineer from a great university with a great GPA, and great knowledge about how to design and create a particular part—but they don't know how to turn the machine on. They have no real-world application of how to actually get that part through the production process."

In addition to general education deficiencies, we frequently heard the more specific problem of a severe national shortage of graduates with backgrounds in science, technology, engineering, and mathematics—collectively referred to as STEM.

"How do I get more American engineers that I can hire?" asked Steve Markmann, vice president at Counterpoint Consulting, a business software firm in Vienna, Virginia. "We're looking to hire—against the tide of the economy. [But] we need way more American kids with degrees in computer science, math, or science."

"There's just not enough engineering talent to go around," said Siobhan Quinn, a former software engineer at Google and currently a product manager at New York–based Foursquare, an online application platform that allows users to explore and share interesting locations around town and around the world. "There are a lot of great ideas, but just not enough people to build them."

"Our STEM problem is serious," said Tim Rowe, chief executive of the Cambridge Innovation Center, which brings together entrepreneurs of all kinds and stages in a single area by offering a wide range of office space options. "What's required for entrepreneurship is money, ideas, and talent . . . and in my view, talent is clearly the toughest piece. We put a lot of energy into it—we use recruiters and we search all over the world. There isn't a day that goes by that someone doesn't say 'Can you tell me how to find someone who knows how to program in Java?' or something like that. We have kids who need jobs in this country and we're not bringing those kids into the workforce in the way we need to in order to capitalize on the money and ideas that we have."[1]

"I own a technology company in Ohio," said Nick Seguin, a partner in Ohio-based Dynamit Technologies and the former manager of entrepreneurship at the Ewing Marion Kauffman Foundation in Kansas City. "We're paying the biggest university in the country with the second ranked math department to help us find and interview engineers and developers, and we can't find them. I don't outsource anything. I want to find people here in my country and my state, but they're just not qualified."

But Rob Lilleness, president and chief executive officer of Seattle-based Medio Systems, a mobile Internet software provider, explained that he has to outsource in order to survive. "Frankly, we can't find enough qualified people. Currently, we have about 70 employees and 20 open spots. And it's a dogfight to find qualified people in Seattle. . . We have to look at India, or Argentina, or Vietnam, or China for a satellite office for software development . . . We need to have more math and science talent coming out of our universities . . . or we are forced offshore to find talent."

Kyle Johnson, founder and chief executive of Audio Anywhere, based in Lawrence, Kansas, agreed: "My graphic designer is in Indonesia, my developers are in Russia. It's less expensive, they're smart, and they're creative. . . I went through multiple developers in Kansas City, firing them one after the other because they couldn't do the job. Ultimately I found an outsourcing firm where I can say, 'Here's what I need and when I need it.' As an entrepreneur with limited capital, there's only so many bullets I can fire."

While particularly acute in the technology sector, the STEM deficiency is also a serious obstacle in other sectors, given the ever-growing importance of high technology across the twenty-first century U.S. economy. "It's really unfortunate," said Neil Amin, chief executive of Shamin Hotels in Richmond, Virginia. "They may have been unemployed for a long time, but they don't have the experience we need. We want to grow our IT department, but we're having a hard time finding people, and we're not even a technology company."

"What really pains me," said Katalin Van Over, chief executive officer of ProLogic IT, a healthcare information technology consulting firm in Los Angeles, "is that there are 12 million unemployed people in the United States and yet there are not enough trained healthcare information technology engineers and technicians who can help providers meet the coming regulatory deadlines. We're going to have to borrow people from overseas."

■ ■ ■

From our roundtables emerged a clear consensus regarding a major and worsening disconnect between the U.S. education system and the needs of twenty-first century American entrepreneurs. Not enough STEM field graduates are being produced, and too often the limited number of STEM graduates lack the specific knowledge base and skill sets needed by employers. Criticism of four-year colleges and universities was particularly harsh, with many of our participating entrepreneurs openly questioning the value of four-year bachelor's degrees, regardless of the college or university.[2]

"We're not training people for the workforce," said a participant in our Kansas City roundtable. "We're putting people through a curriculum that is designed to let tenured professors live a nice lifestyle and put out research papers. But the product is not applicable to most industries now."

Jayson Rapaport, co-founder of Austin-based Birds Barbershop, agreed. "Peter Thiel, one of the founders of PayPal, has launched a movement to convince people to not go to college.[3] It's a waste of money. The return on investment isn't there anymore. School has gotten too expensive. . . If writing [computer] code is your deal and you're able to go to a trade school that enables you to write code, that's far better than a computer science degree from a four-year college or university that looks great on paper, but doesn't give you the skills you need when you graduate."

Mark Mader, a repeat entrepreneur and chief executive at Bellevue, Washington–based Smartsheet, whose cloud-based software enables people to coordinate and manage projects and processes in real time, explained how the scarcity of skilled talent has forced his company to broaden its search beyond colleges and universities. "Number one issue, not enough talent available. We constantly hear about high unemployment rates while we're sitting here wondering, 'How the hell do we fill our next ten positions?' We're much more open today to looking at a diverse experience pool. Finding people who developed their skills in trade school, for example, as opposed to an Ivy League college. That's how the dynamic has changed. We've become much more aggressive and creative about where we find talent."

"We need to think more broadly about making education parallel to actual job requirements," said Rob Quartel, chairman and chief executive officer of NTELX, a data management and information technology company in Vienna, Virginia. "I don't need a college-educated person for every job in my office. We also need mechanics and electricians. And, by the way, some of these guys make $125,000 in these professions—that's twice the income of the average American. We have to be broader about what we need in terms of jobs."

"We've been working with the Austin Chamber of Commerce, the University of Texas, and all the local schools, and they're dying for information from businesses," said Ray Wolf, co-founder and chief executive of Austin-based Green Integrated Services, which provides leadership and strategy services to assist early stage and small businesses. "Who are you going to hire and what skills do you need? . . . We need to get that conversation lined up really quick. The pathway into the economy isn't always through a four-year degree. . . We have about 70 percent [of our students] trying to complete four-year schools and coming out with a $29,000 loan to pay off. . . We need to start thinking about human capital in terms of skills, not titles. Figuring out what skills they need, identifying gaps, and then getting the education to fill those gaps. . . Educators want to do the right thing, businesses want to do the right thing, students want to learn the right thing. Put all their needs together, translate into a common language of skills, and combine with technology to create a dynamic system for aligning education with the needs of business . . . today and into the future . . . resulting in tremendous economic impact."

David Eberhardt, lead faculty for entrepreneurship at North Seattle Community College, agreed. "Partnerships between industry and state and community colleges would really help," he told us. "My college is currently talking with a couple of small businesses about doing specific training for their folks. And I've been talking with a couple of up-and-coming industries about their technology needs so that our electronics and nanotechnology programs can begin training and teaching . . . so that our students, when they graduate, can be prepared. If we don't have those dialogues going on, that's hard to do."

■ ■ ■

To be sure, difficulty finding qualified workers is not limited to new businesses. A 2013 survey by ManpowerGroup, a leading human resources consulting firm, found that 39 percent of U.S. employers reported having difficulty filling "mission-critical positions," up from 14 percent in 2010.[4] Another survey, by Deloitte and The Manufacturing Institute, reported that 67 percent of U.S. manufacturers are experiencing moderate to severe shortages of qualified workers, leaving as many as 600,000 skilled positions unfilled.[5]

As of late 2012, Microsoft reportedly had more than 6,000 open positions in the United States, a 15 percent increase from the year before. Nearly 60 percent of those positions were for engineers, software developers, and researchers.[6] In late 2011, with the unemployment rate at 9.1 percent, Siemens, the German industrial conglomerate, had 3,000 open positions in the United States that the company couldn't fill. Applicants are tested in reading comprehension, math, and mechanical aptitude. Only 10 percent are deemed to have sufficient skills to be trained for jobs. As Peter Solmssen, Siemens' general counsel, told CNBC: "You can't just come in and swing a hammer. You have to be able to operate sophisticated machinery. You've got to have an understanding of what's going on in the manufacturing process. . . As a country we haven't paid enough respect to great manufacturing jobs. We haven't given people the training they need to be able to operate in a modern, competitive manufacturing environment. If you go to our factories in Germany, the guys on the floor can read engineering drawings. They're highly respected. They're well paid."[7]

As Solmssen points out, driving the skilled talent shortage is the extent to which automation and computerized instrumentation are transforming the U.S. economy—a trend accelerated by the recent recession. Over the two years following the end of the recession, spending by U.S. companies on computers, automation, and other high technology equipment surged. Such investments—encouraged by historically low costs of capital and temporary tax breaks—enabled companies struggling to maintain profitability to enhance productivity while putting off more expensive hiring. But such investments have also dramatically raised the required level of technical competency, even for manufacturing jobs that may have only required a high school degree as recently as a decade ago.[8]

The worrisome increase in job vacancies at a time of persistently high unemployment has sparked a debate among economists regarding whether a fundamental shift has occurred in the historical relationship between job vacancies and unemployment. The relationship is most commonly illustrated by what is known as the Beveridge curve—a graphical depiction, named after British labor economist William Henry Beveridge, showing the job vacancy rate along the vertical, or y, axis and the unemployment rate along the horizontal, or x, axis.

As Figure 4.1 shows, the curve slopes downward from left to right as higher rates of unemployment are generally associated with lower rates of job vacancies. An outward shift in the curve—a given level of vacancies associated with higher and higher levels of unemployment—would imply decreasing labor market efficiency due to mismatches between

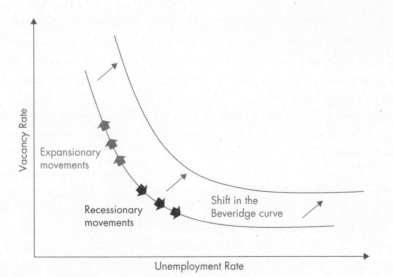

Figure 4.1   The Beveridge Curve
SOURCE: www.clevelandfed.org/research/trends/2010/0810/02labmar-1.gif.

available jobs and the skills of the unemployed.[9] And, indeed, while the number of monthly job openings has increased from a low of 2.2 million in July of 2009 to 3.8 million in April of 2013, the unemployment rate remains north of 7.5 percent, and 12 million Americans remain unemployed.[10]

While the skilled talent shortage is certainly not unique to start-ups, our entrepreneurs explained how the shortage hits new businesses especially hard. For example, in the initial months and years of a new business, skilled talent is the essential ingredient necessary to turn ideas into products and to identify and effectively exploit markets for those new products. Talent and brain power are start-ups' most valuable assets. Without access to highly skilled employees, even great ideas can, and often do, fail as viable businesses.

Moreover, the shoestring circumstances of most start-ups during the initial years typically can't accommodate the training programs necessary to turn high-potential employees into high-value employees.

"My company is small—we're 35 people," said Brenda Hall, chief executive officer of Austin-based Bridge 360. "We do custom application software development—the hard stuff on people's IT list that never gets done. They pass it to us and we take care of it. [But] I'm worried. I'm doing double-digit growth, but how do I find good people? *Good* people. Training is an issue for me because people come in with great resumes, but they just can't do the job. I haven't got the kind of company that gives them time to 'ramp up.' So we've got to hit the ground running with good people and get the job done. And that's a tough one."

And as the scarcity of skilled talent has driven up the price with regard to salaries and benefits, many cash-challenged start-ups simply can't compete.[11]

"I'll give you an example," said Rob Lilleness of Seattle-based Medio Systems. "We had someone who was four or five years out of the University of Washington, total comp somewhere around $125,000. Google hired him away for $225,000."

Dan Sullivan, founder and president of AppsWell, a Cambridge-based developer of iPhone applications, pointed out that even new graduates who want to join a new company may not be able to. "There are a lot of great folks coming out of top schools that would be fantastic adds to young companies, or excellent candidates to start their own companies. But they're coming out hugely in debt. With that burden, they're set on a career path that has to have a certain salary that a lot of start-ups can't match."

Total outstanding student loan debt surpassed $1 trillion for the first time last year, and members of the class of 2013 graduated an average of $35,200 in debt according to a recent survey by Fidelity Investments.[12]

Siobhan Quinn, the former Google software engineer, now at New York–based Foursquare, identified a different sort of talent-related problem faced by many new companies at critical stages of expansion. "At the beginning, there's always some founder, some young visionary. But as [a new business] starts to scale, you may need more experienced specialists. But it's hard because many people aren't comfortable giving up a $200,000-plus salary and lifestyle for less compensation—even if the alternative comes with stock options and has much greater growth potential. They just can't take the risk."

Recent research confirms the feedback from our roundtable participants. A 2010 study published by the Association of American Colleges and Universities found that only 25 percent of U.S. employers think that colleges and universities are adequately preparing graduates for the demands of the global economy.[13] A study by the Federal Reserve Bank of New York and New York University found that as much as a third of the increase in unemployment among college-educated workers between 2006 and 2010 was the result of workers not having the skills for available positions.[14] More recently, an analysis by the Pew Research Center found that less than half of those surveyed between 18 and 34 years old say they have the education and training necessary to advance in their careers.[15]

■ ■ ■

Of course, indictments of American education and alarms regarding the implications for the nation's productive capacity and competitiveness are not new. Perhaps the most notable and influential call-to-arms was the report *A Nation at Risk*, released in April of 1983 by Ronald Reagan's Department of Education—which, ironically, candidate

Reagan had promised to dismantle. The product of a blue-ribbon commission drawn from private industry, government, and education, the report began with memorable assertions that shocked the education establishment:

> [T]he educational foundations of our society are presently being eroded by a rising tide of mediocrity that threatens our very future as a nation and a people. . . . If an unfriendly foreign power had attempted to impose on America the mediocre educational performance that exists today, we might well have viewed it as an act of war. As it stands, we have allowed this to happen to ourselves . . . we have, in effect, been committing an act of unthinking, unilateral educational disarmament.[16]

Called "the most important education reform document of the twentieth century" by education historian Diane Ravitch,[17] the report made 38 recommendations, including raising graduation requirements for students, expanding educational subject areas, increasing the number and length of school days, raising teacher standards and compensation, and ensuring political leadership and fiscal support. Much of the educational establishment regarded the report's findings as exaggerated and overwrought, but the national conversation it launched culminated in the No Child Left Behind Act of 2002, which required public schools to improve students' basics skills and testing performance or face ever-tougher federal sanctions—an approach that has won praise for its focus on eliminating race- and income-based achievement gaps, but also criticism for its emphasis of test scores.

Over the ensuing three decades since the release of "A Nation at Risk," international test scores have repeatedly shown that American students continue to fall farther behind their counterparts overseas. Results from the most recent Program for International Student Assessment (PISA), an evaluation of 15-year-old students' performance in 65 nations administered by the Organisation for Economic Co-operation and Development (OECD), ranked the performance of American students 15th in reading, 23rd in science, and 31st in math. On the same test, students in Shanghai outscored every other school system in the world.[18]

"We have to see this as a wake-up call," Secretary of Education Arne Duncan said, responding to the scores. "I know skeptics will want to argue with the results. . . . We can quibble, or we can face the brutal truth that we're being out-educated."[19]

A recent Harvard University study found that students in Portugal, Hong Kong, Germany, Poland, Liechtenstein, Slovenia, Colombia, and Lithuania are making academic gains at twice the rate of American students, while students in Latvia, Chile, and Brazil are improving three times faster. The report's authors warn: "A country ignores the quality of its schools at its economic peril."[20] Joel Klein, former New York City School Chancellor, wrote in June of 2011, "While America's students are stuck in a ditch, the rest of the world is moving ahead."[21]

Mr. Klein, along with former Secretary of State Condoleezza Rice, recently co-chaired a task force sponsored by the Council on Foreign Relations, which examined the state of U.S. education as a national security issue. They declare in their preface that "American education is vital to sustaining the nation's international leadership and competitiveness" and "is core to upholding the American ideals that our forefathers set out to establish in this democracy." The task force concludes that "[E]ducational failure puts the United States' future economic prosperity, global position, and physical safety at risk."

> In 2012, the sad fact is that . . . despite selective improvement, the big picture performance of America's educational system is all too similar to results from three decades ago. . . By nearly every measure, the United States is falling short of its collective expectations in K-12 public education—leaving individual Americans, communities, and the nation vulnerable. . . The United States will not be able to keep pace—much less lead—globally unless it moves to fix the problems it has allowed to fester for too long.[22]

Economists at Harvard University have estimated that if the math proficiency of U.S. students were raised to levels currently observed in Canada and South Korea, U.S. economic output could be expanded by "nothing less than $75 trillion" over the next 80 years—roughly $1 trillion annually.[23]

Policy Recommendations

The feedback from our participating entrepreneurs is not only consistent with international test scores and the findings of recent academic studies, but is perhaps the most vivid and credible evidence to date that U.S. educational deficiencies are undermining the formation, survival, and growth of new businesses and, thereby, impairing economic recovery, innovation, competitiveness, and job creation. Though not focused specifically on education reform, our roundtables revealed broad support for greater competition among schools and school choice for parents; incorporating more technology in the classroom; giving teachers more freedom to innovate; teacher accountability that rewards excellent teachers financially and gets rid of poor teachers; and a core curriculum focused on fundamental skills like reading, writing, math, and science, but also creative problem-solving, communication, and collaboration—skills increasingly essential to success in the knowledge-based twenty-first century economy, according to our entrepreneurs.

Solving the nation's educational challenges is beyond the scope of this book. We nevertheless recommend the following with the aim of improving the quality and relevance of American education, increasing the number of STEM graduates, and enhancing the marketable skills of those currently out of work.

Incentivize STEM Education

Establish a $50,000 federal tax credit to any student who completes an undergraduate or post-graduate degree in science, technology, engineering, or mathematics. The credit could be deducted from taxable income up to $10,000 per year over the initial five years of post-graduate employment.

Launch a Curriculum-Focused Dialogue Between Business and Education

The Department of Education, in partnership with a consortium of nationwide business groups, should launch an immediate and ongoing dialogue between business and education leaders to examine kindergarten through grade 12, community college, and university curricula to ensure that the nation's education system serves the broader educational needs of students, as well as the skill requirements of twenty-first century U.S. businesses. Businesses represented in the dialogue should include multinational corporations, regionally active firms, small businesses, and young start-ups.

A major focus of the dialogue should be to facilitate business community input into curricula determinations, and to increase opportunities for active business professionals and other practitioners to participate in and outside the classroom as instructors, assistants, advisors, and mentors.

A particular focus of the business-education dialogue should be to more effectively leverage the value of the nation's 1,200 community colleges. Whether serving as an educational "on-ramp" for first generation college-goers or low-wage/low-skill adults, offering cutting-edge occupational training, or working with businesses to provide continuing education and training for their employees, community colleges are the natural backbone of the nation's workforce development efforts.[24]

And yet this great national asset has not been leveraged in the United States anywhere near the degree it has in other advanced economies, especially in Europe. Throughout northern and central Europe, most young people in high school choose vocational education programs that combine classroom and workplace learning for several years, and that culminate in a certificate or credential that has meaning and real value in the labor market. Many of our entrepreneurs referenced Germany's renowned system of vocational education as a potential model for the United States.

Better leveraging of the community college system should focus on business-college partnerships that develop frameworks of "stackable" credentials that are relevant to businesses' needs and portable from the student/worker standpoint, as well as work-study opportunities to complement classroom time and continuously ensure that training curricula are appropriate and relevant. According to Georgetown University's Center on Education and the Workforce, while holders of vocational certificates earn an average of 20 percent more than high school graduates, only 11 percent of Americans workers hold such certificates.[25]

As Robert Templin, President of Northern Virginia Community College, stated in a 2010 Congressional testimony:

> Entry-level skill training represents only one part of what is required for a worker to secure and retain meaningful employment. Without broader foundational knowledge, post-secondary-level training, a portable credential, and actual job experience, narrowly focused skill development too often results in a one-way ticket to entry-level jobs that are the first to be lost at the next technology innovation or economic downturn.[26]

Jay Timmons, president and chief executive officer of the National Association of Manufacturers recently endorsed this approach to vocational education reform:

> We have created an education system that is almost completely divorced from the economy at large. The only way to address this monumental challenge and support the economic recovery is to align education, economic development, workforce, and business agendas to work in concert and develop the talent necessary for success in the global economy. . . The solution . . . is a series of nationally portable, industry-recognized credentials based specifically on those employer-identified skills. These credentials—and the training required to obtain them—certify that an individual possesses the basic skills necessary for a career in manufacturing and ensures that they are useful nationwide and across multiple manufacturing sectors. . . This approach creates more on- and off-ramps in education, which facilitates individuals' ability to obtain schooling when their professional career requires it, and positions them to earn while they learn, applying what they learn in class at night on the job the next day.[27]

At its best, closer collaboration can make employers fully integrated partners with community colleges in producing a highly trained, "ready-on-day-one" workforce. Employers should not only communicate their skill needs to colleges, but also help set aptitude standards, develop study programs, and encourage employees to serve as teachers, instructors, and advisers. This kind of active collaboration would likely produce substantial savings for businesses. U.S. employers currently spend nearly $315 billion each year on informal on-the-job training and an additional $140 billion each year on more formal employer-provided education and training programs.[28]

Launch an Education Reform Dialogue Among America's Educators

The Department of Education, in partnership with national education groups, should launch an immediate and ongoing dialogue among educators at all levels about how to make American education, both at the systemic level and with regard to classroom techniques and methodologies, more flexible, creative, and innovative. This was another common theme at our roundtables. While core skills like reading, writing, math, and science remain essential, our participants told us, skills such as personal motivation, creative problem-solving, communication, and collaboration are just as important to the success of their businesses.

Tony Wagner, co-director of the Change Leadership Group at Harvard's Graduate School of Education, emphasizes such skills in his 2012 book *Creating Innovators: The Making of Young People Who Will Change the World*.[29] Describing himself as "a translator between two hostile tribes"—the education world and the business world—Wagner recently told *New York Times* columnist Tom Friedman that our K–12 and college curricula are not consistently "adding the value and teaching the skills that matter most in the marketplace."[30] The goal of education today, Wagner explained, should not be to make every child "college-ready," but rather "innovation-ready."

> Because knowledge is available on every Internet-connected device, what you know matters far less than what you can do with what you know. The capacity to innovate—the ability to solve problems creatively or bring new possibilities to life—and skills like critical thinking, communication, and collaboration are far more important than academic knowledge. As one executive

told me, "We can teach new hires the content, and we will have to because it continues to change, but we can't teach them how to think—to ask the right questions—and to take initiative."

Every young person will continue to need basic knowledge, of course. But they will need skills and motivation even more. Of these three education goals, motivation is the most critical. Young people who are intrinsically motivated—curious, persistent, and willing to take risks—will learn new knowledge and skills continuously. They will be able to find new opportunities or create their own—a disposition that will be increasingly important as many traditional careers disappear.

We teach and test things most students have no interest in and will never need, and facts that they can Google and will forget as soon as the test is over. Because of this, the longer kids are in school, the less motivated they become. Gallup's recent survey showed student engagement going from 80 percent in fifth grade to 40 percent in high school. More than a century ago, we "reinvented" the one-room schoolhouse and created factory schools for the industrial economy. Re-imagining schools for the twenty-first century must be our highest priority. We need to focus more on teaching the skill and will to learn and to make a difference and bring the three most powerful ingredients of intrinsic motivation into the classroom: play, passion, and purpose.

Finland is one of the most innovative economies in the world, and it is the only country where students leave high school "innovation-ready." They learn concepts and creativity more than facts, and have a choice of many electives—all with a shorter school day, little homework, and almost no testing.

Incentivize Experienced Talent to Consider Joining Growing Start-Ups

Scaling of viable new businesses is critical to significant job creation. And, as Foursquare's Siobhan Quinn pointed out at our New York roundtable, experienced talent is critical to effective scaling, as successful new businesses transition from the informal, kinetic start-up stage to a rapidly growing and maturing business enterprise with more complex operational, human resources, and legal challenges.

With that in mind, we propose meaningfully addressing the significant "life risk" frequently associated with leaving a large, more mature, and secure firm for a growing but fragile new business. Specifically, we propose making the proceeds of all exercised stock options issued to employees of new businesses less than five years old taxable at the reduced long-term capital gain rate. In addition, we propose eliminating the $100,000 per employee annual vesting limit on incentive stock options (ISOs), and eliminating the requirement to pay the ISO strike price at the time of exercise. As an alternative, the cash strike price could be deducted from the eventual capital gain (difference between strike and market) at the time of sale. Net proceeds would be taxed at the reduced long-term capital gains rate.

■ ■ ■

A final thought that, while not a matter of public policy *per se*, may be just as important to the kind of education reform that is necessary to meet not only the challenges of the twenty-first century economy, but also the challenges of twenty-first century life.

A new book entitled *The Start-Up of You: Adapt to the Future, Invest in Yourself, and Transform Your Career* calls on readers to become individual entrepreneurs—not starting a new business necessarily, although that would be great, but adopting into their vision for, and management of, their lives the same ownership, flexibility, and can-do/will-do thinking of the entrepreneur. The book is co-written by Reid Hoffman, the billionaire co-founder of LinkedIn, and Ben Casnocha, an award-winning entrepreneur and writer. As Casnocha recently explained:

> For the past 60 years . . . the job market for educated workers worked like an escalator. After graduating from college, you landed an entry-level job at the bottom of the escalator . . . so long as you played nice and well, you moved up the escalator, and each step brought with it more power, income,

and job security. . . And as a result, you could be rather lackadaisical about managing your career . . . You hop on the escalator at the bottom, you depend on your employer for upward lift, and bank on Social Security when you step off the escalator. That's acting like labor. Of course, the problem is the world has changed. The career story is no longer true, and acting like labor won't cut it anymore.[31]

Co-author Reid Hoffman:

Think about our lives as entrepreneurs. . . Create more value in myself and the world around me by proactively investing in growing my capabilities and adding more to society. . . In a flatter world with more competition, how do you succeed? How do you invest in yourself and gain those skills? You can't do it accidentally.[32]

At first look, this may seem like the kind of "master your destiny" fluff one finds in the Personal Growth section of the bookstore. But we're convinced that Hoffman and Casnocha are on to something—something fundamental, essential, and revolutionary. Their message echoes in remarkable ways what we heard from entrepreneurs all across America. It also captures the still emerging but rapidly growing phenomenon of continuous—and often free of charge—learning that the Internet has made possible. Whether discrete lessons in education basics available through on-line platforms like the Khan Academy, or college and university classes attended not only by the students in the room, but also by millions sitting at computer terminals or watching on smartphones around the world—often called "massive open online courses," or MOOCs—these new approaches to education, and hugely expanded access, are so powerful and consequential that their implications—economic, social, and political—are almost impossible to contemplate.[33] As former hedge fund manager and author Andy Kessler recently wrote in a column for the *Wall Street Journal*: "Online education is about taking the 'best-in-class' teachers and scaling them to thousands or millions of students rather than 25 to 30 at a time."[34]

On May 14, 2013, Georgia Tech announced that it had partnered with AT&T and Udacity, a for-profit provider of MOOCs, to offer the first accredited online master's degree in computer science that students can earn in three years entirely by way of the MOOCs delivery format for just $7,000, a fraction of the cost of traditional, on-campus programs.[35]

The world has changed fundamentally in the course of a single generation. Economic life, as Hoffman and Casnocha point out, is no longer a slowly moving escalator onto which one can hop and ride the rest of one's career to the top floor of comfort, security, and fulfilling retirement. Instead, the U.S. and global economies have been transformed into a much more complex, ever-changing landscape of risk, requirements, and mounting competition. This new world can be bewildering and even frightening, but is also exhilarating in its possibilities and rewards.

Successfully navigating this new economic and socio-political terrain requires schools that produce graduates who are "innovation-ready," which in turn requires a rich and dynamic interaction between those who educate our citizens and those who hire them. It also requires that we as individuals play our part, by committing to lives of continuous learning, accepting the reality of constant change and serendipity, and taking a proactive and entrepreneurial approach to our educations, careers, and relationship networks.

Chapter 5

"Our Immigration Policies Are Insane"

As frustrating as the skilled talent shortage is for our participating entrepreneurs, it is not an exaggeration to report that our nation's immigration policies enrage them. The problem is not merely that the United States does not effectively recruit and welcome the world's best talent. Rather, our roundtable participants insist, current immigration policies in many ways actually obstruct and even actively deter high-skill immigration.

"The real problem is immigration because even if we fix the education system, it's going to take years before you see results," a participant at our Herndon, Virginia, roundtable told us. "In the venture capital industry over the past 20 years, 40 percent of the people who've been funded as CEOs [of new companies] were foreign-born. And that's way more than what immigrants represent in the population by a long shot."

"I've got two co-founders who are not American, along with up to 75 percent of our scientific hires and applicant pool, so visa problems and delays are a major issue for us," said John Sheffield, co-founder of Seven Bridges Genomics, a Boston-based pioneer in the field of bioinformatics, which *Forbes* magazine has estimated could develop into a $100 billion industry.[1] "One of my co-founders graduated a few years ahead of me from Harvard and was in the PhD program. He was the number one student in his country's national exams before he came to Harvard. So he's exactly the kind of guy that you would want in the United States innovating. He's published work that made him one of a handful of people in the world who can find a particular class of genetic variation that's involved in a wide range of cancers and genetic disorders. . . And the struggles that we've encountered to keep him working in the United States and appropriately compensated are just ridiculous. And this is occurring in what we call a 'generative industry,' where the technologies that we're creating will be used in any number of industries downstream."

Such circumstances are highly problematic for several reasons. First, and most tragically, America proudly defines itself as the world's great melting pot of immigrant cultures and talents, a nation whose most recognizable monument is the iconic statue of Libertas, the Roman goddess of freedom, who lifts her torch to illuminate the "golden door" of opportunity.[2]

Second, at a time when official efforts to accelerate economic growth and job creation have focused on fiscal and monetary stimulus—even as the nation struggles to come to terms with staggering levels of government indebtedness—there is ample evidence that targeted, common-sense immigration reforms would significantly accelerate job creation without spending a dime of taxpayers' money.

Most worrisome, our entrepreneurs argue, in an increasingly competitive global economy in which highly skilled talent and brainpower are the resources most sought after, U.S. immigration policies are irrational and self-defeating—exacerbating the serious shortage of skilled American talent that entrepreneurs insist is undermining the formation and growth of new businesses, and, as a result, economic growth and job creation.

Our participants identified barriers in virtually every aspect of U.S. immigration policy. Among the most frustrating are requirements regarding foreign-born graduates of U.S. colleges and universities. The United States remains the top magnet for the world's best and brightest students. More than 760,000 foreign nationals—a record high and the world's largest international student population—enrolled in American colleges and universities last year under the terms of an F-1, or student, visa, an increase of more than 30 percent over the past 10 years.[3] Foreign students contribute more than $20 billion annually to the U.S. economy by way of tuition expenditures and living expenses.[4] Most significantly, foreign students account for almost half of all the graduate students in engineering, mathematics, computer science, and the physical sciences—earning more than 40 percent of all master's degrees in those fields and more than half of all PhDs.[5]

Given the obvious economic value of newly minted, American-trained graduates—particularly in the critical STEM fields—one might expect that U.S. policy would allow or even encourage foreign-born graduates to stay in the United States. After spending four years—or, in the case of graduate students, as many as seven or eight years—educating, training, and cultivating the world's best minds, why would any nation want that intellectual capital to leave?

Unfortunately, in most cases that's precisely what happens. Current policy requires foreign students to return home within 60 days of completing their studies. Under the terms of the F-1 visa, foreign graduates may remain in the United States if they land a job or internship—but only for 12 to 29 months, depending on their field of expertise.[6]

"It's amazing how many international students are in the IT and Engineering programs at Kansas and Kansas State," Keith Molzer, chief executive of Balance Innovation in Lenexa, Kansas, told us. "I think it's over 50 percent. And they are the best and the brightest. But they don't stay here. They graduate and go back to their home countries. We need to find a way to keep those students here to help grow our entrepreneurial talent pool."

"Let's at least let people who come here for higher education stay," said Dr. Kenneth Blaisdell, Associate Dean at Virginia Commonwealth University and Executive Director of VCU's School of Business Foundation. "It's just phenomenally stupid in the extreme that we put students through master's and PhD programs and then we say you have to leave! We bring people in for humanitarian reasons, and that's fine. But, man, are our immigration policies messed up. . . We have foreign grad students at our school who are spectacular. One is cooling her heals in Bucharest right now because her visa required that she leave and reapply. We had one in Islamabad last year, and while she was waiting for a month for a meeting with visa officials at our embassy, extremists blew up a girls' school a block away and actually knocked her to the ground. And this is the best graduate student at VCU! It's absolutely nuts!"

■ ■ ■

There are two other principal pathways by which highly skilled foreign nationals can live and work in the United States—H-1B visas and "green cards." Both entail cumbersome qualifying requirements and strict limitations.[7]

The H-1B visa program allows high-skill immigrants with theoretical or technical expertise in specialized fields such as science, engineering, or computer programming to work in the United States for an initial period of three years. Visas can be extended for an additional three years, but not beyond a total of six years. To qualify, foreign applicants must hold a bachelor's degree from an accredited college or university in the United States, or the equivalent; the prospective U.S.-based employer must sponsor the applicant; and the duties of the prospective job must correspond to the applicant's education and work experience.[8] About 1 million foreigners worked in the United States on H-1B visas in 2012.[9]

The employer-sponsorship requirement of the H-1B visas is cumbersome for all applicants, but particularly problematic for entrepreneurs. First, companies seeking H-1B visas for their employees must be able to demonstrate control over the worker's employment, including the ability to terminate the employee. This requirement is difficult if not impossible for entrepreneurs to demonstrate compliance. It also means that H-1B visitors may not change employers without returning home and reapplying. In addition, sponsoring employers are legally required to pay the filing and processing fees associated with H-1B applications and, though not required, also typically pay legal fees associated with application preparation and petition filings. Such costs can become substantial—often amounting to thousands of dollars—deterring many employers from sponsoring foreign applicants. Start-up businesses, which tend to be small with limited resources, are impacted disproportionately.

"It's very hard to find American citizens with technology degrees," a participant in our Herndon, Virginia roundtable told us. "We're forced to hire people through H-1B arrangements. . . . [But] as a small business, we can't even get one approved. It took us two years to get the last one done. It would be far cheaper to pay a regular salary, but we just can't find enough folks who either have a green card or are a U.S. resident with a technology degree."

Most problematic, the number of H-1B visas is currently capped at just 65,000, with an additional 20,000 set aside for foreign nationals holding a post-graduate degree from a U.S. college or university. Applications frequently exceed the annual cap within weeks or even days of the new allotment being issued.[10] In 2013, visa applications exceeded supply within five days.[11] Two-thirds of annual H-1B applications are for workers in STEM occupations.[12]

A more permanent pathway of entry is the Lawful Permanent Resident Card, or "green card," so-called because of the card's green color between 1946 and 1964, and again since May of 2010. Green cards permit foreign nationals to live and work in the United States indefinitely, subject to compliance with various requirements.[13]

Foreign applicants can acquire permanent residency status in four main categories. The easiest and quickest is to be an immediate relative (i.e., spouse, child, or parent) of someone already a lawful permanent resident or U.S. citizen. Along these lines, one roundtable participant told us a story that would be hilarious were it not so pathetically illustrative of the kind of desperation felt by many foreign-born entrepreneurs who want to build their businesses in America: "I've got two good friends that have an early stage start-up. They actually have investment and they've grown from just the two of them to seven people. They're best friends and former college roommates. But one of them is international. They're two straight guys who are now looking into getting married, just to keep the foreign guy in the country."

Other pathways to permanent residency include winners of a so-called "diversity" lottery, political refugees and asylees, and employment sponsorship.

As with H-1B visas, the application process for an employment-based green card is complicated, cumbersome, expensive, and, depending on the classification of the applicant, can take years. For most employment categories, the sponsoring employer must file documents with the Department of Labor certifying that no qualified American workers are available or willing to do the job that the applicant will perform. To document such circumstances, sponsoring employers must provide proof of advertising for the specific position, skill requirements, verification of the prevailing wage, as well as proof of the employer's capacity to pay that wage.

And, as with temporary H-1B visas, green card applicants must remain with their sponsoring employer until they receive their card and for a period of time thereafter, typically at least a year or two. Altogether, depending on the national origin and classification of the applicant, the required attachment to the sponsoring employer can last years.[14] During that time, careers can stagnate. The spouses of applicants are often prohibited from working and in some states cannot obtain a driver's license. Unsure if they will eventually receive their card or be deported, applicants are reluctant to put down roots, buy a house, or start a business.[15]

"A fellow graduate is trying to get a green card and is working for a large organization who is the sponsor of her application," a participant at our Cambridge, Massachusetts, roundtable told us. "So, in effect, she's being held hostage. She has to stay there for however many years it takes to get that green card, because if she quits her job she'd have to start the process all over again. It's indentured servitude. This person is a brilliant IT talent and she's stuck counting her days where she is."

Most problematic, employment-based green cards are currently capped at just 145,000 annually.[16] Moreover, the quota for each foreign country—regardless of population size—is the same, limited to seven percent of the total allotment. High-skilled applicants from large countries like China or India, therefore, can face delays of a decade or longer. Of the 1 million permanent admissions of immigrants into the United States annually, less than 15 percent are allotted based on the economic skills of the applicants. Other countries—including Canada, South Korea, Switzerland, and Spain—issue as much as 80 percent of their visas for economic reasons.[17]

■ ■ ■

Current immigration policy makes little sense from a number of standpoints. On September 13, 2012, the presidents of more than 150 American universities wrote to President Barack Obama and Congressional leaders, calling current immigration policies "a critical threat to America's preeminence as a global center of innovation and prosperity," and urging bipartisan reform.

> After we have trained these future job creators, our anti-quated immigration laws turn them away to work for our competitors in other countries. . . And while we turn away these American-educated, trained, and funded scientists and engineers, there is a growing skills gap across America's industries. One-quarter of U.S. science and engineering firms already report difficulty hiring, and the problem will only worsen: the U.S. is projected to face a shortfall of 230,000 qualified advanced-degree workers in scientific and technical fields by 2018.[18]

A participant in our Austin, Texas, roundtable pointed out that current policy also squanders taxpayer money. "We're putting a lot of money into research at our universities. Most of the money comes out of DARPA[19]—that's where most of our technology has come from for the last 50 years. But . . . a lot of the folks who are creating the technology are then going back to China, or India, or Thailand, or wherever they come from, and are creating technology for those countries. Keep our research dollars here. Keep the *people* here. Give them citizenship if you need to, but don't let non-American citizens run with this research and technology."

Rob Lilleness, president and chief executive officer of software developer Medio Systems in Seattle, Washington, explained how immigration restrictions often force new companies to outsource jobs the firms would rather create at home. "If there's one thing I think is important, it's that we need to open up work visas to get more people to drive our ability to grow, because we compete on a global level. . . We're growing rapidly, our revenues tripled last year, we're profitable. But to keep that growth up, we need to hire talent. . . We have to look at India, or Argentina, or Vietnam, or China because there's not enough H-1B visas so that we can have a bigger supply pool . . . we need to have more math and science talent . . . or we're forced offshore to find the talent."

Worst of all, by maintaining a skilled talent admission process so narrow, complicated, cumbersome, lengthy, uncertain, and expensive, the United States runs an ever-mounting risk that the world's best and brightest will abandon America, choosing instead to apply their talents and ideas, start their businesses, create wealth and jobs, and pay taxes in their home countries or some other host nation more welcoming of the contributions of foreigners.

And, unfortunately, there is already evidence that foreign students and entrepreneurs are, in fact, looking elsewhere. A 2009 survey of more than 1,200 foreign students attending U.S. colleges and universities conducted by researchers at the Ewing Marion Kauffman Foundation found that only 6 percent of Indian students, 10 percent of Chinese students, and 15 percent of European students hoped to stay in the United States permanently. The vast majority—85 percent of Indian and Chinese students, and 72 percent of European students— cited concerns regarding their ability to obtain work visas. Importantly, more than 70 percent of all foreign students polled indicated that they planned to start a new business within the next decade.[20]

"Talk to anyone in the start-up community, and they all say we've started to run out of talent," Vivek Wadhwa, director of research at Duke University's Center for Entrepreneurship and Research Commercialization, told CNBC in October of 2012. Wadhwa, himself an immigrant from India, is the author of *The Immigrant Exodus*. "What you're seeing is less innovation than you might have otherwise seen. Economic growth is being given away. . . Move forward five years and we'll see what we did wrong. We'll start seeing Google-like ideas in other countries."[21]

"Had I known when I came here what I'd have to do to start my business here, I don't know that I would do it again," said Bettina Hein, founder of Pixability, a web-based YouTube marketing software company in Cambridge, Massachusetts. A German national and repeat entrepreneur, Hein started her first company—SVOX, which developed text-to-speech software for car and mobile device applications— in Switzerland. She sold the company in 2011 for $125 million.[22] "It creates so much uncertainty," she continued. "I'm here on an H-1B.

It was extremely hard and painful to do. And extremely expensive—it cost me $5,000. We looked through the different options, but I would have had to invest $500,000 of my own capital if I had gone with one of the E-visas. . . Right now, my visa is running out and they might not renew it. What would I do with the company? I have enough investors now that I could have them all call their Congressman, I guess. But why do people have to resort to such desperate measures just to stay here? Why do I need to start my company and create jobs here? The thing is, I really don't."

Jonathan Hefter, founder of Neverware, a New York–based start-up whose "Neverware Juicebox" speeds up old computers in schools, expressed similar exasperation regarding his struggle to keep skilled colleagues in the country. "We've launched our business, we've just arranged our first round of financing, we're hiring people—and now they have to leave. Their visas require that they go back to their home countries and reapply for another visa or a green card. That could literally take years. Or it might never happen. The insanity of it is that they've been told that if they had some special talent, like being a model or an entertainer— I'm not kidding—they'd have it renewed, no sweat," he said.

Tim Rowe, founder of the Cambridge Innovation Center, captured the essence of the issue. "It seems to me that our immigration policy is built around the notion that we have to protect American jobs," he said. "But we've got it backwards. We're *threatening* the creation of new jobs by preventing these incredibly talented entrepreneurs from overseas from coming here and building their businesses here. We're in a global economy. From one recent study on Silicon Valley, we learned that fully half of all start-ups have a foreign-born person as a founder—the data is there. Let's get this right."

Recent research confirms Rowe's assertion. Numerous studies show that immigrants are more entrepreneurial than native-born Americans.[23] For example, though representing just 13 percent of the U.S. population, immigrants account for nearly 20 percent of small businesses in America and nearly a third of the increase in the number of small businesses between 1990 and 2010. Immigrant women are twice as likely as U.S.-born women to own a business. Immigrant-owned small businesses employed nearly 5 million Americans in 2010 and generated an estimated $776 billion in revenue.[24]

The Partnership for a New American Economy, a bipartisan group of more than 500 business leaders and mayors united in support of immigration reform, has found that more than 40 percent of Fortune 500 companies—including 7 of the 10 most valuable brands in the world—were founded by immigrants or a child of immigrants. These companies employ more than 10 million people worldwide and generate annual revenue of $4.2 trillion.[25]

Most importantly, immigrants launch half of the nation's top start-ups. A study by the National Foundation for American Policy found that of the top 50 venture capital-backed companies in the United States last year, 23 have at least one foreign-born founder, while 37 have at least one immigrant in a major management position.[26] *The Washington Post* recently observed that "in the decade ending in 2005, the founders of half of the firms in Silicon Valley were born overseas."[27]

Immigrants are also more innovative than native-born Americans. A recent study showed that immigrants were involved in more than 75 percent of the nearly 1,500 patents awarded at the nation's top 10 research universities in 2011—and that nearly all the patents were in the fields of science, technology, engineering, and mathematics. In particular, foreign-born innovators contributed to 87 percent of the patents in semiconductor device manufacturing, 84 percent of the patents in information technology, 83 percent of the patents in pulse or digital communications, and 79 percent of the patents in pharmaceutical drugs or drug compounds.[28]

The net result of immigrants' propensity for innovation and entrepreneurship is more American jobs. According to the American Enterprise Institute, immigrants—whether permanent or temporary, high-skill or less-skill—boost employment among Americans. This effect is most pronounced for immigrants with advanced degrees from U.S. universities working in STEM fields. According to the study, over the period 2000 to 2007, each additional group of 100 foreign-born workers with STEM backgrounds was associated with 262 additional American jobs.[29]

"What people don't understand is the leverage effect," said Bettina Hein of Cambridge-based Pixability. "All the other jobs in the companies we start are held by American citizens. If we weren't here, our American colleagues wouldn't have these jobs."

In a speech before the U.S. Chamber of Commerce in September of 2011, New York City Mayor Michael Bloomberg called current U.S. immigration policies "national suicide:"

> We've become the laughingstock of the world with this policy. In China, the government offers tax breaks, cheap loans, and start-up capital to Chinese citizens who are educated overseas and then return to start a business. . . In Israel, the government is spending hundreds of millions of dollars on a program to attract thousands of Israeli ex-pats, particularly scientists, researchers, and doctors, by offering them tax breaks, health insurance, and free tuition for further education.
>
> In Chile, a pilot program for the founders of new technology companies offers start-up capital, free office space, reduced red tape, and access to mentors. And many of our English-speaking competitors—from Canada and the U.K. to Australia and New Zealand—have visa programs designed to attract entrepreneurs to create jobs. All these countries know . . . that there's no chance they'll stay competitive unless they can attract top talent from around the world—and that certainly goes for the United States.[30]

President Obama has also addressed the senselessness of current policy. In a speech in El Paso, Texas, on May 10, 2011, the President stated:

> Immigration reform is an economic imperative. . . Today, we provide students from around the world with visas to get engineering and computer science degrees at our top universities. But our laws discourage them from using those skills to start a business or power a new industry right here in the United States. So instead of training entrepreneurs to create jobs in America, we train them to create jobs for our competition. That makes no sense.
>
> Look at Intel and Google and Yahoo! and eBay—these are great American companies that have created countless jobs and helped us lead the world in high-tech industries. Every one was founded by an immigrant. We don't want the next Intel or Google to be created in China or India. We want those companies and jobs to take root in America.

In his State of the Union address eight months later, the President implored Congress: "Let's at least agree to stop expelling responsible young people who want to staff our labs, start new businesses. . . Send me a law that gives them the chance to earn their citizenship. I will sign it right away."[31]

In response, a number of bills have been introduced in both chambers of Congress with the aim of attracting and retaining the world's best talent. The most meaningful progress to date came in the House of Representatives on November 30, 2012. The STEM Jobs Act, introduced by Rep. Lamar Smith (R-TX), then-chairman of the House Judiciary Committee, would end the "diversity lottery" for green cards and reallocate 55,000 cards for foreign applicants with advanced degrees in STEM fields.[32] After failing to pass the House just a month before, the bill passed 245-139 with 27 Democrats joining all but five Republicans in favor.

Unfortunately, the bill had no chance in the Senate, as most Democrats and the Obama Administration have insisted that any effort to retain foreign talent be part of comprehensive immigration reform that also includes increased enforcement of immigration laws, tighter border security, and a designated pathway to citizenship for undocumented immigrants.[33]

At his first post-election news conference on November 14, 2012, President Obama signaled that comprehensive immigration reform would be an early priority of his second term in office:[34]

> [W]e need to seize the moment. And my expectation is that we get a bill introduced and we begin the process in Congress very soon after my inauguration. . . And when I say comprehensive immigration reform. . . I think it should include a continuation of the strong border security measures that we've taken because we have to secure our borders. I think it should contain serious penalties for companies that are purposely hiring undocumented workers and taking advantage of them. And I do think that there should be a pathway for legal status for those who are living in this country, are not engaged in criminal activity, are here simply to work. . . I am a believer

that if you've got a PhD in physics or computer science who wants to stay here and start a business here, we shouldn't make it harder for him to stay here; we should try to encourage him to contribute to this society. . . And I think that's something that we can get done.[35]

On April 16, 2013, a bipartisan group of Senators known as the "Gang of Eight"—Republicans John McCain (R-AZ), Jeff Flake, (R-AZ), Marco Rubio (R-FL), and Lindsey Graham (R-SC), and Democrats Chuck Schumer (D-NY), Michael Bennet (D-CO), Robert Menendez (D-NJ), Richard Durbin (D-IL)—introduced an 800-page comprehensive immigration reform bill that addressed border security, high-skill immigration, low-skill workers, and a path to citizenship for the estimated 11 million undocumented immigrants currently in the United States. After debating hundreds of offered amendments, the Senate Judiciary Committee approved the bill on May 21, 2013, by a vote of 13 to 5, with Republican Orrin Hatch (R-UT) and gang members Lindsey Graham (R-SC) and Jeff Flake (R-AZ) joining the Committee's Democrats in support of the bill.

On the afternoon of June 27th, following three weeks of floor debate, the full Senate passed the Border Security, Economic Opportunity, and Immigration Modernization Act by a vote of 68 to 32. As of this writing, however, the bill's prospects in the House of Representatives are far from certain.[36]

Policy Recommendations

Despite the clear benefits to U.S. economic growth and job creation, reform of U.S. immigration laws to more effectively attract and retain the world's best talent remains fraught with political complexity and difficulty. Most significantly, the debate has been overshadowed— some would say held hostage—by the imperative of improving border security and the vexing challenge of what to do about 11 million undocumented workers already in the United States, some for many years. Moreover, an underperforming economy and persistently high unemployment continue to stoke fears that higher numbers of skilled immigrants will cost native-born Americans scarce jobs.

As compelling as such concerns may be, they should be substantially allayed by repeated research showing that skilled immigrants contribute to high quality job creation in America, and the reality that other nations are vigorously competing for the same skilled talent.

With these realities in mind, and given the critical importance of immigration reform to new business formation, growth, and job creation as emphasized by our roundtable participants, we recommend the following with the intention of attracting and retaining the world's best talent.

Eliminate the Cap on H-1B Visas

The Senate-passed legislation would raise the annual cap on H-1B visas from 65,000 currently to 110,000. It would also allow for as many as 180,000 visas based on a new formula, the High Skilled Jobs Demand Index, which would consider the number of petitions filed in excess of the cap in the previous year and the unemployment rate in the "management, professional, and related occupations" category of Bureau of Labor Statistics data.[37] If enacted into law, that would certainly be progress.

But why cap such visas at all? By limiting the number of highly skilled foreign workers that U.S. businesses can hire, the cap on H-1B visas is an arbitrary and self-defeating curb on innovation and job creation.

While participating in a technology panel at the Library of Congress in April of 2005, Bill Gates, the chairman and former chief executive of Microsoft, was asked how he would reform U.S. immigration laws. "I'd certainly get rid of the H-1B cap," Gates replied. "The whole idea of the H-1B thing is don't let too many smart people come into the country. It doesn't make sense."[38]

In an address to the Council on Foreign Relations in June of 2011, New York City Mayor Michael Bloomberg agreed:

> Make no mistake about it: If companies can't hire the workers they need here, they will move those operations out of the country. . . . There's lots of west coast companies that now

have offices in Canada because they can't get the engineers into this country. . . [W]e not only lose those jobs, we lose their spending, and we lose their taxes. Again, this makes no sense. We are stabbing ourselves in the back even as our economy is in critical condition. . . We should end these arbitrary limits on high-skilled H–1B visas. Let the marketplace decide.

An analysis by the Technology Policy Institute found that, had H–1B visas not been capped between 2003 and 2007, foreign students who would not have been required to leave the United States after graduation, together with H–1B workers whose visas would not have expired, would have contributed nearly $40 billion to GDP in 2008 alone, and would have paid almost $10 billion in federal income taxes.[39] In a budget-conscious era, common-sense immigration reform offers a means of boosting GDP and federal revenues without spending a dime of taxpayer money.

Award "Graduation" Green Cards

A permanent residency card—or green card—should be automatically awarded to any foreign-born student meeting national security requirements who completes an undergraduate or postgraduate degree in science, technology, engineering, or mathematics. About 60,000 foreign students earn undergraduate and graduate degrees in science and engineering from American universities each year.[40] As previously discussed, most are forced to return home after graduation, taking their U.S.-acquired human capital with them.

Create a "High-Skill Immigrant" Green Card

An additional green card category of at least 50,000 annually should be established to specifically attract top international graduates in STEM fields who meet national security requirements. These preferential green cards should be awarded based on a points system that rewards skills, level of education and training, entrepreneurship, English proficiency, and other key metrics in order to attract applicants with desired economic backgrounds.

Create a Start-Up Visa

Unlike other countries, the United States does not have a visa category explicitly for foreign-born entrepreneurs. "It's the single stupidest policy the U.S. government has around high-tech immigration," Eric Schmidt, executive chairman and former CEO of Google, recently told the *Wall Street Journal*. "These people will create billions of dollars in investment in the economy and provide us with the ability to be world class in every industry."[41]

A special "start-up visa" should be created for foreign-born entrepreneurs meeting national security requirements who want to start a business in the United States and who have secured at least $100,000 in initial funding. Such people would be admitted on a temporary basis, say two years. If by the end of that period their business has been successfully launched, is producing verifiable revenue, and has produced a job for at least two nonfamily members, the temporary visa would be extended by an additional three years. Authentic, demonstrable revenue is important to ensure that sham companies aren't set up to gain entry. If the new business continues to be successful and produce verifiable revenue, and has created jobs for at least five nonfamily members by the end of the initial five-year period, the foreign-born entrepreneur would be granted permanent residency.

Our proposal is similar to legislation introduced in 2010 by former Senators John Kerry (D-MA) and Richard Lugar (R-IN), and to aspects of "The Start-Up Act" proposed by the Ewing Marion Kauffman Foundation in July of 2011.[42] A recent study by the Kauffman Foundation concludes that a start-up visa would create between 500,000 and 1.6 million new American jobs within 10 years.[43]

Our proposal is also similar to provisions of the Start-Up Act 3.0, introduced in February of 2013 by Senators Jerry Moran (R-KS), Mark Warner (D-VA), Chris Coons (D-DE), and Roy Blunt (R-MO)—with two key differences.[44]

First, the Senators' proposed legislation would require prospective recipients of start-up visas to already be in the United States on an H-1B visa or an F-1 student visa. While we applaud the Senators' leadership and support the general thrust of their proposed legislation, we view such criteria as too restrictive. Why limit potential foreign-born entrepreneurs to those already working here or attending a U.S. college or university?

Among the foreign-born founders of U.S. companies who would likely fail to meet the standards of the Start-Up Act 3.0 for potential admission are Steve Chen, the Taiwanese founder of YouTube, who dropped out of the University of Illinois-Urbana Champaign; Elon Musk, the South African co-founder of Tesla Motors and PayPal, who dropped out of the applied physics graduate program at Stanford; and Janus Friis, the Danish co-founder of Skype, who dropped out of high school.

We also note that, had they not been born in the United States, neither Bill Gates, Steve Jobs, nor Mark Zuckerberg would have made the cut—all three dropped out of college to pursue their start-up ideas.[45] In our view, start-up visas should be available to any foreign-born entrepreneur of any academic field or background who meets security and outside funding requirements.

Second, whereas the Start-Up Act 3.0 would limit visas issued to foreign-born entrepreneurs to 75,000, we see no reason to cap the number of immigrant entrepreneurs who want to start their businesses in America and who meet security and outside funding requirements.

In the Start-Up Act 3.0, the Senators do make a major improvement to the previous version of the bill—they expand eligibility to include foreign students in *any* field, not just STEM fields. While STEM graduates are of enormous value to U.S. economic growth, competitiveness, and job creation—which is why we propose awarding such graduates with permanent residency cards upon graduation—they are not the exclusive source of new business ideas.

At an Apple event to unveil the iPad 2 in March of 2011, Steve Jobs declared: "It's in Apple's DNA that technology alone is not enough—it's technology married with liberal arts, married with the humanities, that yields us the result that makes our heart sing."[46]

Indeed, after dropping out of Reed College after just six months, Jobs spent the next 18 months sitting in on various art classes, including a calligraphy class. As he recounted in a commencement address to Stanford's class of 2005:

Reed College at that time offered perhaps the best calligraphy instruction in the country. Throughout the campus every poster, every label on every drawer, was beautifully hand-calligraphed. Because I had dropped out and didn't have to take the normal classes, I decided to take a calligraphy class to learn how to do this. I learned about serif and sans serif typefaces, about varying the amount of space between different letter combinations, about what makes great typography great. It was beautiful, historical, artistically subtle in a way that science can't capture—and I found it fascinating.

[T]en years later, when we were designing the first Macintosh computer, it all came back to me. And we designed it all into the Mac. It was the first computer with beautiful typography. . . If I had never dropped out, I would have never dropped in on that calligraphy class, and personal computers might not have the wonderful typography that they do.

Create CitizenCorps

The challenge of whether and how to construct a pathway toward citizenship for undocumented immigrants is very different from how to attract and retain the world's best talent. It is also the most controversial and politically difficult aspect of the immigration reform debate. But given the political imperative of comprehensive reform, it seems clear that the proposals outlined above depend on the formulation of an effective and politically acceptable means for dealing with the reality of an estimated 11 million undocumented workers in America.[47]

With that in mind, we call attention to an idea we think deserves consideration: creation of a new federal program called CitizenCorps. First proposed by veteran Washington journalist Major Garrett—Chief White House Correspondent for CBS News and Correspondent at Large for the *National Journal*—CitizenCorps would be modeled on AmeriCorps, the federal program created by the National and Community Service Trust Act of 1993 in which participants serve their communities through a network of partnerships with local and national nonprofit groups, and can earn an Education Award of up to $5,500. More than 75,000 individuals serve in AmeriCorps annually, more than 540,000 since 1994.[48]

According to Mr. Garrett's proposal:

> The idea is to use the existing 50-state bureaucracy of AmeriCorps to link undocumented workers with community service projects where they live—to use community service as

a means of accelerating the legalization process. Undocumented residents who volunteer can earn residency/citizenship credits that could shorten their wait for a green card and, ultimately, citizenship. . . AmeriCorps knows the projects that need to be done and could find a ready supply of volunteers under a CitizenCorps model. The projects could be large-scale— refurbishing schools, sprucing up low-income housing, and clearing parks and streams of garbage—to small-bore tasks of mentoring, teaching English, or logging hours at after-school programs . . . A CitizenCorps identification card could be the first rung on a ladder of legal residency and citizenship.[49]

A service-toward-citizenship model offers something for all sides: undocumented workers want a reasonable and sanctioned means of obtaining legal residency or citizenship; Democrats want a credible pathway for undocumented workers from illegal status to citizenship; and Republicans want a solution consistent with the rule of law that is much more than simple amnesty.

CitizenCorps could be part of the answer.

■ ■ ■

Finally, we recently learned of a new start-up that is itself a remarkable testament to human creative genius—and to the abject stupidity of America's current immigration policies. You've heard of start-ups being launched in garages or in dorm rooms? How about on a ship?

Blueseed Company, based in Sunnyvale, California, is a start-up with a unique solution to a big problem. Max Marty, the company's co-founder and chief executive officer, and the son of Cuban immigrants, plans to anchor a decommissioned cruise ship off the coast of California near Silicon Valley to house up to 1,000 foreign-born entrepreneurs who want to start their companies in the United States but haven't been able to obtain visas. Marty told the *Associated Press* that he thought of the idea after hearing international classmates at the University of Miami business school complain about having to leave the country after graduation.[50] The floating office park will anchor in international waters 12 nautical miles southwest of San Francisco Bay—just a ferry ride away from Silicon Valley.

"We're enabling people from all around the world to connect into Silicon Valley," Marty told *Marketplace*, which airs on National Public Radio.[51] "People live and work out there on their start-up for about six to nine months. When they are in the right position and those companies gain a little bit of traction, they look at moving into Silicon Valley itself."

The ship will be equipped with all the high-tech amenities that modern entrepreneurs require and will have the open, employee-friendly feel similar to the corporate campuses of companies like Google and Facebook. According to an early draft of Blueseed's business plan, the company will make money by charging tenants $1,200 a month and by taking a 6 percent stake in the companies it accepts aboard.

The company has reportedly raised over $9 million from investors so far, and hopes to raise $30 million. If all goes according to plan, Blueseed will set sail in the second quarter of 2014.

"The real value for us—and really, the real value for the world—is the value that those companies are going to produce as they grow, as they produce new technologies, and as they create jobs," Marty said.

Chapter 6

"Not All Good Ideas Get Funded Anymore"

S tarting a new business requires money. In the initial days of a start-up, capital needs may be limited to the bare essentials—money to purchase supplies, computers, and other office equipment. Falling costs for computers, software, and other office technologies in recent years, together with the establishment, distributional, and promotional powers of the Internet, have dramatically lowered the cost of getting a new business off the ground. Starting a new business from scratch costs, on average, about $30,000.[1]

But that's just the beginning. As new businesses begin to grow, capital needs multiply. Entrepreneurs need money to pay bills, to move out of the garage or dining room into office space, and, hopefully, to begin paying initial employees. Most importantly, entrepreneurs need capital to further develop their product or service idea, research the marketplace, and develop and implement a strategy for identifying and targeting customers.

Because such costs typically arrive long before the first dollar of revenue, capital and credit are the lifeblood of any new business. Difficulties in accessing sufficient capital and credit at reasonable terms can delay or prevent the launch of a new business, disrupt the further growth and development of an existing business, or even kill an otherwise healthy and viable business.

While securing financing has always been a major challenge for entrepreneurs, our roundtables made clear that circumstances have become significantly more difficult in the wake of the 2008 financial crisis and may account, at least in part, for the declining rate of new business formation. Access to capital difficulties were mentioned by our roundtable participants as much as any other challenge they confront.

"There's a theory that all good ideas eventually get funded," said Joni Cobb, president and chief executive officer of Midwest-based Pipeline, an entrepreneurship fellowship organization for high-growth entrepreneurs. "Well, they don't all get funded anymore."

In this chapter, we examine the various sources of start-up capital, advantages and disadvantages of each, and how and why the recent financial crisis has made securing entrepreneurial capital more difficult.

■ ■ ■

Entrepreneurs have traditionally pursued a variety of financing alternatives, including personal savings, family and friends, home equity, credit cards, bank loans, venture capital, and angel investors:

Personal savings and assets: One's own resources are the easiest and fastest to access. No forms to fill out, no applications to submit, no interest rate to pay or equity stake to give away. Putting one's own money at risk has the additional benefit of clarifying the mind regarding just how confident and passionate an entrepreneur really is about his or her idea. Moreover, other potential sources of funding—family and friends, banks, or outside investors—are more willing to listen to an entrepreneur who has put his own money on the line. Recent business survey data indicate that more than 70 percent of new businesses are launched using the entrepreneur's personal savings or assets.[2] Steve Jobs financed the 1976 launch of Apple in his parents' garage by selling his Volkswagen van.[3]

Family and friends: Other than the entrepreneur herself, the people who know her best—her background, skills, and character—are the most likely to be willing to risk some of their own money to help her pursue her idea.

Home equity: Tapping into the equity in one's home by way of a second mortgage or home equity line of credit (HELOC) is a common route to start-up financing. For many entrepreneurs, like many Americans, their home is their largest asset, and HELOCs can be easier to get than business loans and typically entail lower interest rates. According to Federal Reserve data, home equity debt of small-business-owning households rose by 110 percent between 1998 and 2007, while the home equity debt of households led by those employed by someone else grew by only 46 percent.[4] Sam Walton launched Walmart in 1962 with a loan backed in part by his home.

Personal credit cards: More than half of all new businesses rely on some form of debt financing, and the vast majority of those rely to some degree on credit cards.[5] Credit cards are ideally suited for entrepreneurs in a number of ways. As a form of revolving credit, cards are similar to a line of credit, yet don't require collateral, a business plan, or months waiting for approval. They are generally obtainable with very little paperwork, and credit card companies—unlike other providers of capital—don't care how the money is spent. Cards are accepted virtually everywhere and so are ideal for securing supplies and equipment, and most cards offer cash advances.

Cards also have downsides. Most notably, they are an expensive way to finance a business, with interest rates on personal or business cards commonly set at 15 percent or higher. High interest rates, coupled with the relative ease of obtaining and using cards, means that credit cards can be dangerous for new businesses. A 2009 study by the Ewing Marion Kauffman Foundation estimated that every additional $1,000 in credit card debt increases the probability that a new business will fail by 2.2 percent.[6] Despite these disadvantages, credit cards remain a popular source of financing for entrepreneurs. Larry Page and Sergey Brin launched Google in 1997 with $15,000 generated by maxing out their credit cards.

Banks: Banks can, and occasionally do, serve start-ups, but obtaining initial financing from banks can be difficult for entrepreneurs—and for good reason. New businesses typically lack the assets, collateral, cash flow, and track record that banks look for in order to secure credit. Moreover, while all business lending entails risk, start-ups are particularly risky. More than 20 percent of new businesses fail within the first year, half within the first five years. A 2010 survey of business owners showed that only about 6 percent of new businesses are launched using a personal loan from a bank, and just 3 percent by way of a business loan.[7] Bank credit becomes more easily obtainable once new firms have established consistent revenues or acquire inventories or other assets that can serve as collateral.

Venture capital: Venture capital firms pool money from outside investors (wealthy individuals and institutional investors) and provide larger dollar—generally more than $1 million—early-stage funding for new and rapidly growing companies in exchange for an equity stake in the young company. Virtually synonymous with American entrepreneurship for decades, venture capital has helped finance thousands of successful companies. Since the Internet bust in 2000, however, the number of venture funds, the amount of capital raised and invested, and returns on those investments have plummeted, raising many questions about the industry's future.

Angel investors: Wealthy individuals—many of them successful entrepreneurs themselves—are an increasingly important source of early-stage "seed" funding for entrepreneurs. Known as "angel investors," such individuals invest relatively small amounts, typically between $25,000 and $500,000, in exchange for an equity stake in the new business.[8] Many, particularly those who are current or former entrepreneurs, also provide mentoring to the new businesses they invest in. Jeff Bezos launched Amazon.com in 1995 with $1 million provided by 20 angels who invested $50,000 each.

The range of start-up financing alternatives is itself a testament to the creativity and resourcefulness of American entrepreneurs.

■　■　■

Securing financing has always been a critical challenge for entrepreneurs. But our roundtables made clear that, in the wake of the 2008 financial crisis, access to capital has become a major obstacle to success. For example, the personal savings of many would-be entrepreneurs have been diminished or even depleted due to financial losses, the loss of a job, or stagnant salaries. Family and friends have experienced similar financial setbacks, leaving them with fewer resources to share with entrepreneurs. According to an analysis by the Federal Reserve, the 2008 financial crisis and the economic downturn that followed slashed the median net worth of American households by 40 percent, wiping out nearly two decades of household wealth accumulation.[9]

Meanwhile, millions of Americans, including many would-be entrepreneurs, have had their credit cards cancelled or credit limits cut as many issuers have reduced exposures, limiting or eliminating a traditional source of start-up capital.[10] Total outstanding credit card debt has dropped 17 percent since 2008.[11]

Following the collapse of the U.S. housing market, most Americans have far less equity in their homes—if any. According to the Federal Reserve, the 30 to 40 percent drop in home prices nationwide between 2006 and 2011 destroyed more than $7 trillion in home equity wealth. Eleven million homeowners—more than one in five, and nearly half of homeowners under 40—owe more on their mortgage than their home is currently worth, according to mortgage data firm CoreLogic.[12] In aggregate, American homeowners currently owe $715 billion more than their homes are actually worth.[13] Moody's Analytics has estimated that home equity borrowing by small business owners fell from about $75 billion in 2006 to just $20 billion in 2012.[14]

"We started from a home equity line, and that HELOC now sits like this dark entity in our lives," Kim Wills, chief financial officer of Richmond, Virginia-based Milestone Counseling Services, told us. "If we had found sufficient funding somewhere else . . . that would have helped us along. It's a challenge for someone just trying to keep her doors open."

Brett Coffee, general counsel at Computer Systems Center Inc., an information systems integration and hardware development firm in Springfield, Virginia, explained another way the plunge in home equity is undermining job creation: "I can't tell you how many entrepreneurs have told me that the seizing up of the housing market has affected their ability to tap into their houses for capital to start businesses. But it's also about workers not being able to move to where the jobs are. It's absolutely critical. I hear it all across the country. There are people out of work who can't afford to move because they can't sell their house, can't afford to take the jobs where they are, and they're just stuck."

■ ■ ■

Many roundtable participants across the country expressed frustration with banks, both large and small. Complaints generally fell into two principal categories, the most common and fundamental of which is that many banks simply won't lend to new businesses.

"The banks wouldn't talk to me because I'm a start-up," said Sharon Delay, founder and president of Adjunct Solutions in Westerville, Ohio, a niche staffing agency that places adjunct faculty in schools, colleges, and universities. "They wouldn't even look beyond the first couple of pages. I'm a start-up—I'm risky. There's absolutely nothing to benchmark it to, so I'm an unknown. It's too scary."

As mentioned above, start-ups typically lack the assets, collateral, and track record that banks look for in order to secure credit, and the reliable cash flow to service the loan. And following severe losses sustained during the recent financial crisis, and confronted with the risks associated with a still-fragile economy and much higher capital requirements, many banks have tightened lending standards and raised terms, making bank credit even more difficult for entrepreneurs to obtain.

Nita Black, managing partner at MAP Momentum, a management consulting firm serving women- and minority-owned businesses in Memphis, Tennessee, and a former loan work-out officer at a local bank, explained at our Memphis roundtable the dilemma from the banks' perspective: "Start-ups—nobody wants to take that risk because it's like Jell-O. It's like lending to Jell-O. It disappears and then you can't find it. . . It's almost impossible for a company in the early stages of commercialization, because you don't have the operating history yet. Banks check boxes, they do their tests and credit scores, and these new companies fail miserably because they don't have the history."

"Who has a history?" asked an exasperated Tony McGee, who launched HNM Enterprises, an Orlando, Florida–based freight logistics and warehousing company, in 2004 following an 11-year career in the National Football League. "A lot of us newbies in terms of being a business owner just don't have the history. And when you're a new business . . . your credit history isn't going to be representative of the business you might become. That's been the hardest thing. I played in the NFL, so I've had my savings to tap. But as a small business owner, I'm asking myself—if I hadn't had a little nest egg, how would I deal with that? And even as I move forward, my wife keeps looking at me and asking how long I'll have to keep tapping our savings until payables and receivables catch up to each other. . . I've spoken to the banks, but I think from their perspective, if you can absolutely prove that you absolutely don't need the money, then you can get it."

"The banks really suck at helping start-ups," said Bryan Janeczko, founder of New York–based Wicked Start, a web-based platform to help entrepreneurs plan, fund, and launch new businesses. "Banks are in the business of minimizing risk, so I think it's an antiquated model for us. I believe that a lot more could be done by banks to really foster start-ups and think about that particular model in a different way."

We agree. For some ideas regarding what banks and other financial institutions can do to support start-ups and entrepreneurship, see the box beginning on page 104.

Another bank-related challenge reported by a number of our entrepreneurs is sudden changes to credit terms, or the freezing or elimination of credit lines.

"I had my credit line frozen a couple of years back, and being a manufacturer, you live and breathe by your credit line," Sheryl Batchelder, founder and chief executive officer of NIS Print in Orlando, Florida, told us. Batchelder was also president of the Orlando chapter of the National Association of Women Business Owners in 2011. "So, I've taken personal funds and put them into the business. That's really scary, but you do what you have to do to keep your business afloat. . . Entrepreneurs' entire lives are based on taking risks, but banks want absolutely no risk themselves."

Kirsten Dermer, chief executive officer of Spohn Ranch Inc., a Los Angeles–based designer and builder of municipal skateboard parks, and president of the Entrepreneurs Organization in Los Angeles, told a similar story. "Our main challenge is access to capital because we're growing pretty dramatically. We're on track to definitely double and possibly triple revenues over last year. But we had our credit line pulled two years ago by our bank. We had always paid on time, always within terms. And then, basically, they just suddenly decided they wanted their money back—immediately. They needed it because they made all these bad mortgage loans, and now I'm suddenly in the workout group because I needed some time to pay back money that I was told had to come back instantly. It's definitely made me shy away from ever working with banks again. Who can build a business when the bank can decide at any time 'I need the money back?' That's no way to plan for the future."

In a speech on new businesses financing in November of 2011, Dennis Lockhart, President of the Federal Reserve Bank of Atlanta, addressed the disconnect between commercial banks and start-ups:

> [B]anks are not natural financial backers of a new business. . . The data showing the incidence of failure among startups reinforces this point. . . The more reasonable domain for banks is loans of moderate risk to more established businesses that can demonstrate a track record. Because banks make loans using mostly depositors' money, they have to be right in their credit decisions virtually all the time.[15]

The mission of the Small Business Administration (SBA) is to help small businesses obtain bank credit by guaranteeing a portion of loans. But many of our roundtable participants reported that SBA paperwork, requirements, and restrictions simply don't work for entrepreneurs.

Nancy Simmons, president of AERO Industries in Orlando, Florida, told us: "I launched my business with an SBA-backed loan and it tied my hands so much that I paid it off in two years. I couldn't move my business forward. They told me 'we own all your accounts receivables.' I tried to work within their regulatory requirements and it was unsuccessful. I pulled all the cash out of my business and paid off the loan, just to get them off my back and out of my way."

Brad Silver, chief executive officer of Quire, a Memphis, Tennessee–based healthcare analytics company, explained how the SBA's focus on asset-based collateral simply doesn't work for most information technology companies. "SBA is so tied up in asset-based lending and loan guarantees backed by inventory or real estate. I'm not really an asset-based, inventory-based business, right? Maybe I could get an SBA loan or guarantee to build a building or put in some factory equipment. But getting some working capital or a line of credit to chase the market? Not there."

"For the smallest businesses—less than 10 employees—the SBA is broken," said Jerry Ross, Executive Director of the National Entrepreneurial Center in Orlando, Florida. "It usually takes twice as long to deal with the SBA and costs twice as much, if they consider funding the company at all. . . We met with a member of Congress after the 2009 stimulus and told her that the stimulus money isn't making it to small businesses. And her staff said, 'Yes it is, we swear it is.' And we said, no, actually it's not. And so we hosted her and her staff, along with with seven banks and seven entrepreneurs, and the folks here that coach new businesses. And the banks said, 'If we make the loans the regulators show up and punish us for it and we have to call a credit line. We don't have the regulations from the SBA that we need to avoid the classification of the loan.' . . So it all comes back to the SBA. . . There's this hope that the money is going to come, that you're going to get the loan, that they're going to meet you where you are . . . but the cavalry never arrived. It stopped somewhere at the SBA."

■ ■ ■

Read any recent analysis of the venture capital industry and you are likely to encounter terms like "inflection point," "paradigm shift," and even "broken." After decades of success and a spectacular crescendo during the 1990s, the venture capital industry experienced a virtual collapse in the early 2000s, and then, following something of a recovery, the devastating impact of the financial crisis. Though circumstances have improved since 2009, venture capital continues to face a number of significant challenges. For entrepreneurs, the net effect of those challenges is a venture industry whose appetite for risk has diminished significantly—along with the volume of venture financing itself.[16]

"One of the big issues we see now is that new companies get started—and that's hard enough—but then getting to the next level is really tough because the banks aren't lending to start-ups and venture capital is often not available," Ken Woody told us at our Memphis, Tennessee, roundtable. Woody is president of Innova Memphis, Inc., a seed and early-stage venture firm focused on high-growth companies in bioscience, technology, and healthcare technology. "It's just a simple fact," he said. "It's a very big issue and it needs fixing."

Venture capital firms are long-term investors that provide early-stage funding to new and rapidly growing companies in exchange for an equity stake in the company. Venture firms raise investment capital from outside investors—wealthy individuals, pension funds, insurance companies, university endowments, and foundations—referred to as "limited partners," while the fund professionals who make and manage the investments are called "general partners." Venture firms also assist in the management and professionalization of the young companies in which they invest, typically taking seats on the board. Investment capital is recovered and returns realized when the new firms either go public—that is, issue shares in the company by way of an initial public offering (IPO)—or are bought by another company, transactions referred to as "exits" or "liquidity events."

Virtually synonymous with American entrepreneurship for decades, venture capital has helped finance thousands of successful companies, including such marquee names as Intel, Federal Express, Apple, Microsoft, Google, Cisco, Home Depot, and Starbucks.[17] While this track record speaks for itself, it also tends to overstate the importance of venture capital. Of the hundreds of thousands of new businesses launched annually, less than 1 percent ever receives venture financing. A recent analysis of *Inc.* magazine's annual list of the 500 fastest growing companies over 10 years—900 companies over the period 1997 to 2007—found that just 16 percent had received venture funding.[18] Still, being a principal source of financing for nearly a fifth of America's fastest growing companies makes venture capital a vital resource to new business formation and job creation.

Venture investing is also risky business. According to the National Venture Capital Association (NVCA), 40 percent of venture-backed companies fail, another 40 percent generate only moderate returns, and less than 20 percent produce high returns. Shikhar Ghosh, a successful technology entrepreneur and senior lecturer at Harvard Business School, has shown that as much as 95 percent of venture-backed start-ups fail to deliver expected returns.[19] Even before the 2008 financial crisis, venture capital had suffered a stunning reversal of fortune. According to many industry observers, venture capital became a victim of its own success.

Most industry historians cite the 1946 formation of the American Research & Development Corporation in Boston as the official launch of the venture capital industry. ARDC was founded by Georges Doriot, a professor of industrial administration at Harvard Business School and considered the "father of venture capital."[20] But the industry developed principally alongside the technology industry in the Silicon Valley area south of San Francisco in the late 1950s. In the early years, most limited partners were wealthy individuals and funds were comparatively small. Prior to 1980, the total amount of new money raised annually by the industry averaged around $200 million.[21] For example, when prominent venture pioneer William H. Draper III joined Franklin P. "Pitch" Johnson to form Draper & Johnson Investment Company in Palo Alto, California, in 1962, the firm launched with just $450,000.[22]

Over time that changed, particularly after the Department of Labor liberalized rules in 1979 to allow pension funds to make venture investments. By the mid-1990s, individual funds were able to raise hundreds of millions of dollars.

This remarkable growth was driven by profitability. Over the period 1980 to 1997, venture capital consistently outperformed the S&P 500 on a capital-weighted basis,[23] with the best funds generating quarterly returns as high as 20 percent or more.[24] The Internet boom and the prospect of outsized returns produced a tidal wave of venture capital—a wave that crested in 2000, with the industry raising more than $100 billion in new money, up 2,400 percent from 1990 levels.

But as funds swelled in number and size, industry critics say, general partners became less focused, less disciplined, and, ultimately, less effective. Flush with cash, many funds became less discriminating with regard to their investments, and, spread too thin, less active in helping to nurture the developing companies in which they invested.[25] Exacerbating the deterioration was the industry's standard "2-and-20" compensation structure—a 2 percent management fee on committed capital plus 20 percent of any realized profits—that incentivized the

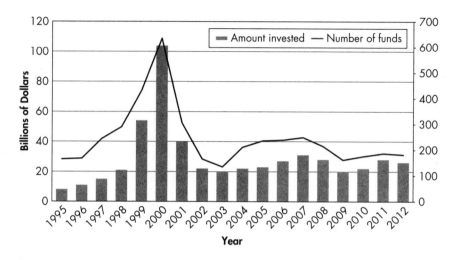

Figure 6.1　Venture Funds and Capital Invested
SOURCE: National Venture Capital Association.

creation of larger funds and enabled general partners to earn high fee-based income regardless of investment performance.[26]

After riding the Internet bubble to all-time highs in terms of the number of active funds, total amounts of capital raised and invested, and multi-year returns, the industry was devastated by the dot-com bust. As Figure 6.1 shows, between 2000 and 2002, the number of active funds dropped by half, while the amount of new money raised, and the amount of money invested, plunged by 95 percent and 80 percent respectively.[27]

Another significant challenge emerged in 2002 with the passage of the Sarbanes-Oxley Act (SOX) following a series of financial reporting scandals involving companies such as Enron, Tyco, and WorldCom. Among other new requirements intended to enhance the quality and reliability of reported financial data, section 404 of SOX requires publicly traded companies to disclose the findings of an external audit of the scope, adequacy, and effectiveness of the company's internal control structure and procedures for financial reporting. Though just 170 words in length, section 404 has accounted for the majority of the cost of complying with SOX, estimated to be well over $1 million per company annually.[28]

The substantial cost and burden of complying with SOX has amounted to a major obstacle for many new and rapidly growing companies hoping to access the capital markets to secure the substantial financing they need to continue growing and creating jobs. In a recent interview, Steve Case, co-founder and former chief executive of America Online, said: "When AOL went public 20 years ago, we only raised $10 million. Nobody could do that now because of the cost of Sarbanes-Oxley."[29]

In a 2007 report, New York City Mayor Michael Bloomberg and Senator Charles Schumer (D–NY) warned:

> [O]ur regulatory framework is a thicket of complicated rules, rather than a streamlined set of commonly understood principles, as is the case in the United Kingdom and elsewhere. The flawed implementation of the 2002 Sarbanes-Oxley Act (SOX), which produced far heavier costs than expected, has only aggravated the situation . . . if we do nothing, within 10 years, while we will remain a leading regional financial center, we will no longer be the financial capital of the world."[30]

"As a technology entrepreneur, when I started my career I had the aspiration of going public," said Bettina Hein of Cambridge, Massachusetts–based Pixability. "Sometimes I think about that. I have friends who have, and mentors who have. But it's so onerous now I don't know if I want that. It's what I aspired to as an entrepreneur—you know, ringing the opening bell at the stock exchange—but it's kind of been taken away. The reality is that when I hear how onerous Sarbanes-Oxley is, I'm thinking that's not something I want to do right now."

According to several of our entrepreneurs, other factors relating to stock market structure and regulation—changes intended to protect investors and reduce costs—have also complicated the prospects for venture capital. Perhaps most significantly, following the decimalization of stock prices in 2001, tick sizes—the minimum increment by which a stock's price can change when shares are bought or sold—have been slashed.[31] Inadequate tick sizes, according to many industry analysts, produce trading revenue for investment banks that is insufficient to support the research and sales force needed to promote small capitalization stocks, and to attract the liquidity necessary to support the shares of small companies once they go public.[32]

"Trading in small cap stocks has been decimated," Steve O'Leary told us. O'Leary is co-founder and managing director of Aeris Partners, a Cambridge, Massachusetts–headquartered M&A advisory firm serving high-growth software, digital, media, and business information companies. "It's just not profitable anymore. And the result is a huge change in the number of small companies going public since the mid-1990s. Think about Intel, which went public in 1971 with about a $50 million market valuation. Like Intel, many of the pre-decimalization IPOs, even in the 1990s, had $100 million market caps or less. Could a $30, $40, or $50 million company go public today? That would be a rare event. Restoring the spreads on trading is a key element in making the small cap IPO market profitable. Decent spreads enable smaller underwriting firms to do smaller deals. It keeps them issuing research, supporting trading activity, and finding growth investors after new companies go public."

Other market experts agree. In March of 2011, just a month before we conducted our first roundtable, the Treasury Department sponsored a conference entitled *Access to Capital: Fostering Growth and Innovation for Small Companies*. Following that conference, a number of the participants formed the "IPO Task Force" to examine IPO-related challenges to emerging growth companies and to develop recommendations to address those challenges.[33] The Task Force produced a report, many of the recommendations of which became the substance of the JOBS Act of 2012.[34] In its report, the Task Force stated:

> In the new, low-cost, frictionless environment promulgated by electronic trading and decimalization, investment banks now generate revenue primarily by executing a high volume of low-priced trades meant to capitalize on short-term changes in the price of highly liquid, very large-cap stocks . . . by contrast, emerging growth stocks do not fit this model. They begin their "public" lives with modest liquidity levels and small floats. . . . Due to this relative lack of liquidity and float, emerging growth companies simply don't produce enough trading volume to make money for the investment bank's trading desk and, therefore, the investment bank as a whole. This undermines the incentive for the investment banks to underwrite and make markets for newly public companies.

The Task Force report also observed that the impact of decimalization on the economics of small company IPOs has been exacerbated by the Global Analyst Research Settlement, an agreement reached in 2003 between the securities industry and then–New York Attorney General Elliot Spitzer, which prohibited compensating research analysts with revenue generated from investment banking.[35] The settlement, according to the IPO Task Force, reduced analyst coverage of smaller capitalization companies, leading to diminished visibility and market interest.

In testimony before Congress last year, David Weild, former vice chairman of NASDAQ, noted that, between 1991 and 1997, nearly 3,000 small companies went public with deals valued at less than $50 million, representing 80 percent of all IPOs in the United States over the period. Between 2001 and 2007—a period over which tick sizes were slashed by 95 percent—small company IPOs fell by 92 percent and currently represent only 20 percent of total U.S. IPOs. "We now have a stock market that covers the cost of trade-execution only," Weild testified.[36]

The combined effect of the dot-com bust, SOX, and the market structure issues discussed above is dramatically fewer IPOs, as young companies either choose to remain private or wait much longer before going public. As Figure 6.2 shows, initial public offerings by venture-backed companies plunged from 270 in 1999 to just 23 in 2003.

The number of IPOs recovered somewhat between 2004 and 2007, averaging about 60 each year. But plunging stock prices during the 2008 financial crisis slashed IPOs to single digits in 2008 and 2009. In the second quarter of 2008—for the first time in 30 years—not a single venture-backed company went public. Only six companies went public the entire year.

Because venture funds get their investment capital back and realize returns only when financed companies go public or are bought by other firms, the collapse in the number of IPOs made venture investments less liquid, and reasonable returns far less certain. A 2009 poll of more than 100 venture capital executives found that a majority, 53 percent, agreed that the industry is "broken." Asked which industry trends they were most worried about, 93 percent of respondents indicated uncertainty regarding exit markets.[37] As one prominent VC explained to the *New York Times*: "There is no venture industry if there is no IPO market."[38]

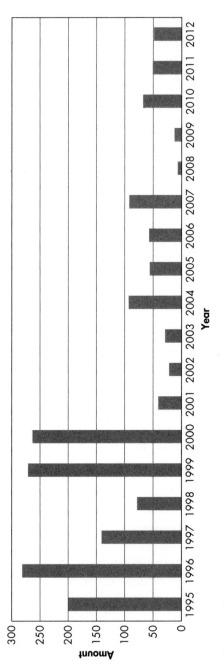

Figure 6.2 Annual IPOs

Source: National Venture Capital Association.

By 2010, the amount of venture capital invested in new companies had fallen nearly 80 percent from the peak in 2000, and the 10-year average return for venture funds had fallen to *negative* 4.6 percent—the first negative 10-year return in industry history.[39]

While certainly bad for venture capitalists and their investors, such circumstances are even more worrisome for the companies who depend on them. When capital is tied up in existing investments for longer periods, and producing lower or even no returns, the recycling of that capital into newer companies is delayed or even eliminated, sending ripple effects through the entrepreneurial ecosystem. And without the reasonable prospect of going public, new businesses, often unable to offer competitive initial salaries, can't use stock options to attract talented employees. As discussed in Chapter 4, stock options become particularly critical in attracting more experienced personnel needed to successfully scale a new company—people already in senior positions and enjoying lucrative careers at more established companies.

Mark Heesen, president of the National Venture Capital Association, called the 2008 collapse in IPOs "a crisis for the start-up community."[40] According to NVCA, the average time between initial venture investment in a new company and venture-backed IPO more than doubled between 1999 and 2009, from less than five to 10 years. "Limited partners are saying, 'Don't call me,'" Heesen commented at the time, "and general partners are saying to entrepreneurs, 'We're not funding anything.' Caution is not normally a word in venture capitalists' vocabulary, but it's being used today."[41]

The impact of venture's decline appears to vary from region to region, as some cities have more sophisticated and active financing networks than others. The Boston/Cambridge area, for example, enjoys one of the most developed and diverse entrepreneurial financing networks in the nation, as angel investors and venture capital firms have innovated to accommodate the needs of the new technologies and businesses regularly generated by the area's many research universities.[42]

Other regions of the country are not so fortunate. "I'm coming from high-tech, so banks are not a classic source of funding until a company is fairly far along," said Shannon Blake Gans, co-founder and chief executive officer of New Deal Studios, Inc., a full-service visual effects production facility in Los Angeles, California. "And what we're seeing is that venture capital, which is the classic source of funding for companies like us, is just not there. . . Since the crash in 2008, investors in the funds have gotten really skittish. They took a big hit, so for all of 2009 there was basically no venture capital at all. And since then, it's either very small amounts, or, in companies much farther along, much more advanced."

We heard about similar challenges at our Richmond, Virginia, roundtable. "My office commercializes inventions that are developed at the university," said Ivelina Metcheva, executive director of the technology transfer office at Virginia Commonwealth University. "We license with existing companies and spin off new businesses. . . If you're a start-up, one of the problems in this region is a lack of early-stage financing. Real seed financing. Most VCs are looking at more mature companies. . . In the last five years we've started eight companies—and most of them went elsewhere, only two in Virginia. So we really need a base of entrepreneurs here, or a way to attract them. And the way to attract them is to have funding for their companies."

Fewer IPOs, and new companies waiting much longer to go public, also reduce the opportunity for millions of investors to share in the wealth created by high-growth companies, concentrating vast wealth in the hands of fewer people. As Steve O'Leary of Aeris Partners pointed out, Intel's IPO in October of 1971, just two years after the company's founding, issued 350,000 shares at a price of $23.50, raising just $8 million, or $44 million in today's dollars. Intel's market capitalization has since grown to more than $120 billion, creating wealth for millions of employees and investors. By contrast, Facebook's IPO in May of 2012— eight years after the company's founding—issued 421 million shares, raising $16 billion and creating vast fortunes for comparatively few insiders.[43]

Companies waiting longer to go public can also mean fewer successful IPOs. Many more mature companies taken public in recent years have seen the value of their shares fall dramatically after the IPO. The share prices of two-thirds of the companies taken public in 2011, and 40 percent of those taken public in 2012, ended the year trading lower than their initial offering price.[44] Perhaps the most dramatic recent example is Facebook, whose IPO was probably the most anticipated since Google's in 2004. Priced at $38 when trading began on May 17, 2012, the stock dropped 54 percent by early September.

Most importantly, fewer IPOs mean fewer jobs. From the standpoint of job creation, IPOs are far more important than the sale of new companies to larger companies. When purchased by existing companies, new firms are absorbed into the culture and operation of the purchasing firms, and typically don't grow or create jobs at rates that independent companies do. In fact, mergers often result in job cuts. Many buyouts of new firms are done for defensive reasons, to head off or even shut down a competitive threat.

"I find that many of the new companies today are being built really well," one venture capital executive told us. "They have great cultures and the quality of people that can really take them a long way. But, unfortunately, the venture capitalists are constrained today. They have a limited window to create value and realize a return. Some of these companies could be billion-dollar companies in 10 years, but they're too small to go public for the foreseeable window for the venture investors, and so guess what happens? I think we lose a lot by helping to put these great cultural organisms together brick by brick, only to destroy them by ultimately integrating them into a larger company."[45]

"A structurally compromised IPO market leaves a lot of shareholder return, economic growth, and job formation on the table," David Weild, former vice chairman of NASDAQ, wrote in 2008. "Big corporations are eating our young as they starve for capital before they have the opportunity to reach adulthood. Their true potential will never be known."[46]

By contrast, following the issuance of shares to the public, young companies are flush with cash to buy equipment, research potential markets, and develop and launch new products—all of which requires additional staff. Over the past four decades, more than 90 percent of the jobs created by rapidly growing new companies were created after the companies went public.[47] According to research by audit and tax consulting firm Grant Thornton, the decline in IPOs since the late 1990s has cost the U.S. economy between 10 and 20 million new jobs.[48]

Conditions for venture capital have improved since 2009, with 68 venture-backed companies going public in 2010, 51 in 2011, and 49 in 2012—but the three-year trend is down. Initial IPO filings with the SEC as of late-2012 suggested the downward trend would likely continue in 2013,[49] but activity in the first half of the year has been more encouraging.[50] Still, annual IPOs remain only a fraction of those in previous years, even before the dramatic increase in the mid- to late-1990s. Between 1990 and 1994, an average of 160 companies went public annually, three times the current rate.

According to most industry insiders and observers, venture capital continues to work through a period of consolidation and reorientation that, in the end, will leave far fewer, better firms raising and investing less money, and focused on fewer, later-stage deals.[51] At least one prominent VC, Matt McCall of New World Ventures, has argued that for venture capital to produce returns sufficient to compensate investors for risk and years of illiquidity, no more than $10 billion to $15 billion should be invested annually.[52]

The industry has a long way to go. Venture funds invested $26.5 billion in 2012, and, over the past 15 years of poor performance, have continued to invest between $25 billion and $30 billion annually—about what was invested *in total* between 1985 and 1995.

"The venture capital asset class does not scale," prominent New York–based venture capitalist Fred Wilson wrote in a 2009 blog post. "You cannot invest $25 billion per year and generate the kinds of returns investors seek from the asset class. . . I think 'back to the future' is the answer. . . Less capital in the asset class, smaller fund sizes, smaller partnerships, smaller deals, and smaller exits. The math works as long as you don't put too many zeros on the end of the numbers you are working with."[53]

Other insiders worry about the impact of a smaller, more risk-averse industry. "What's the long-term impact of that?" asked Geoff Mamlet, a principal at New Atlantic Ventures in Boston, Masachusetts, and a participant in our Cambridge roundtable. "You're already seeing the beginning of that impact. The Washington, DC, market, for example, currently has only three or four early-stage venture funds writing checks. So you're already seeing a market that had been much more vibrant drying up."

With the personal resources of many would-be entrepreneurs depleted, home equity slashed, banks focused on lending to more established businesses, and a diminished venture capital industry increasingly targeting less risky, later-stage start-ups, "angel" investors—wealthy individuals who invest in young promising companies—have emerged as a critical source of funding for start-ups.[54] According to the Center for Venture Research (CVR), which has monitored and analyzed the angel market since 1980, there are currently more than 300,000 active angel investors in the United States.

In recent years angel investing has also become more organized, with more angels participating in groups. Such groups allow angels to conduct more rigorous analysis of potential ventures, and, occasionally, to spread risk by syndicating investments.[55] They also help entrepreneurs identify and connect with active angel investors. According to the Angel Capital Association, the number of angel groups across the country has tripled since 1999 to more than 350.

In a number of ways, angel investors are similar to venture capitalists. Like VCs, angels invest in new, high potential companies in exchange for an equity stake in the new business. Many angel investors—particularly those who are current or former entrepreneurs—also provide advice, mentoring, and other support to the management team of the new businesses they invest in. As with venture capital, angel capital is recovered and returns realized when financed firms either go public or are bought by another company. And, like venture investing, angel investing is risky. According to a 2007 analysis of angel capital returns, more than half of angel investments lose money and just 7 percent account for 75 percent of total returns.[56]

Angel investors also differ from venture capitalists in significant ways. For example, unlike VCs, who invest institutionally-raised capital in amounts of $1 million or more, angels invest their own money, typically in amounts between $25,000 and $500,000. Despite smaller individual investments, aggregate angel capital rivals that of venture capital. In 2011, angels invested $23 billion in more than 66,000 new companies, while venture firms invested $28 billion in 3,800 companies. For every new company that receives venture capital, nearly 20 others receive angel capital.

Perhaps most importantly, whereas venture capital is typically invested during a later growth phase after initial financing has helped create a viable company, angel investors have emerged as the principal source of outside "seed" and early-stage funding, after entrepreneurs have exhausted their own resources and those of family and friends.[57] Of the approximately 45,000 new companies that received outside seed-stage funding in 2012, 97 percent were funded by angel investors, who provided 80 percent of the total seed capital committed by outside investors.[58]

In this way, angel investors and venture capital funds complement each other in the financing pipeline for new companies. Angel investors provide critical seed financing for new companies, while venture funds—at least ideally—provide follow-on financing that fuels the company's further development and accelerates its growth. Unfortunately, as venture capital funds have become more risk averse, focusing on more developed companies, the financing necessary to bridge young companies from the start-up stage to the early expansion stage is increasingly difficult to get. A recent study of more than 4,000 companies that secured seed investments since 2009 found that more than a quarter have or will fail to secure follow-on financing from venture funds, generating losses for angel investors of $1 billion.[59]

"Support and incentives for early-stage investors is key, along with education for angels," said Margo Shiroyama, executive director of Northwest Energy Angels and a participant in our Seattle, Washington, roundtable. "In the Seattle area we have several industry-targeted angel groups. One focused on medical device and technology companies, others focused on IT software and life science companies, and then our group, which is focused on clean technology. And the issues and challenges for those industries are all different. . . Our members invest independently, but they go through the due diligence process as a group when they identify a company that they might want to invest in. So the groups support our members. We also provide roundtables for investors to help them manage their existing portfolios—understanding how to work with the companies they've invested in, provide the best support, and contribute to their growth—which is probably just as important as looking at new opportunities."

Despite the growing importance and rigor of angel investing, capital provided by angel investors also fell dramatically in the wake of the financial crisis, as wealthy individuals, like everyone else, sustained significant financial losses.[60] According to CVR, capital committed by angel investors fell 32 percent, from $26 billion to $17.6 billion, between 2007 and 2009. Over the same period, the average investment also fell by a third, as investors' risk appetite diminished.

"The recent turmoil in financial markets has scared off a lot of angel investors and reduced the number of exits—either IPOs or buyouts in recent years—which makes the circumstances for financing new start-ups even more difficult," Hall Martin, director of the Austin Entrepreneur Network, told us.

CVR data also revealed that as angels reduced their overall commitments following financial crisis losses, they also shifted their reduced investing away from seed-stage funding to less risky, later-stage companies. Commenting on this worrisome trend, CVR director Jeffry Sohl warned in October of 2010:

> Historically angels have been the major source of seed and start-up capital for entrepreneurs and this declining interest in seed and start-up capital represents a significant change in the angel market. Without a reversal of this trend in the near future, the dearth of seed and start-up capital may approach a critical stage, deepening the capital gap and impeding both new venture formation and job creation."[61]

Karen Wilson, vice president for business development at the Intego Group in Lake Mary, Florida, explained at our Orlando roundtable just how stark the change had been. "I was recently with a start-up company and we were looking for capital. . . I had another company 10 years ago and raised $5 million by myself in a year and a half. I was not a professional fundraiser, but it wasn't very hard, really. My first investment was $300,000. I made a pitch to a group of angel investors and got the money. Today, those same angel groups have dried up. Winter Park, which is a wealthy area here in town, had a large angel group of about 45 members, and they've disbanded. And the last two years that they were technically operating, they made no investments. They'd hear pitches, but then say, 'Thanks a lot, goodbye.' I've heard the same thing has happened in Naples. . . I looked very aggressively for our company—and I'm pretty good at looking—but it's just not in central Florida anymore."

Brad Silver of Memphis, Tennessee–based Quire agreed. "The universal theme is an overall reduction in the appetite for risk. Whether it's a bank, a venture capital firm, or an angel investor . . . the reduced appetite for risk is pervasive. The psychology is 'we got clobbered,' so it takes a while to get over that. And one of the most acute areas you see that is the angels. A lot of high-net-worth people, who had a lot of risk capital in play, all of a sudden are worried about lifestyle issues. How do I keep that condo in Vail or the house at the beach? So they're cutting back on everything that doesn't support those kinds of things. And that pulls a ton of risk capital out of the pipeline. I've heard it from a lot of other entrepreneurs who are trying to raise capital."

The angel investor market has recovered significantly since 2009, with total capital invested, the average size of commitments, and the number of active investors all increasing. Still, total investments by angels in 2012 remained down 12 percent from pre-recession highs, with the size of the average investment down 25 percent, and the number of angels actively investing down 16 percent from 2011.[62] Angel investors have also become more cautious, according to our participating entrepreneurs, demanding more information, more research, and more advanced prototypes before investing.[63]

Policy Recommendations

The Jumpstart Our Business Start-ups ("JOBS") Act was signed into law by President Obama in April of 2012 and is specifically intended to enhance new companies' access to capital.[64] Among other provisions, the Act lowers the regulatory burdens and costs of going public for "emerging growth companies" (EGCs), defined as companies with less than $1 billion in revenue and a market capitalization of less than $700 million. Among the regulatory relief provisions, EGCs planning to go public will be permitted to submit regulatory disclosures to the SEC confidentially, in order to protect sensitive proprietary information. The Act also provides a so-called "on-ramp" to compliance with section 404 of SOX by exempting EGCs for up to five years.[65] According to Kate Mitchell, co-founder and managing director of Scale Venture Partners, and chairman of the IPO Task Force, the recommendations from which served as the basis of the JOBS Act, the regulatory relief provided by the Act will reduce the average cost of going public, currently about $2.5 million, by 30 to 50 percent.[66]

Perhaps the most significant, and controversial, aspect of the Act is that it permits entrepreneurs, without registering with the SEC, to leverage their online presence and contact networks to raise up to $1 million in small investments from unaccredited investors[67] collected by way of online "crowdfunding" platforms. To implement the crowd-funding provisions, the SEC must amend restrictions regarding "general solicitation"—public communications regarding upcoming stock offerings—and draft other regulations pertaining to online fundraising sites, as well as new investor protection rules.

The Act set a deadline of year-end 2012 for the new rules, but concern within the SEC that crowdfunding could become an opportunity for investor abuse and fraud has delayed implementation.[68] In a public statement, SEC Commissioner Luis Aguilar said that crowd-funding could be "a boon to boiler room operators, Ponzi schemers, bucket shops, and garden variety fraudsters, by enabling them to cast a wider net, and making securities law enforcement much more difficult."[69] Before stepping down as SEC Chairman in December of 2012, Mary Schapiro delayed release of proposed rules implementing the crowdfunding provisions. Internal e-mails released as part of a Congressional inquiry revealed that Ms. Schapiro feared being "tagged with an anti-investor legacy."[70]

In a speech in November of 2012, Commissioner Elisse B. Walter, who briefly succeeded Schapiro as SEC Chairman, stated:

> A vital prerequisite to efficient capital formation is a market in which investors have confidence. If allowing general solicitation results in increased incidence of fraud or sales in securities to investors that do not have the sophistication to understand the risks and merits of a particular investment, we will have failed not only investors, but small businesses as well.[71]

We agree. A major lesson of the recent financial crisis is that even laudable policy objectives—helping more American families own their own home, or helping entrepreneurs secure the financing they need—cannot be achieved at the expense of market integrity or investor protection. Moreover, it is an unfortunate fact that over the past decade the U.S. capital markets, admired for decades around the world for transparency and robust investor protection, have been badly tarnished by a series of scandals or regulatory breakdowns—the dot-com bust, the corporate accounting and financial reporting scandal, the Wall Street analyst scandal, the mutual fund market-timing and trading scandal, the Bernie Madoff Ponzi scheme, the collapse of MF Global, and, of course, the worst financial crisis in 80 years. America's capital markets cannot afford another devastating blow to investor confidence, and Groupon's pre- and post-IPO accounting challenges demonstrate that concerns raised by some provisions of the JOBS Act are well-founded.[72]

Crowdfunding has enormous conceptual and intuitive appeal, and might well be a "potential game changer," as President Obama called it, transforming millions of users of social media into venture capitalists and opening vast new resources for America's entrepreneurs.[73] But it also raises significant challenges that must be addressed. As one consumer advocate told the *New York Times*, "The thing about crowdfunding is that it brings together unsophisticated issuers with unsophisticated investors. What could possibly go wrong?"[74]

We remain hopeful that the SEC can successfully resolve the challenges that crowdfunding presents and that the Internet might yet become a new and important source of start-up finance. In the meantime, additional steps can and should be taken to enhance the financing alternatives for young companies.

Make the SBA More Entrepreneur-Friendly

As discussed earlier, we heard complaints about the SBA at virtually every roundtable across the country. Entrepreneurs cited the burden of dealing with its bureaucracy, daunting paperwork, restrictions on the operation of their businesses, and the agency's focus on asset-based lending, which overlooks many technology and information-based start-ups.

In the SBA's defense, it's in the business of facilitating bank lending to new and small businesses by guaranteeing a portion of the loans, and, as discussed above, bank lending to start-ups is fraught with risk, whether or not the loan is partially backed by the SBA. Moreover, it should be acknowledged that SBA-backed lending hit an all-time high in 2011, with the agency facilitating loans worth $30.5 billion to nearly 62,000 small businesses, including more than 16,000 start-ups. The SBA posted similar numbers in 2012.[75]

Record loan figures notwithstanding, the problems cited by our participating entrepreneurs are real. We know because upon completing our roundtables, we had the opportunity to sit down with a dozen of the nation's most active business-lending banks at the Washington offices of the Consumer Bankers Association. After hearing from us the issues and complaints cited by entrepreneurs, the banks unanimously agreed that the SBA's approach and requirements are unnecessarily cumbersome, burdensome, and restrictive—undermining the potential impact of SBA assistance to new and small businesses and discouraging banks from participating in SBA-guaranteed lending.

With these problems in mind, the SBA should be directed to initiate a detailed and comprehensive dialogue with lending banks and entrepreneurs with the aim of making SBA lending more available, less complex and cumbersome, less physical asset–based, and less restrictive of new businesses' tactical and strategic decision making.

Incentivize the Formation and Commitment of Angel Capital

Early-stage financing is essential to the formation, survival, and growth of new businesses. And, as mentioned above, angel investors account for more than 80 percent of outside seed- and early-stage funding for new companies—an already impressive figure, and one likely to increase as venture capital funds increasingly target later-stage companies. Moreover, angel investing is high risk, with more than half of all investments losing money, and just 7 percent of investments generating 75 percent of returns.

Given the importance of angel investors to start-ups—and the importance of start-ups to job creation—the formation and commitment of angel capital should be reasonably and effectively incentivized. In our view, this objective can be best achieved by way of a federal tax credit, coupled with relief from capital gains taxes. A federal tax credit equal to 25 percent of investments in start-ups would lower investment risk by providing an immediate return. In addition, exempting any gains on investments in start-ups held for at least three years from federal income tax would maximize the pay-off on any successful investments.[76]

Total capital gains tax revenues have historically represented less than 5 percent of federal tax revenues, so exempting any gains on angel investments would have almost no impact on federal tax revenue while having a potentially dramatic effect on job creation.[77] And, since most angel investors reinvest most or all of their returns into the next generation of innovative new companies, exempting such gains from federal taxes would have the further benefit of increasing the amount of seed capital available to start-ups.[78]

Twenty-two states have enacted tax credits of various kinds to incentivize angel investing. Details vary from state to state regarding the size of the credit, limits per investment, caps on total investments, and qualifying businesses. About half the states offer credits of between 25 and 35 percent.[79]

And the evidence is clear—tax credits work. For example, since Ohio created its Technology Investment Tax Credit in 1996, the program has been used by 4,800 angels to invest more than $160 million in 668 companies, according to the state economic development agency.[80] Similarly, since Wisconsin enacted a 25 percent tax credit in 2005, total angel investments have jumped more than 10 times and the number of angel investor groups in the state has increased from just four to more than 20.[81] Other states have experienced similar success.

Virginia has enacted one of the most aggressive tax incentives for angels, and, as Mark A. Herzog told us at our Richmond roundtable, the favorable tax treatment has had a significant impact. Herzog is the former executive director of the Virginia Biotechnology Association and is currently Senior Vice President for Corporate and Government Affairs at Health Diagnostic Laboratory, Inc., a laboratory testing and health management company in Richmond. Launched in 2010, HDL has grown to nearly 700 employees, and chief executive Tonya Mallory was named Ernst & Young's 2012 Entrepreneur of the Year. "Three years ago, we worked on improving the angel investor tax credit so that it's truly valuable,"Herzog told us," and now we have investors that are willing to make decisions they might not have otherwise. Now they can get a 50 percent tax credit on their investment. So if they invest $100,000 in a start-up advanced technology company, they get $50,000 in credits back from the Commonwealth. By de-risking the investment by 50 percent, this incentive policy really gets people off the sidelines."

Tax credits are better policy than government co-investment funds, an approach tried in a few states and a number of countries around the world. While tax credits encourage investment, the majority of the angel's money remains at risk, preserving the investor's incentive to carefully examine potential projects and ensuring that scarce investment capital will be directed to only the most promising business ideas.

Fix Venture Capital by Fixing the IPO Market

The challenges confronting venture capital do not relate to taxation or other structural incentives. In fact, as discussed earlier, some within the industry maintain that annual amounts of venture capital invested need to be reduced by as much as half to generate returns sufficient to compensate investors for risk and years of illiquidity.

But such calculations are based on expectations regarding the likely number of available exits, especially IPOs, and the number of IPOs in recent years remains a fraction of previous averages, even before the dramatic Internet bubble. Increasing the number of venture-backed IPOs back to healthy levels—somewhere between 150 and 200 per year—will not only hasten the right-sizing of the venture capital industry, but also establish market conditions supportive of higher levels of profitably invested capital.

Acknowledging that IPO activity is driven principally by economic growth and the associated rate of new company formation, our roundtable participants identified two major obstacles to more IPOs— SOX and the collapse of the economics of smaller IPOs associated with the decimalization of stock prices.

A 2009 survey by the Securities and Exchange Commission found that 70 percent of small public-company respondents had considered returning to private control due to the costs and burdens of complying with section 404 of SOX, while 77 percent of small U.S.-listed foreign firms said they had considered abandoning their U.S. listings due to SOX.[82]

The JOBS Act of 2012 provides relief from compliance with section 404 for "emerging growth companies"—those with less than $1 billion in annual revenue during the most recent fiscal year—for at least one year and potentially up to five years.[83] This so-called "on-ramp" replaces the IPO obstacle of immediate compliance with SOX with phased compliance.

The JOBS Act's on-ramp is an excellent start. But given the scale of America's jobs emergency, we recommend that policymakers go farther—by widening and lengthening the on-ramp, and by building a permanent off-ramp. Specifically, we propose that companies with annual gross revenue of less than $500 million be exempt from compliance with section 404 of SOX, with no limits as to time or other metrics. In addition, we recommend that companies with annual gross revenue of between $500 million and $5 billion be able to opt out of compliance with section 404, based on a majority vote of the company's shareholders, for a period of five years.

The JOBS Act also required the SEC to conduct a study of the effects of decimalization on IPOs and the liquidity of small- and mid-capitalization securities. SEC staff released its report in July of last year.[84] The staff found that, while very little academic research has been done on the impact of decimalization on capital formation, "the decline in smaller public company IPOs, and IPOs in general, coincides with the implementation of decimalization." The staff also found that the U.S. system of uniform decimalization of stock prices stands in stark contrast to stock pricing frameworks in other industrialized nations:

> In contrast to the United States, with its essentially flat, "one size fits all," tick size regime, many other countries have adopted tiered regimes that provide greater variability for tick sizes based on the price level of a stock. These include Hong Kong (11 price levels), Japan, (11 price levels), Taiwan (6 price levels), South Korea (4 or more price levels), United Kingdom (4 or more price levels), Germany (4 price levels), Australia (3 price levels), and Singapore (3 price levels) . . . the average U.S. percentage tick size based on the offer price of small IPOs is relatively narrow compared to many other countries with significant smaller company IPO activity. Specifically, many countries have percentage tick sizes that are four or more times wider than the United States.

Despite concluding that uniform decimalization "may not necessarily be optimal for smaller capitalization securities," and that "there may be viable, and perhaps preferable, alternatives to uniform decimalization rules," the SEC staff, in the end, recommended only that the agency conduct additional study and "solicit the views of investors, companies, market professionals, academics, and other interested parties."

In our view, the evidence presented in the SEC staff report, combined with the stark contrast between uniform decimalization in the United States and varied pricing regimes around the world, and the dramatic decline—92 percent!—in small capitalization IPOs since 2001, amounts to sufficient reason for U.S. policymakers to act now.

Specifically, we recommend that Congress direct the SEC to create an optional pricing regime for companies with a market capitalization of less than $700 million (borrowing from the definition of "emerging growth company" established by the JOBS Act).[85] The new regime would establish fixed minimum tick sizes—say, 10 cents for stocks under $5 per share, 20 cents for stocks valued at $5 or higher. Specific increments could be reviewed and, if necessary, recalibrated by the SEC annually with input from issuers and other market participants.

Participation in the alternative pricing regime would be optional—small issuers could choose to list under the new alternative pricing regime or under the current regime. Companies already public with a market capitalization of less than $700 million could also choose to move into the alternative pricing regime. The new smaller cap market would be subject to the same disclosure, oversight, and enforcement standards as the market for larger companies, and investors would be free to buy and sell stocks in either market.

The two parallel regimes, operating side-by-side, would preserve the pricing and other benefits to investors of one-penny spreads in the market for larger company stocks, while also preserving the economics necessary to support the research, underwriting, and liquidity upon which a thriving market for smaller IPOs depends. In doing so, a two-tiered system would restore the broken link between emerging growth companies and investors who want to invest in them, helping more young companies access the public markets, with all the associated implications for growth, wealth creation, and job creation.

Ways Financial Institutions Can Support Entrepreneurship

Banks can, and occasionally do, serve start-ups, but obtaining initial financing from banks can be difficult for entrepreneurs—and for good reason. Start-ups typically lack the assets, collateral, and track record that banks look for in order to secure credit, as well as the reliable cash flow to service the loan. Moreover, while all business lending entails risk, start-ups are especially risky.

Nevertheless, banks and other financial institutions have an enormous stake in the strength and vitality of the entrepreneurial economy. Start-ups account for virtually all net new job creation and a disproportionate share of innovation—and, if they survive and grow, start-ups are the future clients of banks and other financial institutions.

With these realities in mind, we offer the following ideas as ways that banks and other financial institutions can promote new business formation, survival, and growth—even if that assistance is not in the form of initial financing.

Cultivate the Formation of Viable New Businesses

- Provide financial support to entrepreneurship incubators and accelerators across the nation. Such facilities provide personal and business finance instruction, technical assistance, and mentoring of entrepreneurs by experienced business executives and current and former entrepreneurs. The intention of such support would be to cultivate new business formation, increase the survival rate of newly formed businesses, and identify scalable companies capable of high-rate growth as possible candidates for angel or venture capital investments.
- Sponsor "seats" in entrepreneurship training facilities around the country and conduct competitions among local entrepreneurs for a chance to win seats in the sponsored training programs.
- Provide incentives to financial institution employees to volunteer their time and expertise to entrepreneurship facilities, and to enhance the professionalization, strategic management, and

Ways Financial Institutions Can Support Entrepreneurship (*Continued*)

operational effectiveness of new companies by serving on the boards and other management committees of young companies graduating from incubators and accelerators.

- Coordinate the documentation and distribution of incubator and accelerator best practices, drawing on the best techniques, methods, and programs at facilities across the nation.

Increase Start-Ups' Access to Capital

- Expand the national network of angel investors—who provide more than 80 percent of the outside, early-stage funding to new businesses—by informing the private wealth clients of financial institutions about the potential opportunity to become angel investors and educating those inclined regarding how to effectively engage with local or national angel networks.
- Offer regular workshops that would provide the pro bono training and other assistance of top industry sector analysts employed by financial institutions to angel investor groups around the country seeking to improve their due diligence and vetting expertise with regard to new or unfamiliar industry sectors.
- Organize and sponsor regular "rocket pitch" business plan competitions, whereby high-promise graduates of entrepreneurship training centers around the nation would be invited to pitch audiences of angel investors and venture capitalists.
- Expand the pool of venture capital—a critical catalyst for scaling growing new businesses into large companies that create many jobs—by committing capital to a number of early-stage venture capital funds across the country. The provided allotments should be available for "first close" of new funds, so that those funds can be immediately invested and, importantly, so that fund managers can raise additional investment capital many times the initial commitment. Venture industry experts tell

(*Continued*)

Ways Financial Institutions Can Support Entrepreneurship
(*Continued*)

us that $1 billion provided by financial institutions and allocated across 100 funds around the country could help create several hundred new, high-growth companies.

Enhance the Science and Technology Capacity of the U.S. Workforce

- Establish and underwrite a selective program of paid internships for community college and university students seeking cooperative education arrangements with local employers, with an emphasis on high technology and manufacturing.
- Underwrite a sustained nationwide public service announcement (PSA) campaign designed to enhance the standing and reputation—the "coolness"—of math and science among American elementary and high school students. The campaign could entail athletes, entertainers, and other high-profile celebrities introducing, explaining, and praising the work of noted scientists and engineers.

Chapter 7

"Regulations Are Killing Us"

Regulation is essential to market economies. It establishes the rules of competition, ensures a level playing field, governs participants' behavior, and protects consumers, public health and safety, private property, and environmental resources. In this important sense, economic growth and wealth creation depend on the promulgation and enforcement of regulation.

Indeed, two of our roundtable participants cited regulatory enforcement deficiencies as one of their principal challenges. The first, the owner of an environmental engineering and construction firm outside York, Pennsylvania, told us that spotty local enforcement of immigration and labor regulations, and unscrupulous competitors who take advantage of such breakdowns, frequently rob him of business.

Similarly, Catherine Figueroa, owner of Redi Pedi Cab Company, a rickshaw enterprise catering to Orlando's tourists and conventioneers, told us that frequent violations of tax, insurance, and safety regulations by her competitors damage the reputation and prospects of her operation, despite her strict compliance. "We operate on International Drive, the tourist district here in Orlando," she explained. "We offer short-haul transportation and outdoor advertising opportunities on our rickshaws. Exhibitors will come in and sponsor 20 of our pedicabs to ride around the property and promote their business. . . I'm all for government regulation. I know a lot of companies are not. But in my view, if there isn't regulation, then there's going to be abusers. We have insurance. We do our business tax receipts. We do everything we need to do to make sure we're operating safe and at the professional level we're trying to portray. But there are others who don't buy insurance and don't do their tax receipts. So they don't have the same expenses we do, and we're competing with them."

Without question, sound and consistently enforced regulation is an essential aspect of any fair, efficient, and effective marketplace.

But regulation isn't free, or without consequence. Regulation imposes costs—costs borne by businesses. A wave of new regulations, inconsistent or outdated regulations, or complex and confusing regulations can distract business owners' focus and time away from their product line and the marketplace, and impose costs that consume resources that could otherwise be invested back into businesses. Regulation can create economic distortions, entrenched interests, and powerful constituencies, and can lead to cronyism and dependency. Regulation can also entail unintended consequences, as incentives created or destroyed by new rules can lead to unforeseen outcomes that negate or even more than offset the intended benefit.

If overdone or unwisely implemented, therefore, regulation can cease to be a facilitator of economic activity and, instead, become an obstacle, stifling innovation and investment and undermining economic growth and job creation—"hardening the arteries" of the nation's economy.

Michael Mandel, chief economic strategist at the Progressive Policy Institute, has pointed out that the sheer accumulation of regulations over time can begin to suppress innovation and growth—even if every individual regulation, considered in isolation, is determined to be sound and reasonable.

> The problem is that it's possible for every individual regulation to pass a cost-benefit test, while the total accumulation

of regulation creates a heavy burden. . . The number of regulations matter, even if individually all are worthwhile. I call this the "pebble in the stream" effect. Throw one pebble in the stream, nothing happens. Throw two pebbles in the stream, nothing happens. Throw one hundred pebbles in the stream, and you have dammed up the stream. Which pebble did the damage? It's not any single pebble, it's the accumulation.[1]

The stifling effect of regulatory burden, complexity, and uncertainty is particularly acute for new businesses. New firms lack the resources and scale of larger firms over which to absorb and amortize the costs of compliance. Moreover, their very survival, especially during the initial years, depends on the energy, focus, and flexibility of their leaders.

"Entrepreneurs succeed or fail based on our momentum, our speed to the market," explained Alan Blake, founder and chief executive officer of Yorktown Technologies, L.P., an Austin, Texas-based biotechnology company. Blake has also served as president of the Austin chapter of the Entrepreneurs Organization, a global network of more than 8,700 successful entrepreneurs. "It's hard to do anything those first few years except try to keep revenues ahead of expenses. It's a constant battle. We're trying to blaze new trails and there's a constant underbrush of regulations. They can be federal, state, or local—and sometimes they conflict. Sometimes they're just dead-stop barriers. You walk up and there's a canyon, and you just have to turn around. In other cases, it just slows you down. A lot of those struggles involve employment-related regulations, which can be very challenging. Exempt versus nonexempt. Contractor versus employee. Fair Credit Reporting Act. Worker's Compensation. Payroll taxes and 1099s. Then there's the new healthcare law, and nobody understands yet how that's going to effect business. Identifying, understanding, and complying with all of these regulations results in a huge loss of productivity. And the important thing is that entrepreneurs—particularly in the early years when they're at that 'succeed-or-fail' point—don't have the resources to hire an HR person or in-house counsel or a chief financial officer. They're trying to do all of it themselves."

"It's as if the politicians and regulators in Washington want me to fail—and spend all their time thinking up new ways to ensure that I do," said Sharon Delay, founder and president of Adjunct Solutions in Westerville, Ohio. "What it amounts to is we can't build our businesses because we're fighting. We're fighting regulations. . . We're fighting the government. We're like boxers who don't stand a chance of winning. . . Quit throwing ridiculous roadblocks in front of me! You either want me to be the engine of the economy or you don't."

Sitting across the table from Sharon, Mark Luden, chief executive of the Guitammer Company and a former chairman of the Small Business Council, agreed: "Some of these regulations coming out—you'd almost think that my teenage son was reading it out of *The Onion* and it wasn't real. You read some of these and go, 'They can't be serious!' You're basically putting a tax on small businesses."

That regulation coming up at our roundtables as a challenge and source of frustration did not surprise us. The degree of exasperation and even anger expressed by so many of our participants did surprise us. According to our roundtable participants, the U.S. economy is currently mired in a period of over-regulation that, more than ever, is threatening their businesses and obstructing their ability to grow and create jobs.

■ ■ ■

Some participants spoke of the sheer burden of regulatory compliance and uncertainty. "You just never know what's coming down the pike," said David Wysocki, founding principal at Hoefer Wysocki Architects in Leawood, Kansas. "My attorney called just this morning and said, 'There's this new regulation that you're probably unaware of but you need to comply with it. It's about registering new employees with the state.' I never knew I had to register new hires with the state. Well, now I do and there are fines if I don't do it. How do you even keep up with all this?"

"Whenever we go to hire someone, there's dealing with the state fund or worker's comp, or teeny changes in other regulations," said Kate Pletcher, principal at Mom Corps, a Los Angeles–based professional staffing and recruiting firm focusing on flexible work schedules. "In California they're now requiring our employees to mark their time down by the minute, and soon they're going to start making sure that they clock out on breaks. Or documenting someone who's working from home. Keeping up to date with all the regulations, for both California and federally, it's really half our job. And it's a total headache."

Other participants pointed out the complexity and redundancy of many regulations. "It's not just federal government," said Chuck Kirkpatrick of Orlando-based ThePeoplesVote.com, a nonpartisan, online platform that allows visitors to cast votes on the issues of the day. "You've got to think about the different layers of regulation. We've got federal regulations, state regulations, county regulations, city regulations. We have to deal with every level."

Kenneth Blaisdell, Associate Dean of the School of Business at Virginia Commonwealth University in Richmond, agreed: "There is a bewildering alphabet soup of agencies that overlap like a Venn diagram. I can't imagine any business navigating that easily."

"I can tell you that the federal, state, county, and local regulations that we have to adhere to in our work, which is civil/site design of land development projects, are constantly changing, making it harder and harder for us to get projects approved in a reasonable time frame," said J. Michael Brill, P.E., P.L.S., owner of J. Michael Brill & Associates, Inc., a civil engineering firm in Mechanicsburg, Pennsylvania. "The entitlement process has made it hard for any small developer to stay in the game, as the design, application, and permitting costs just to meet the regulations in order to obtain approvals from the various government agencies are outrageous. The vast majority of our projects entail the use of various professionals, including various disciplines of engineers, attorneys, architects, and landscape architects—and that's just to obtain the various government approvals. Obviously, the design items then translate into construction costs. It's a very expensive endeavour."

Others highlighted the burden of antiquated regulatory requirements. "We see on a daily basis the number of outdated and outmoded rules that are really crushing innovation for small government contractors trying to bring technology to the government market," said Brett Coffee, general counsel at Springfield, Virginia–based Computer Systems Center Inc. Coffee is also a former chairman of the Fairfax County Small Business Commission. "[The government's] technology is 10 years old to begin with. Just being able to work on innovative projects, there are so many hurdles."

Kim Wills, chief financial officer of Milestone Counseling Services in Richmond, Virginia, agreed. "We have the ability to capture data electronically, but the regulators say there has to be a binder somewhere that they can check to make sure that something has been done."

"A lot of the regulation has good intent, but the unintended consequences can actually defeat their exact purpose," said a participant at our Seattle, Washington, roundtable. "We had a kid who came to us and said 'Hey, I want to work with you guys.' We said, 'One, we don't have an open job and, two, we couldn't pay you even if we did.' He said, 'It doesn't matter; I don't have any technology experience. I can't get into the field unless I get some experience, and you guys have a great track record and great name in the community. I want to be in your company.' So, since training someone isn't free, we said, 'Fine, you can come here. But you're going to do everything from crap work to interesting stuff—and you have to commit to be here for at least three months.' He said, 'Great.' So three months came and went, and we said, 'Max, you've done fabulous work. You're free to go. You've got our recommendation. But you're welcome to stay if you want to be here. At some point when we're profitable and have a job opening, you can compete for it.' Which is exactly what happened. He's got a job now, great experience, and he's making good money. And none of that would have happened had we followed all of the mandates of regulation."[2]

Patrick Flynn, president and chief executive officer of Flynn Construction, Inc. in Austin, Texas, explained how heavy regulation or new rules imposed on one industry can ripple across the economy. "I don't think it's isolated. I was with a CEO of a credit union two weeks ago. He'd been building new locations, and I said to him, 'How are you doing? Are you still expanding?' He said, 'Absolutely not. We shut all that down.' I asked him why, and he said, 'The new regulations that are coming out of Washington for smaller banks. We're going to stay status quo.' He was going to build a lot of branches in town over the next several years, but now he says, 'We're just going to stay with what we have.' So there's a trickle down, because you're crushing the market. . . Either the subcontractor, the builder, is going to get hurt, or some other guy is going to go down and take a bunch of people with him. And the only people who are making money out of it are the bankruptcy attorneys. Meanwhile, people are running as hard as they can on a treadmill to keep people employed."

Jerry Ross, Executive Director of the National Entrepreneur Center in Orlando, Florida, explained how regulatory uncertainty can interfere with businesses' access to bank financing. "Even the banks are uncertain. I remember when one of the loan programs was launched—I think it was the Patriot Express Loan program [for veteran-owned businesses] from the SBA. You didn't have to make a payment for a year, but not all the regulations had been completed and sent to the banks yet. I was told that the regulators showed up at one bank and made them classify that particular loan as a nonperforming asset because they're not getting paid for a year. They had to call in a credit line to get their ratios back in order. So, for every loan the bank considered under that program, it was going to be punishing someone else. So the bank was facing the same uncertainty with regulation that small businesses face. With regulators showing up, and not knowing what the policies are going to be when they're finally written, they're afraid to make loans under the new program that has already been announced, and that entrepreneurs are seeking."

The Boston/Cambridge area—with MIT, Harvard, and several other research universities nearby—is a leader in the formation of new biotech and life science products and businesses.[3] But David Verrill, founder of Hub Angels, a Boston-based angel investor group, explained how Food and Drug Administration regulations can be an obstacle to such promising ventures securing capital from non-bank sources. "We've been around 11 years, made 26 investments, about a third of which were in life sciences—but not lately. The FDA approval process is very problematic, both in time and cost. So we tend to stay away from those companies that, because of regulation, have a longer time horizon and larger capital costs than we can support."

Other participants at our Cambridge roundtable explained that the FDA's lengthy and uncertain approval process often leads pharmaceutical and other life science companies to pursue the testing, licensing, and marketing of new drugs in Europe and other more accommodating jurisdictions rather than here in the United States. According to a 2011 survey by the National Venture Capital Association, 85 percent of the polled venture-backed healthcare companies expected to seek regulatory approval of their new products outside the United States.[4]

Regulatory statistics confirm that the message from our roundtables is more than mere griping—that, in fact, regulation of the U.S.

economy has dramatically increased in scale and scope in recent decades, and particularly in recent years. For example, the number of pages in the *Federal Register*—the government publication in which new regulations must be posted and explained and which, therefore, serves as a proxy for regulatory activity—has expanded more than six-fold since 1950. In the 1950s, regulatory agencies published an average of about 11,000 pages per year in the *Federal Register*. By stark contrast, federal agencies published an average of more than 73,000 per year from 2001 to 2009.[5] Published pages expanded by 19 percent in 2010 alone.

Between 2009 and 2011, 106 new major regulations were issued, with "major" defined as having an expected economic impact of at least $100 million per year, at a cost of more than $46 billion annually and one-time implementation costs of $11 billion—four times the number of major regulations issued in the preceding four years, at five times the cost to the economy, amounting to one of the most intensive periods of new regulation in U.S. history.[6]

The Federal Code of Regulations hit an all-time high of 174,545 pages in 2012, up more than 20 percent over the past decade and up 145 percent since 1975. Federal regulatory agencies issued 1,172 final rules in 2012, up 16 percent from 1,010 new rules in 2011, which was a 40 percent increase over the 722 issued in 2010. Federal agencies also proposed 2,517 new rules in 2012, the highest number since 2003. These increases came on top of a pipeline of more than 4,000 regulations at various stages of implementation—854 of which will have a significant impact on small businesses, as determined by the relevant regulating agency. [7]

Not surprisingly, the bureaucracy required to administer the expanding array of regulations has also grown significantly. The combined budgets of federal regulatory agencies have grown to $60 billion, up 26 percent since 2008 and up 50 percent over the past decade. Between 2000 and 2010, staffing levels at federal regulatory agencies jumped 54 percent—the largest increase in five decades.[8] Indeed, according to *Investor's Business Daily*, if the federal government's regulatory operations were a business, it would be one of the 50 largest corporations in the country in terms of revenue and the third largest in terms of employees, with more staff than McDonalds, Ford, Disney, and Boeing combined.[9]

In Washington, Republicans and Democrats alike have acknowledged the problem. For example, during remarks before the Economic

Club of Washington on September 15, 2011, John Boehner (R-OH), Speaker of the House of Representatives, stated:

> We all know some regulations are needed. We have a responsibility under the Constitution to regulate interstate commerce. There are reasonable regulations . . . and then there are excessive regulations that unnecessarily increase costs for consumers and small businesses. . . The current regulatory burden coming out of Washington far exceeds the federal government's constitutional mandate. And it's hurting job creation in our country at a time when we can't afford it.

In January of 2011, President Obama announced an executive order launching a government-wide review of "rules already on the books to remove outdated regulations that stifle job creation and make our economy less competitive."[10] Eight months later, on August 22, 2011, the Administration released the final plans of 26 regulatory agencies to implement more than 500 reforms the Administration said would save $10 billion over the next five years.[11]

Regulatory streamlining that saves American businesses $10 billion over five years is a step in the right direction—but only a very small step. According to the Small Business Administration (SBA), the cost of complying with federal regulations exceeded $1.75 *trillion* annually, nearly 12 percent of GDP and more than $10,500 per American worker, as of 2008—*before* the historic expansion of regulation over the past four years! Even more alarming from the standpoint of new businesses and job creation, the SBA has also found that regulatory compliance costs small businesses 36 percent more per employee than larger firms.[12]

"Look, I believe in regulation," said Chuck Kirkpatrick of Orlando–based ThePeoplesVote.com. "I've actually lobbied for regulation. But it has to be responsible and the government has to be accountable; but it's not. In many ways, America is no longer a business-friendly country. We like to say we are, but we're not."

"Reduce the number of regulations, especially around employment," said Alan Blake of Yorktown Technologies in Austin, Texas. "Ironically, while they were designed with good intentions—to protect employees and prospective employees—the result is that companies have a very difficult time navigating them. Small businesses in particular struggle with the complexity and risk associated with employment-related regulations. The result is that many companies are much more reluctant to hire than they would be otherwise. Simplifying the regulations in favor of making it easier and less risky to hire would be a huge help."[13]

Policy Recommendations

With the intention of significantly reducing regulatory burden, complexity, and uncertainty—especially for job-creating new businesses—we recommend the following.

Devise a Preferential Regulatory Framework for New Businesses

The Congressional Budget Office (CBO) and Office of Management and Budget (OMB) should be directed to co-develop a preferential regulatory framework to which fragile new businesses would be subject for the first five years after formation. The framework should be comprised of only the most essential product safety, environmental, and worker protection regulations. Co-development of the preferential framework by CBO and OMB is important since regulation is the implementation of Congressional intent by Executive branch agencies.

To minimize regulatory uncertainty, the new-business framework should also protect new businesses from new regulations for the critical first five years. To be sure, the preferential framework would need to be updated, improved, and refined from time to time by CBO and OMB. But any changes should apply only to new firms the following year and not to young firms already operating within the five-year window of protection.

To avoid abuse of the preferential regulatory framework—such as business owners simply renaming or reconstituting existing companies every five years—the Internal Revenue Service (IRS), working with the CBO and OMB, should develop appropriate definitions, characteristics, and limitations regarding the meaning of "new business."

Require Third-Party Review of All Proposed Regulations

CBO and OMB should be directed to co-conduct third-party analysis of the economic costs and benefits of all proposed new regulations. The third-party review should require analysis of the costs of the proposed regulation in relation to other federal regulations as well as in relation to existing state and local regulations. In particular, the third-party review should focus on the impact of the proposed new regulation on new and small businesses. Proposed regulations determined to have economic costs, or costs to new and small businesses, that exceed identifiable benefits should require Congressional approval for enactment.

Create a Regulatory Improvement Commission

The federal government has a large, complex, and effective process for generating new regulations, but no mechanism for systematically addressing unnecessarily burdensome, ineffective, inefficient, duplicative, or outdated regulations. Therefore, Congress and the President should create through signed legislation a federal Regulatory Improvement Commission (RIC), as proposed by Michael Mandel of the Progressive Policy Institute.[14] By way of his "pebble in the stream" analogy, Mandel has illustrated not only the problem of cumulative impact of even sound and reasonable regulations, but also, and importantly, the inherent flaw of regulatory review exercises that focus on the merits of individual regulations: No particular pebble in the pile is to blame for damming the stream.

Building on President Obama's January 18, 2011, executive order *Improving Regulation and Regulatory Review*, and modeled on the Base Closure and Realignment Commission (BRAC)—which provided independent, objective, nonpartisan review and analysis of U.S. military installations—the RIC's purpose would be to serve as a procedural mechanism for the regular evaluation, simplification, streamlining, consolidation, and even elimination of selected existing regulations in pursuit of objectives such as encouraging innovation, enhancing competitiveness, and accelerating economic growth and job creation, as stipulated in the RIC's establishing statute.

The RIC should be comprised of a bipartisan group of highly qualified stakeholder appointees and staffed by experts seconded from various regulatory agencies, Congress, and independent organizations. After selecting a portion of the regulatory code for review—a "scoop" of pebbles from the pile in the stream—the RIC should solicit input from individuals, businesses, other affected stakeholders, and outside experts, hold public hearings, and carefully and objectively examine the evidence in an open and transparent manner. Upon completion of its analysis, the RIC should submit a package of recommended improvements to Congress for a "fast-tracked" up-or-down vote. Following Congressional approval, the package would be sent to the White House for the President's approval and signature, ensuring that the reforms carry the force of law.

Such an independent RIC framework would provide a politically feasible alternative to ideological and indiscriminant deregulation efforts, and would avoid the obvious flaws and limitations of regulatory agency self-review. Moreover, by considering the cumulative impact of regulations across agencies, the RIC would also escape the self-defeating trap of focusing on individual regulations that, considered in isolation, often appear perfectly sound and reasonable. And by requiring Congressional approval by way of a fast-tracked up-or-down vote, the RIC process would provide legislators with sufficient political cover to deliver authentic regulatory reform and improvement, safe from the conflict and interest group pressure that consideration of individual regulations would provoke.

Rank States' Regulatory Environment

The Department of Commerce should be directed to launch a nationwide initiative—in partnership with entrepreneurship organizations and facilities around the country—to develop a research framework by which all 50 states will be ranked as to their regulatory friendliness to new business formation, survival, and growth. Metrics and rankings should be published online for easy and widespread use by entrepreneurs.

Importantly, state-based versions of the federal Regulatory Improvement Commission discussed above would significantly enhance a state's ranking.

To further incentivize a "race to the top" among states, the federal government might consider allocating economic development block grants to states based on their annual ranking for the purpose of funding enhancements of their entrepreneurship ecosystem.

Chapter 8

"Tax Payments Can Be the Difference between Survival and Failure"

t's difficult to embark on a project of this kind completely free of expectations regarding what you're likely to hear. As we set out to ask entrepreneurs across the nation about the issues and challenges that complicate their efforts, one of our expectations was that taxes might come up as a source of frustration. After all, any business owner would naturally prefer to keep as large a portion of the business' earnings as possible—to reinvest into the business or to simply enjoy more of the fruits of one's labor.

And, indeed, as we expected, the subject of taxes came up frequently—but not in the way we expected. In fact, all over the country we heard entrepreneurs make comments such as: "I understand that we all have to pay taxes," and "I'm fine paying taxes," and even,

"I didn't get into business to avoid paying taxes." And yet our roundtables made clear that taxes are a source of frustration and even anxiety for many of our participants.

For a while, we were puzzled by this nuanced, even seemingly contradictory feedback regarding taxes. But as we continued to listen, we began to understand.

"We literally spend thousands of dollars a month on accountants," said Mark Casey, president and chief executive officer of CFN Services, a telecommunications networking company based in Herndon, Virginia. "Sometimes the issue is getting bills for taxes that we're not even aware that we owe. How do you find out about these things? I've raised my hand and said 'I'm doing business in your state—have someone call me.' We're not trying to be noncompliant. But we need a little help to make sure that we're not missing something. Large businesses have huge accounting departments to take care of this, but for smaller firms it's a real burden."

"Here's the problem with taxes," said Bob Burns, president of RL Burns, Inc., a construction management company in Orlando, Florida. "We do the work and then we wait to get paid. So cash flow is extremely important. It's where we're most vulnerable. When you have a good year, you get hit hard with taxes. When you have a bad year that extra cash you paid in taxes would really be great to have. And so taxes make things difficult, especially given how volatile things have been."

Our roundtables revealed that entrepreneurs often think about taxes the way they think about two other critical challenges—the burden and distraction of regulation, and access to capital. Tax complexity and uncertainty—like regulatory complexity and uncertainty—divert the time, attention, and energy of entrepreneurs away from the essential tasks required to successfully launch and grow their businesses. Even more important, tax payments drain new businesses of critical cash flow and operating capital.

Taxes are a business reality, and our roundtable participants are "fine" with paying them. But tax complexity and uncertainty, together with the loss of precious capital, can amount to mortal threats to new businesses, particularly in the critical early years.

"Cash flow is the lifeblood of start-ups," Reggie Chandra, president and chief executive officer of Rhythm Engineering in Lenexa,

Kansas, told us. "People around the table have talked about the importance of access to capital in the context of outside investors. But it's
also about holding onto the capital you generate internally through
sales. Young businesses barely scrape by in the beginning and then the
government takes a third of their profit in taxes—money that could
have been invested back into to the business. That money can be the
difference between survival and failure."

Chad Gummer agreed. "Our biggest challenge that we run into is
tax issues." Gummer is president of Gummer Wholesale, Inc., a family-
owned and -operated wholesale distribution company based in Heath,
Ohio, that supplies convenience stores in Ohio, Kentucky, and West
Virginia. "We're in a high sales dollar, low net profit kind of business.
So when they come and take the money from your net sales, it kills
you."

"My big frustration, and what I see as the big issue affecting not
only women-owned businesses but small businesses in general, is that
business only works when you can project," said Laura Yamanaka,
president and founder of LA-based teamCFO, and chairwoman of the
National Association of Women Business Owners. "These days, it feels
more like Vegas—so much unpredictability . . . the tax rules have to
change so we have more predictability. So that it's attractive to invest
and so that the economy is working."

■ ■ ■

Research supports the feedback from our participating entrepreneurs.
For example, higher tax rates have been shown to reduce investment
spending by entrepreneurs and to deter their hiring of additional workers.[1] And, indeed, a survey of more than 900 chief executives of small
businesses conducted by the *Wall Street Journal* in December of 2012
found that, due to anticipated tax increases associated with the "fiscal
cliff" negotiations in late 2012, 32 percent of respondents indicated
they planned to reduce investment spending, while another 30 percent
planned to hire fewer workers.[2]

During the 2012 tax policy debate leading up to the year-end
expiration of tax cuts passed during the Bush Administration, an analysis by Ernst & Young found that raising top individual tax rates would

be associated with a loss of approximately 710,000 jobs because more than 2 million U.S. businesses organized as S corporations,[3] partnerships, limited liability companies, and sole proprietorships would be affected.[4] Such businesses are referred to as "pass-through" businesses because their profits are passed through to owners and investors who pay taxes on those distributions by way of their individual returns.[5] Nearly 95 percent of U.S. businesses,[6] 85 percent of small businesses,[7] and virtually all new businesses are organized as pass-throughs.

Such firms employ more than half of the private sector workforce.[8] A recent analysis of the Federal Reserve's Survey of Small Business Finances by George Haynes of Montana State University reveals that small-business owning families who earn more than $250,000 per year employ 93 percent of the people employed by small businesses.[9] Because the vast majority of new and small businesses are organized as pass-throughs, raising taxes on wealthy individuals also raises taxes on millions of start-ups and other small businesses, leaving them with less money to reinvest, expand, and create jobs.[10]

The American Taxpayer Relief Act of 2012, signed into law by President Obama on January 3, 2013, following month-long negotiations between the Administration and Congress to avoid the so-called "fiscal cliff"[11] raised tax rates on personal income above $400,000 for individuals and $450,000 for couples from 35 percent to 39.6 percent. As a result, businesses organized as pass-throughs that earn income above those levels now pay a tax rate 4.6 to 10 percentage points higher than businesses organized as corporations.[12] According to Doug Elmendorf, Director of the Congressional Budget Office, the higher rates mean 750,000 fewer new jobs in 2013.[13]

In Chapter 7, we explained that the stifling effect of regulatory burden, complexity, and uncertainty is particularly acute for new businesses. New firms lack the resources and scale of larger firms over which to absorb and amortize the costs of compliance. Moreover, their very survival, especially during the initial years, depends on the energy, focus, and flexibility of their leaders. According to the Small Business Administration, the cost of regulatory compliance for small businesses is 36 percent higher per employee than for larger firms.[14]

For similar reasons, new businesses are much more vulnerable to the impact of tax complexity and uncertainty than larger businesses.

According to the National Federation of Independent Business (NFIB), tax compliance costs are 67 percent higher for small businesses than for larger businesses, costing small businesses nearly 2 billion hours and more than $18 billion each year. Nearly nine out of 10 small businesses are forced to rely on outside tax professionals to ensure compliance. A recent NFIB survey of 12,500 of its member businesses found that 85 percent want Congress to "fundamentally revise" the tax code in 2013, with 78 percent supporting a simpler tax code with fewer exemptions and preferences.[15]

"Take some of the tax burden off!" an exasperated Brent Frei of Smartsheet in Seattle, Washington, told us. "When this state was talking about slapping a 10 percent tax on the 'wealthy,' what that really means is small businesses. If that had passed, I would have moved our business out of the state, because it would have paid to do so—and might have made the difference."

Frei went on to explain another way that taxes can undermine new businesses, or even discourage them from ever launching. "I've started three companies and I know a lot of successful entrepreneurs. They succeeded by clawing and scratching at the dirt. A lot of hours and a lot of personal risk. They look for a longer-term payout after a lot of short-term pain. That's the culture. And it's fundamental. I didn't go without a wage for the entire founding phase of my businesses and put all my personal capital into them in hopes of an eventual payout only to have that hurdle raised unexpectedly down the road. I mean, that's crazy. Make the incentives better for people and they'll go out and take the risk."

An additional issue we heard is that the tax code is often irrational—punishing, or not sufficient rewarding, business activity that should be encouraged, and encouraging activity that should be minimized. For example, the research and development tax credit was created by way of the Economic Recovery and Tax Act of 1981 and is intended to incentivize technological progress and innovation by allowing businesses to deduct a portion of the cost of research and product development from their taxable earnings. Unfortunately, the original credit was temporary and, while Congress has renewed the credit 14 times, it has never made it permanent, creating year-to-year uncertainty for firms that need to plan their R&D spending coherently over time.[16] Moreover, even when renewed, the formula for calculating the credit has changed many times.

"We took a third of our profits last year and invested in R&D," said Brent Gendleman, president and chief executive officer of 5AM Solutions, a life science and healthcare software engineering company in Reston, Virginia. "This is how the tax credit worked: Take 50 percent of the money that we invested, then take 20 percent of that 50 percent. That's the tax credit we got. Just 10 percent of what you invest. And only off the top line of your tax burden, so the actual value is minimal. Maybe a laptop. For a state to claim that's an incentive to entrepreneurship is nonsense."

We propose two broad reforms of the R&D tax credit in the next chapter.

Rob Lilleness, president and chief executive officer of Seattle-based Medio Systems explained how the tax code virtually requires him to invest offshore: "The U.S. rewards companies for having people and assets offshore. In a prior company we opened in Singapore—zero taxes. We opened in Hong Kong—12 percent taxes. Before long, the majority of our revenues were outside the United States, even though I might not want it that way or even believe in it. We serve our shareholders and they want the best return on their capital. We offshored, that lowered our tax base, and boosted our earnings per share. And now that the money is banked offshore, it makes more sense to buy companies and talent overseas because you can't repatriate that capital or you'll face a 35 percent hit."

But the most common complaint we heard from entrepreneurs regarding taxes is that they are too complex and constantly changing, requiring far too much time, energy, and other resources, and making it virtually impossible for young businesses to effectively plan. This feedback from our roundtable participants is consistent with the results of the 2012 Small Business Taxation Survey released by the National Small Business Association. Asked what tax-related issue is the most significant challenge to their business, 56 percent of respondents said the administrative burden of the tax code. Eighty-five percent said the tax code is so complex they have to hire an external tax practitioner or accountant to handle their taxes.

Another survey conducted in January of 2013 asked senior executives at 600 start-up companies across the nation: "What piece of advice would you give to President Obama with regard to supporting the innovation economy?" The top response, offered by nearly a third of survey respondents, was to simplify the tax system. Attracting and retaining the world's best talent was the second most common response.[17]

"Just give me a number!" said an exasperated Rhonda Pressgrove, founder and chief executive officer of Help Me Rhonda Cleaning Services in Southaven, Mississippi, and a participant at our Memphis, Tennessee, roundtable.

"And don't change it!" echoed Rick Leung, vice president of development and chief technology officer at Austin, Texas–based Vyopta, Inc., a developer of applications for business video. "If we have a number we can count on, we can build a business around that. What we can't manage is the goal posts constantly moving. We don't have the time or the money to keep up with changes year after year that force us to rethink our business model and what our tax liability is going to be."

"We just want [the government] to make taxes easy to handle," said Mary McCarthy, co-founder and president of Your Management Team, a Westerville, Ohio–based management consulting firm serving entrepreneurs and small business owners. "And the employment laws and healthcare laws, too. The things that impact us. Make them as simple as possible so that we can just focus on our business."

A number of our participants went so far as to say that they would pay higher tax rates—despite the impact on their businesses—in exchange for certainty.

Policy Recommendations

With the intention of significantly reducing tax burden, complexity, and uncertainty for new businesses, we recommend the following:

Establish a Preferential Tax Framework for New Businesses

In Chapter 7 we proposed that the Congressional Budget Office (CBO) and the Office of Management and Budget (OMB) be directed to co-develop a preferential regulatory framework to which fragile new businesses would be subject for the critical first five years after formation. The preferential framework would be comprised of only the most essential product safety, environmental, and worker protection regulations in order to minimize regulatory burden on new firms. To minimize regulatory uncertainty, the new-business regulatory framework should also protect new businesses from new regulations for the first five years after formation.

To this preferential regulatory framework, we propose adding preferential tax treatment of new businesses. Specifically, we propose that the Internal Revenue Service (IRS) be directed to establish a new entrepreneur—or "e-corp"—tax status, whereby newly launched businesses would be subject to a flat 5 percent income tax for the first five years after formation. Call it the "Five for Five" plan. Such favorable and predictable tax treatment will help cultivate new business formation, survival, and growth by allowing new businesses to retain and reinvest most of what they earn, preserving critical cash flow, and eliminating the distraction and burdens of tax complexity and uncertainty.

As we mentioned in Chapter 7, the IRS, working with CBO and OMB, should develop appropriate definitions, characteristics, and limitations regarding the meaning of "new business" to avoid abuse of the preferential regulatory and tax framework, such as business owners simply renaming or reconstituting existing companies every five years.

Allow Cash Method of Accounting for the First Five Years

Current law generally permits businesses with gross receipts of $10 million or less to use the cash method of accounting. The cash method is simpler, less costly, and easier for new businesses to understand than accrual accounting or other more complex accounting methods to which some businesses are subject. As part of the proposed framework of favorable and predictable tax treatment of new firms, we also propose that all new businesses, regardless of revenue levels, be permitted to use the cash method of accounting, if they choose to, for the first five years of their operation.

Allow 100 Percent Expensing of Business Investment for the First Five Years

The Small Business Tax Revision Act of 1958 created for the first time a special first-year depreciation allowance whereby small businesses could deduct or "expense" from their taxable earnings a portion of the total cost of capital and equipment investment, pursuant to section 179 of the Internal Revenue Code. The purpose of the provision was to reduce the tax burden on small businesses, stimulate small business investment, and simplify tax accounting for smaller firms. The original deduction was limited to $2,000 of the cost of new and used business machines and equipment.[18]

Expensing is the most accelerated form of depreciation, allowing businesses to write off the cost of business investment immediately rather than over time. Future deductions are not as valuable to businesses due to the time value of money and because deductions are not indexed for inflation. Expensing stimulates business investment by maximizing the tax benefit of depreciation and thereby effectively lowering the cost of the capital required to make the investment.[19]

Since 1958, the limits and details of the special expensing allowance have changed many times—most typically to raise the expensing limit as a means of stimulating economic growth by incentivizing business investment. Most recently, in the midst of the accelerating economic downturn in 2008, Congress raised the allowance to $250,000 as part of the Economic Stimulus Act of 2008, and then to $500,000 as part of the Small Business Jobs Act of 2010. The American Taxpayer Relief Act of 2012, signed by President Obama to avoid the "fiscal cliff," preserved the $500,000 allowance for 2013.

As part of our proposal to provide preferential tax treatment for new businesses over the critical first five years after their formation, we also propose that new firms be allowed 100 percent first-year expensing of the total cost of business-related capital, equipment, off-the-shelf software, and real estate investment. According to an analysis by the Treasury Department, 100 percent expensing lowers the average cost of capital on new investments by more than 75 percent.[20] Such savings are enormously significant, especially for new businesses for whom access to sufficient capital at reasonable terms remains a principal challenge. We also propose that new businesses with no taxable earnings in particular years during their initial five years be permitted to carry forward the deduction of such expenses for 15 years beyond the year in which the capital expenses were incurred.

Together with the proposed 5 percent flat income tax for the first five years after formation, such favorable and predictable tax treatment will help cultivate new business formation, survival, and growth by allowing new businesses to retain and reinvest most of what they earn, preserving critical cash flow, and eliminating the distraction and burdens of tax complexity and uncertainty.

Pass the Start-Up Innovation Credit Act

On January 31, 2013, Senators Chris Coons (D–DE) and Mike Enzi (R–WY) reintroduced a bill to help start-ups access the research and development (R&D) tax credit.[21] As mentioned briefly above, the credit was created by way of the Economic Recovery and Tax Act of 1981, and is intended to incentivize technological progress and innovation by allowing businesses to deduct a portion of the cost of research and product development from their taxable earnings.

The credit is particularly relevant for new businesses, which often incur substantial costs in their early years researching and developing new products and services, methodologies, and techniques—and for whom preservation of cash flow and operating capital is crucial.[22] But because many new businesses experience operating losses in their early years, there may be no income tax liability against which to claim the credit.

The Start-Up Innovation Credit Act would allow companies less than five years old with less than $5 million in revenue to deduct the total amount of R&D spending up to $250,000 from the payroll taxes they pay on employee wages in the following year, rather than against income taxes.[23]

In reintroducing the bill on the floor of the Senate on January 31, 2013, Senator Coons stated:

> Companies that invest in R&D generate new products, which spark new industries with spill-over benefits for all kinds of sectors. . . The R&D credit has helped tens of thousands of American companies succeed and create jobs. But there is a critical gap in the existing R&D credit. It isn't available to start-ups, because they are not yet profitable, and thus they don't have an income tax liability against which to

take a credit. In fact, more than half the R&D credit last year was taken by companies with revenue over $1 billion, well-established, profitable companies. . . [T]his bipartisan Start-up Innovation Credit Act . . . opens this credit to new companies who don't yet have an income tax liability. . . Rather than shutting our start-ups out of the R&D tax credit, let's open the doors to these innovators and see what they can do.[24]

We agree. If new businesses are both the engine of job creation and the source of most innovation in the economy—and they are—an R&D tax credit that overlooks new businesses, however important and well-intentioned the credit may be, is off-target.

As we mentioned in Chapter 2, a recent study by the Small Business Administration found that, between 2002 and 2006, firms with fewer than 500 employees registered 15 times more patents per employee than large firms.[25] We strongly suspect that, as with job creation, start-ups are responsible for the vast majority of small business innovation and registered patents. Small companies are also more likely to explore technology subfields in which large firms are less active, and more likely to do their R&D in the United States.[26] Senator Coons' bill sharpens the aim of the R&D tax credit, rewarding research and development in the most innovative sector of the economy.

But we suggest one change—to maximize the impact of the Senator's proposal, we recommend lifting the $5 million in revenue limitation and simply allowing all new firms to deduct their R&D spending up to $250,000 from payroll taxes for the first five years after formation.

Chapter 9

"There's Too Much Uncertainty—and It's Washington's Fault"

Our moderator began each roundtable by inviting participants to comment on local economic conditions and recent circumstances for their business. We began our discussions this way both as an easy icebreaker—folks were eager to introduce and talk about their businesses—and because, as mentioned in Chapter 3, we understand that the U.S. economy is not a monolithic whole, but rather an amalgam of many regional and local economies, with certain cities or regions often closely associated with particular industries. For example, Seattle is known for web-based technology and clean energy companies, while Memphis is known for healthcare, bioscience, and medical device companies.[1] Starting our discussions by focusing on local conditions helped us get a good read on the area and set the context for what we would hear over the next couple of hours.

While some participants reported steady or even growing business, particularly in the technology space, most reported that conditions— both for the local economy and their business—remained very challenging. As one participant succinctly put it: "There's just no demand out there."

That message is, of course, consistent with broader economic indicators. As we discussed in Chapter 1, though the recent recession officially ended in June of 2009, the subsequent recovery has been remarkably weak and fragile. The economy expanded by just 2.4 percent in 2010, 1.8 percent in 2011, and 2.2 percent in 2012. In the fourth quarter of 2012, growth slowed to an annualized rate of just 0.4 percent. An analysis by the Associated Press showed that of the 10 post-recession recoveries of three years or more since World War II, the current recovery is the weakest "by just about any measure."[2] At year-end 2012, economic output was just 7.2 percent larger than it was when the recovery began, compared to double-digit increases during other multi-year recoveries since World War II. Had economic growth remained on trend since 2007, the economy would be more than 12 percent larger than it is today.[3] As Neal Soss, chief economist at Credit Suisse, commented to the *New York Times*: "This is the weakest recovery we've ever seen, weaker even than the recovery during the Great Depression. . . If you're not scared by that, you're not paying attention."[4]

As much as any other factor discussed at our roundtables, the return to anemic growth so soon after the worst economic downturn since the Great Depression jarred and frightened many of our participating entrepreneurs, causing them to second-guess, postpone, or even cancel plans to expand and hire.

"There are a lot of businesses in this area that barely survived the recession and are hanging on by their fingernails," said Brenda Hall, chief executive of Bridge360, an Austin-based software developer. "If the economy takes another leg down or doesn't get better soon, there's going to be a huge second wave of failures as those barely-alive firms are swept away."

The lack of business, and the uncertainty regarding future business, is the principal obstacle to accelerated hiring, according to many of our roundtable participants.[5] "We can't afford to have another full-time employee, so we're doing a lot of the work ourselves," said Elizabeth Barrios, president of Office Wall Solutions in Richmond, Virginia. "It's one of those vicious circles. We need to get the construction jobs coming in so we can go out and install. If we have the business coming into the company and the money coming in, we can put that into another employee. [But] we're just not getting the business in."

"I don't see a light at the end of the tunnel," said Suman Saripalli, founder and president of Intellispeak, LLC in Lawrence, Kansas, a research and development venture specializing in the physical sciences and engineering. "I think we have structural problems that are getting more difficult. For example, there are whole classes of jobs that I think will never come back. Classes of jobs that have long been considered the foundations of the middle class. If those jobs are hit and stay deflated, can we really expect any kind of recovery? Another problem is that the housing industry remains down because people don't have jobs. That's why they're not buying, and because they're not buying other people don't have jobs. And it just goes round and round."

"To effectively grow and create jobs, businesses have to think strategically," said Jerry Ross, Executive Director of the National Entrepreneur Center in Orlando, Florida. "Today, no one is thinking strategically. Everyone is thinking tactically because they have to in order to get through this. So that they're still around when it's time to do a strategic plan and think about hiring."[6]

A participant in our Austin, Texas, roundtable spoke for many of our entrepreneurs: "I'm about to sign a lease to triple my space because I see growth, but I'm scared. I don't need another 2008. I'm not normally doom and gloom, but I'm worried."

And like a dense fog that settles over an area given the right conditions of temperature and humidity, continued economic weakness combined with regulatory burden and complexity, access to capital difficulties, a shortage of qualified talent, and tax complexity have produced a profound uncertainty among many of the entrepreneurs we met.

"There's a lot of uncertainty and angst out there about the long-term direction and health of the economy," said Jeff Cornwall, Director of the Center for Entrepreneurship at Belmont University in Nashville, Tennessee. In January, Cornwall was named the Entrepreneurship

Educator of the Year by the United States Association of Small Business and Entrepreneurship. "I work with lots of young entrepreneurs and we're creating a lot of start-ups in our program. These young folks are really thinking about long-term viability and what's going to sustain them. And quite honestly, many are very pessimist about the next 10 to 20 years—and yet they're still trying."

"So much unpredictability is driving decisions," said Laura Yamanaka, president of teamCFO in Los Angeles. "Our clients are pulling back, sitting on a lot of cash because they don't know. The patterns aren't there. They can't rely on their customers, can't rely on their vendors, can't rely on the market, and now we can't rely on the government."

And, of course, this psychology of apprehension and hesitation only further reinforces the problem of insufficient demand, as worried business owners postpone spending, investment, expansion, and hiring.

"For us and for most people I talk to, it's no more business as usual," said Bob Burns, president of construction management firm RL Burns, Inc. in Orlando, Florida. "We've made some pretty good investments in our business in the past—equipment, staff, training, education, and so on. But taking the risk of those investments today is not very wise, and I don't think many others do it either. It's very difficult to consider investing money in a future you just can't see. There's no way to gauge it or really know what the next year is going to look like. . . So today we're looking to cut back, get lean, and stay lean. . . We have absolutely no plans to upgrade our equipment or purchase new computers. They're going to hang around until they blow up. Any kind of long-term investment is off the table."

Bobbie Kilberg, president and chief executive officer of the Northern Virginia Technology Council in Herndon, Virginia, pointed out an additional source of uncertainty facing businesses in the greater Washington, DC, area: "Many of our members, a lot of whom are small companies, are federal contractors or subcontractors. The inevitable [government] cutbacks are simply going to have to come in defense as well as civilian agencies, given the budget situation. And that will hit particularly hard on small businesses. Those businesses don't have the ability to put people on the sidelines and wait for those contracts to come back along."

Travis McCready, former Executive Director of the Kendall Square Association in Cambridge, Massachusetts highlighted a similar problem: "There is great uncertainty about what the federal government will do regarding R&D dollars. If you look back at the history of Kendall Square, MIT, and how some of our best companies have been built over the years, many of them have their roots in R&D dollars from some aspect of the federal government. We have no certainty now, no predictability about federal research dollars. And that's going to be an issue going forward."

Rodney Hughes, Managing Partner of Orlando-based South Star Distribution Services, which designs and installs energy reducing roofing materials, explained how protracted economic weakness and uncertainty has changed the way businesses make decisions, including hiring. "Rather than making longer-term decisions about investing in their business and hiring and training people based on trends and what they see coming from farther down the road, now it's job to job. We hire people as independent contractors based on the jobs we get, rather than hiring full time."

Perhaps the most fascinating aspect of the problem of too little economic dynamism and too much uncertainty was what, or rather who, the vast majority of our entrepreneurs blame for such debilitating circumstances. While a range of factors were cited as contributing to the halting recovery—the still struggling housing market, continued deleveraging by the American consumer, political turmoil and recession in Europe—most of our participants insistently and even angrily blamed the sluggish U.S. economy on what they perceive as poor leadership, dysfunction, and outright incompetence in Washington, DC. Many cited policymakers' inexplicable inability or unwillingness to address problems they see as threatening the future of the nation itself, most notably federal budget deficits and the national debt. Others railed against policymakers' apparent ignorance regarding the needs and priorities of business.

"I could have all the tax credits in the world," said Craig Sonksen, owner of Krema Natural Peanut Butter and Crazy Richard's Natural Peanut Butter brands in Dublin, Ohio, "but if I don't have more business, I'm not going to hire a soul. I cashed my Bush check happily a number of years ago, and I get a payroll tax break now from Obama.

But here's my personal soapbox—quit gerrymandering the economy. How about we get back to some basic free-market capitalism? Stop trying to use this lever and that lever. If they just left us alone to do what we do best, we'd all be much better off."

Jamie Rhodes, chief executive officer of National NanoMaterials, Inc. in Austin, Texas, and vice chairman of the Angel Capital Association, agreed. "The people in power in Washington not only don't understand business, they don't have a clue. When we go to war, I want the generals up there leading. And when the war is kick-starting the economy, I want the people who run businesses, not the career politicians, to be the leaders. Someone who understands business, who understands how to rebuild a healthy middle class—that's who I want leading. Especially right now when we're in this economic crisis."

Still others were more cynical, dismissing policymakers as hopelessly conflicted and, therefore, incapable of making decisions in the best interest of the country. "The politicians are largely ignorant and make decisions based on short-term political considerations," lamented Laura Yamanaka of teamCFO in Los Angeles. "Or they know the consequences of their decisions, but just don't seem to care."

As context, it should be remembered that our roundtables took place over the summer of 2011, with most occurring as Congressional Republicans and the White House were negotiating a deal to raise the nation's debt ceiling.[7] Negotiations became increasingly intense, and as the days ticked down to the deadline of August 2, the date the Treasury Department said it would likely run out of money, the unthinkable—that the United States might default on its national debt—became all too imaginable. Finally, on July 31, President Obama and Speaker of the House John Boehner announced that an agreement had been reached. President Obama signed the Budget Control Act of 2011 into law on August 2.

Four days later, on August 6, Standard & Poor's downgraded the credit rating of the U.S. government for the first time in our nation's history. In a press release, S&P stated:

> The downgrade reflects our opinion that the fiscal consolidation plan that Congress and the Administration recently

agreed to falls short of what, in our view, would be necessary to stabilize the government's medium-term debt dynamics. More broadly, the downgrade reflects our view that the effectiveness, stability, and predictability of American policymaking and political institutions have weakened at a time of ongoing fiscal and economic challenges to a degree more than we envisioned when we assigned a negative outlook to the rating on April 18, 2011. Since then, we have changed our view of the difficulties in bridging the gulf between the political parties over fiscal policy, which makes us pessimistic about the capacity of Congress and the Administration to be able to leverage their agreement this week into a broader fiscal consolidation plan that stabilizes the government's debt dynamics any time soon.

Following S&P's downgrade, markets around the world experienced their most volatile week since the 2008 financial crisis, with the Dow Jones Industrial Average plunging 635 points on August 8.

■ ■ ■

In expressing pessimism regarding the ability of Congress and the Administration to work together constructively to address the nation's fiscal challenges, S&P proved prescient. The Budget Control Act of 2011, which resolved the 2011 debt-ceiling crisis, cut more than $900 billion in discretionary spending over 10 years and created a Joint Select Committee on Deficit Reduction, commonly referred to as the "Supercommittee," to produce bipartisan legislation by November of 2011 to reduce the deficit by an additional $1.2 trillion over 10 years. If the Committee failed to achieve that objective, the Act required deep across-the-board spending cuts—referred to as "sequestration"—split evenly between defense and nondefense spending. The cuts were to total $110 billion per year, or $1.2 trillion over 10 years.

Sequestration was intended to be so unthinkable given the fragility of the economic recovery, and therefore so painful politically, that it would force members of the Supercommittee to make the hard choices necessary to reach a bipartisan agreement.

But in the end, the Supercommittee, perhaps predictably, failed to reach agreement, triggering sequestration to begin on January 2, 2013. That timing happened to coincide with the expiration of legislation[8] that had extended for two years tax cuts from 2001 and 2003, commonly referred to as the "Bush tax cuts."[9] Expiration of all the relevant tax cuts was estimated to amount to an aggregate tax increase of about $400 billion.[10] The Tax Policy Center estimated that 80 percent of American households would experience some form of increase, with the average household facing a tax increase of about $3,700.

The coincident timing of the sequestration spending cuts and expiring tax cuts became known as the "fiscal cliff," a term first used by Federal Reserve Chairman Ben Bernanke.[11] According to the Congressional Budget Office (CBO), the total fiscal impact of the cliff would be about $500 billion annually, or about 4 percent of GDP. The CBO also estimated that the spending cuts and additional tax revenue would reduce the federal budget deficit from more than $1 trillion in 2012 to about $640 billion in 2013—and by as much as $7 trillion over the next 10 years, reducing the federal debt-to-GDP ratio to 58 percent in 2023, compared to 90 percent without the cliff. But the CBO also predicted that the fiscal contraction would push the United States back into recession, with the economy likely to contract by 3 percent in the first half of 2013, eliminating some 2 million jobs and raising the already elevated unemployment rate to more than 9 percent.

Business and consumer anxiety provoked by the threat of the cliff likely worsened economic conditions far in advance of the year-end deadline. In July of 2012, CBO Director Doug Elmendorf warned reporters that uncertainty caused by the cliff could reduce economic growth by 0.5 percent. "We think it's an issue now, and it will be increasingly an issue in the second half of the year for people's decisions."[12]

A report released in October of 2012 by the National Association of Manufacturers concluded that business anxiety in the months approaching the year-end cliff had in fact cost 0.5 percentage points in economic growth in 2012—and as many as 1 million jobs.[13] As mentioned in the previous chapter, a survey of more than 900 chief executives of small businesses conducted by the *Wall Street Journal* in December of 2012 found that, due to anticipated tax increases associated with the fiscal cliff negotiations, 30 percent of respondents indicated they planned to hire fewer workers, while another 32 percent planned to reduce capital and equipment spending.[14] In the weeks leading up to the year-end cliff, surveys of consumer and business confidence plunged.[15]

Following month-long negotiations between the Administration and Congress, a deal was finally reached to avoid the cliff just three hours before the midnight December 31, 2012, deadline.[16] President Obama signed the American Taxpayer Relief Act on January 3, 2013. The Act raised tax rates on personal income above $400,000 for individuals and $450,000 for couples from 35 percent to 39.6 percent. According to CBO Director Elmendorf, the higher rates mean 750,000 fewer new jobs in 2013.[17] The Act also postponed—until March 1—the deep spending cuts known as sequestration.

March 1st arrived with no further agreement on taxes and spending. And so what was intended to never happen, indeed what was designed to be unthinkable both economically and politically, actually happened. Sequestration, the indiscriminate, across-the-board cuts in government spending, totaling $1.2 trillion over 10 years, went into effect.[18] In the weeks and months that followed, furlough notices for thousands of government workers and contractors were issued, a third of the nation's air traffic control towers were closed, national parks made plans for reduced public access and security during the coming summer, and even public tours of the White House were suspended. In announcing the failure of negotiations to avoid sequestration, President Obama said:

> Washington sure isn't making it easy. At a time when our businesses have finally begun to get some traction—hiring new workers, bringing jobs back to America—we shouldn't be making a series of dumb, arbitrary cuts to things that businesses depend on and workers depend on, like education, and research, and infrastructure and defense. It's unnecessary. And at a time when too many Americans are still looking for work, it's inexcusable. . .This is not a win for anybody. This is a loss for the American people.

According to the CBO, sequestration will shave 0.6 percentage points off economic growth in 2013 and eliminate another 750,000 jobs.[19] Other estimates project job losses as high as 1.9 million by year-end 2014.[20] Looking ahead, the nation will hit the recently raised debt ceiling sometime in late 2013, raising the specter of yet another dangerous partisan showdown.[21]

■ ■ ■

Reading the previous section—which summarizes what has happened in Washington regarding debt and taxes since our roundtables—one can understand the frustration, exasperation, and even anger expressed by so many of our entrepreneurs.

"We're on the verge of becoming a third world country," declared a participant in our Herndon, Virginia, roundtable. "The politicians are playing Russian roulette and they don't have any damn idea who's holding the gun. I try to be optimistic about America, but right now I think they're going to plunge us into the biggest unknown this country has ever seen—and I'm including in that the Civil War. . . The debt ceiling is just a symptom of the disease, which is that we're spending far more than we bring in. Fix the problem! Do something!"

"Small business owners need customers feeling confident about the economy to start spending their money," said Clay Banks, director of Economic Development at the Chamber of Commerce in Bartlett, Tennessee, outside Memphis. "When we talk about the fact that we're already borrowing 50 cents of every dollar we spend, and now we're talking about borrowing even more, that money has to come from somewhere. It's coming out of the pockets of consumers that entrepreneurs need out there spending money."

Patrick Flynn, president of Flynn Construction in Austin, Texas, agreed. "I talked to a buddy of mine last night who has a plant here in Austin—100,000 square feet. He's a good-sized manufacturer. He said 'I've got a million dollars to invest in equipment right now but, hell, I'm not going to do it. So I'm shedding jobs instead.' It's the uncertainty, the lack of stability and consistency. . . This isn't high school politics. We've got to get on with it! We have to lead! We need Washington to lead because you've got 315 million people in this country that are scared to death about what's going to happen tomorrow."

The National Federation of Independent Business (NFIB) polls its members monthly regarding business conditions, expectations, and confidence. In its January 2013 poll, the first following the fiscal cliff threat, the survey revealed expectations regarding business conditions six months forward to be at their fourth lowest level since the NFIB began its survey 40 years ago. In a press release, NFIB chief economist Bill Dunkelberg stated:

> If small businesses were publicly traded companies, the stock market would be in shambles. . . Owner pessimism is certainly not surprising in light of higher taxes, rising health care costs, increasing regulations, and just plain uncertainty."[22]

Our roundtable participants' expressions of acute uncertainty, and the impact of that uncertainty on their ability to expand their businesses and create jobs, are consistent with recent work done by economists Scott Baker and Nicholas Bloom of Stanford University and Steven Davis at the University of Chicago.[23] The trio has constructed an index of "policy uncertainty" and analyzed the relationship of the index relative to previous levels of economic output, investment, and employment.[24]

As Figure 9.1 shows, their index reached its historic high in August of 2011—higher than following the terror attacks of September 11, 2001, or the bankruptcy of Lehman Brothers in September of 2008—due principally to the protracted U.S. debt ceiling negotiations. The index spiked again in the weeks approaching the fiscal cliff. As the economists explained in a *Bloomberg* editorial:

> When businesses are uncertain about taxes, healthcare costs, and regulatory initiatives, they adopt a cautious stance. Because it is costly to make a hiring or investment mistake, many companies will wait for calmer times to expand. If too many businesses wait, the recovery never takes off.

Astonishingly, Baker, Bloom, and Davis estimate that if policy uncertainty were restored to 2006 levels, U.S. businesses would create 2.5 million new jobs within 18 months![25] A similar analysis recently conducted by economists at the Vanguard Group concluded that policy uncertainty since 2011 has created a $261 billion "uncertainty tax" on the economy, without which economic growth would have been 3 percent rather than 2 percent, and more than 1 million additional jobs would have been created.[26]

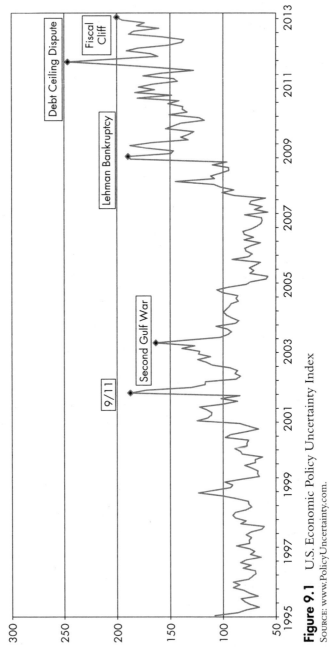

Figure 9.1 U.S. Economic Policy Uncertainty Index

SOURCE: www.PolicyUncertainty.com.

The paralyzing effect of economic uncertainty is not unique to new and small businesses. On October 25, 2012, the chief executives of more than 80 large corporations issued a statement urging policymakers to avoid the fiscal cliff and reduce the federal budget deficit.[27]

> Policymakers should acknowledge that our growing debt is a serious threat to the economic well-being and security of the United States. It is urgent and essential that we put in place a plan to fix America's debt. An effective plan must stabilize the debt as a share of the economy, and put it on a downward path. This plan should be enacted now, but implemented gradually to protect the fragile economic recovery and to give Americans time to prepare.

At a CEO Council event sponsored by the *Wall Street Journal* in November of 2012, nearly three-quarters of the chief executives attending listed the approaching fiscal cliff as the their biggest worry—above continuing political and financial turmoil in Europe, slowing economic growth in China, and conflict in the Middle East.[28]

Another letter, signed by the chief executives of 160 corporations, was released by the Business Roundtable on December 11, 2012.[29] The previous quarter, the Roundtable's CEO Economic Outlook survey had plunged to its lowest level since the third quarter of 2009, immediately following the end of the Great Recession.[30] Jim McNerney, chief executive of Boeing and chairman of the Roundtable told the *Financial Times*: "The continued inaction in Washington is holding up much-needed tax, fiscal, entitlement, and regulatory reforms that would provide certainty for business, reassure markets, and enhance U.S. economic growth."[31]

According to the Federal Reserve, U.S. corporations have $1.8 trillion in cash and liquid securities parked unproductively on their balance sheets. In early February of 2013, prominent hedge fund investor David Einhorn sued Apple to force the company to return some of its $137 billion in cash—an amount larger than Intel's entire market value—to investors.[32] While economists disagree about the precise nature, motivations, and implications of such cash stockpiling,[33] there is broad consensus that continued economic uncertainty looms large in the minds of corporate leaders.

A recent analysis by the University of Massachusetts concluded that if corporations channeled their "excess liquid asset hoards" into productive investments, approximately 19 million new jobs would be created, pushing the unemployment rate below 5 percent.[34]

But as debilitating as Washington-produced uncertainty clearly is for small businesses and larger corporations, start-ups are particularly vulnerable. As we have discussed, new businesses, given their inherent fragility and limited resources, are disproportionately impacted by burdensome regulations and tax complexity. No doubt Washington-created economic uncertainty inflicts a similarly disproportionate blow.

"Where's the leadership?" asked an exasperated Mark Luden, chief executive of the Guitammer Company in Westerville, Ohio. "It's the uncertainty out there. When people are uncertain, those with capital sit on their hands. Those who are trying to sell decide to wait. And buyers who are able to wait just wait. It's the uncertainty that's killing us. And, yeah, I hear President Obama and people in Congress talk about how innovation is the driver of growth and job creation, but where's the follow-up? My response to uncertainty is 'Where's the leadership?' Until someone leads and gets rid of some of the uncertainty out there, you're going to have problems getting people to buy and invest. If you're a big company like Walmart, you can wait it out. But if you're new and small, all of this makes it harder to stay afloat."

Policy Recommendations

The following recommendations are not specifically targeted at start-ups—except that they have everything to do with enhancing the prospects for start-ups in that they are intended to minimize Washington-produced policy uncertainty and to significantly accelerate economic growth, from which businesses of all types, sizes, and ages benefit.

The first two recommendations are rather obvious, and yet sometimes—particularly in Washington, DC—it's important to have a firm grasp on the obvious.

Gradually But Significantly Reduce the Federal Budget Deficit and National Debt

As recently as 2007, U.S. publicly held debt amounted to just 36 percent of GDP. As shown in Figure 9.2, however, since 2007 the nation's debt has increased by 125 percent. A ccording to the CBO, federal debt will exceed 76 percent of GDP in 2013, and chronic deficits could push debt levels to 87 percent of GDP within 10 years and 200 percent of GDP with in 25 years.[35]

Over the course of repeated collaborations, including their widely noted 2009 book *This Time Is Different* and a 2010 paper entitled "Growth in a Time of Debt," economists Carmen Reinhart and Kenneth Rogoff have argued that high levels of government debt tend to impede countries' economic growth, weaken their ability to respond to unexpected challenges, and leave them more vulnerable to financial crisis.[36] Drawing on public debt data encompassing 44 countries and spanning two centuries, Reinhart and Rogoff contend that government debt levels of 90 percent of GDP or higher are associated with lower median annual growth of 1 percent. High debt levels undermine economic growth by putting upward pressure on interest rates and inflation, and by crowding out private investment.[37] Higher debt may also undermine growth by influencing businesses' expectations with regard to taxes. Indeed, numerous participants in our roundtables made clear that they view high government debt levels as deferred taxes that will have to be

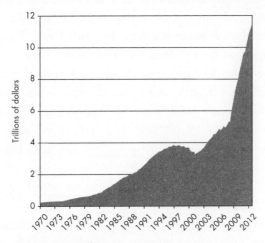

Figure 9.2   Federal Debt Held by the Public
SOURCE: Congressional Budget Office.

paid at some point. Recent studies by the Bank for International Settlements and the International Monetary Fund have also concluded that similarly high levels of debt have a "significant" and negative impact on economic growth.[38]

Slower growth by an average of 1 percent per year is no small matter over an extended period. Consider the following.

According to CBO's baseline economic forecast, GDP is projected to grow to $26 trillion in 2023. That same year, according to CBO's alternative fiscal scenario, U.S. publicly held debt could reach 90 percent of GDP. If the economy grew by an average annual rate of 3 percent over the next 25 years, by 2048 GDP would have expanded to $54 trillion. If, however, the economy grew at an average annual rate of just 2 percent—one percentage point less each year—GDP would grow to $42 trillion by 2048, or $12 trillion less than otherwise. In other words, just one percentage point less in average annual growth would cost America more than 20 percent of projected GDP over 25 years.

It should be noted that Reinhart and Rogoff's thesis came under intense scrutiny last spring following the revelation of an apparent error in their data by Thomas Herndon, a graduate student in the economics department at the University of Massachusetts Amherst.[39] While conceding "a spreadsheet coding error," Reinhart and Rogoff have vigorously defended their work, arguing that the conclusions of Herndon and his two colleagues "are less dramatic than they would have you believe" and "do not overturn [our] fundamental finding."[40]

Beyond the academic debate, a review of the actual relevant figures reveals the extent of American's debt dilemma Over the past 20 years, federal spending has nearly doubled, increasing 71 percent faster than inflation.[41] Spending in fiscal year 2012 reached $3.7 trillion, or 22.8 percent of GDP, significantly above the 40-year average of 21 percent. In 2012, the U.S. spent more than $1 trillion more than it collected in tax revenues, for the fourth year in a row. Spending is projected to increase to $5.5 trillion within 10 years and reach 36 percent of GDP within 25 years.[42]

Principally responsible for increased federal spending are America's entitlement programs. Less than half of federal spending 20 years ago, entitlements accounted for 62 percent of federal spending in 2012. The three major entitlement programs—Medicare, Medicaid, and Social

Security—accounted for 44 percent of all federal spending. With expenditures of $773 billion in 2012, Social Security is the largest entitlement, larger than Medicare ($478 billion) and Medicaid ($255 billion) combined. Medicare is the fastest growing entitlement program, expanding by 68 percent since 2002, while Social Security and Medicaid grew by 37 percent.[43] Spending on these largest entitlements alone is projected to increase from 10.4 percent of GDP in 2012 to 18.2 percent in 2048. Such levels of spending would consume all federal tax revenues, implying that all other government operations—national defense, transportation, education and training, federal law enforcement, and veterans' benefits—would have to be financed through additional borrowing.

As sobering as such figures are, they're not the whole story. Looking out over the next 75 years, the federal government has promised entitlement benefits, as yet unfunded, of an estimated $87 trillion—more than five times current GDP.[44]

Clearly, current trends are unsustainable. If America is to avoid national bankruptcy, and if the U.S. economy is to grow at rates necessary to create millions of new jobs and generate the tax revenue necessary to pay down the nation's accumulated debt, the rate of government spending must be significantly reduced.

Importantly, the pacing of that needed reduction in spending can and, in our view, should be gradual. As we've already noted, the current economic recovery is the weakest post-recession recovery since World War II and remains fragile. Jeopardizing the recovery with sharp and sudden reductions in government spending is not only ill-advised but self-defeating, as even slower growth or a return to recession would reduce tax receipts and lead to even higher levels of debt. Nevertheless, a credible framework for accomplishing meaningful long-term reduction of the nation's debt is essential if economic growth and job creation are to accelerate.

How can that be achieved?

It's clear to us that U.S. policymakers must come to terms with a simple reality pointed out by one of America's most notorious criminals, Willie Sutton. Asked by FBI agents after his capture in 1934 why he robbed banks, Sutton is said to have responded: "That's where the money is."

Entitlements are where the money is. No doubt spending can be reduced in other areas of the budget, and sequestration, while hardly an ideal approach, has already begun that process. Moreover, comprehensive reform of the nation's immensely complex and grossly inefficient tax code would likely produce additional tax revenue (see the next section).

But current debt levels and the government's future promises have far outstripped the capacity of additional tax revenues to make any meaningful difference. Chris Cox, former chairman of the Securities and Exchange Commission, and Bill Archer, former chairman of the tax-writing House Ways and Means Committee, have pointed out that the combined annual earnings of U.S. households and corporations amount to about $7 trillion per year, while the annual accrued expenses—taking into account current and future spending—of America's entitlement programs totals over $8 trillion. In other words, even if the government confiscated the entire gross income of all American households and corporations, it wouldn't be enough to meet accrual basis government spending for a single year.[45]

America's runaway entitlement spending is nothing less than a clear and present danger to America's economic viability—and even to our national security.

In August of 2010, Admiral Michael Mullen, Chairman of the Joint Chiefs of Staff, told CNN: "The most significant threat to our national security is our debt . . . the strength and the support and the resources that our military uses are directly related to the health of our economy."[46] In December of 2012, Mullen, now retired, announced the formation of the Coalition for Fiscal and National Security, the purpose of which is to urge Washington policymakers to lay the foundation for long-term deficit reduction—including new revenue, entitlement reform, and further cuts to nonentitlement spending, including defense. Other members of the coalition include former Secretaries of State Henry Kissinger, George Schultz, James Baker, and Madeleine Albright, as well as former Senators John Warner and Sam Nunn.[47]

Recent academic research suggests that gradual but substantial reductions in government spending promote economic growth because expectations on the part of businesses of lower future debt and taxes, and therefore higher incomes, encourages private spending and investment.[48]

The sooner policymakers act, the less severe the required steps need to be and the more gradually they can be implemented.

Enact Comprehensive Competitiveness-Enhancing Tax Reform

The most significant overhaul of the U.S. tax code was signed into law by President Ronald Reagan on October 22, 1986. In the years prior, the tax code had become a monstrosity of complexity, inefficiency, and unfairness, characterized by high individual and corporate tax rates and countless deductions, exemptions, and shelters. In short, the U.S. tax code was a mess and an impediment to economic growth. The basic reform idea was simple: lower rates and broaden the base by eliminating complexity and loopholes.[49] The Act and the tax clarity it delivered helped revitalize the U.S. economy and laid the foundation for one of the longest periods of economic expansion in American history.

But, for democratically elected policymakers, the temptation to use the tax code to reward special causes and constituencies is a powerful one. Efforts to undo the historic progress achieved by the Tax Reform Act began almost immediately. As the *Wall Street Journal* observed on October 23, 1986:

> Yesterday, shortly after 11 A.M., Ronald Reagan signed HR 3838, the landmark tax-reform bill of 1986. The battle to get tax reform is over; the battle to keep it is just beginning. Mr. Reagan recognized this in his statement at the signing ceremony, pledging to stop rate increases, and laying out a remarkably thoughtful explanation of the principles behind the movement to cut tax rates. Enjoy it while you can. Congress will be back on January 6, and the movement to take away tax reform will start.

In the years since, Congress has passed nearly 15,000 changes to the tax code and many of the loopholes, deductions, special credits, and expenditures are back.[50] Certain tax breaks are referred to as "expenditures" because they reduce tax revenue and subsidize certain activities—like homeownership—just as government spending programs do. According to the Joint Committee on Taxation, the lost revenue associated with just the top 10 tax expenditures totaled $576 billion in 2010.[51]

Higher marginal rates are also back. The Tax Reform Act of 1986 reduced the rate on ordinary income from 50 percent to 28 percent.

The American Taxpayer Relief Act of 2012, signed by President Obama to avoid the fiscal cliff, raised rates on personal income above $400,000 for individuals and $450,000 for couples from 35 percent to 39.6 percent.

Once again, the U.S. tax code has become a monstrosity of complexity, inefficiency, and unfairness, and an impediment to economic growth and job creation. Another overhaul is long overdue.

Modernization of the tax code is also badly needed because the U.S. economy and the world have changed dramatically since Reagan signed the Tax Reform Act. In 1986, a young company called Microsoft had just gone public; Steve Jobs had just been fired from Apple; there was no Internet; and Amazon, Google, Yahoo!, and Facebook were far on the horizon. The U.S. and global economies have been transformed since 1986 by rapid advancements in computing and telecommunications technology, and by the resulting forces of globalization. Cross-border foreign direct investment among all countries has expanded from less than 6 percent of the world's GDP in 1980 to 33 percent by 2009.[52] The global economy of 2013 is more integrated and competitive than could have been imagined in 1986.

This final observation is of crucial importance because the U.S. corporate tax rate, at 35 percent, is the highest in the developed world. Including state and local taxes, the top corporate tax rate is 39.2 percent, nearly 14 percentage points higher than the average of the 33 other members of the Organisation for Economic Cooperation and Development (OECD). Over the past 20 years, every member of the OECD has significantly reduced its corporate tax rate, except the United States. Indeed, the United Kingdom plans to further reduce its corporate tax rate in 2014, from 28 percent to 23 percent.[53] Even after adjusting for various deductions, credits, and expenditures, America's average effective corporate tax rate, at 27.7 percent, significantly exceeds the average of the world's 58 largest nations (19.5 percent), OECD nations (22.6 percent), and non-OECD nations (16.5 percent).[54]

The dubious distinction of imposing the highest corporate tax rate in the world not only undermines the competitiveness of U.S. corporations in an ever-more competitive global economy, it undermines the attractiveness of the United States as a place for multinational companies to locate and invest. In 1960, 17 of the world's 20 largest companies were headquartered in the United States. By 1985, the number had fallen to 13, and by 2010 only six of the world's 20 largest companies were headquartered in the United States.[55]

It should also be pointed out that American workers bear an enormous share of the burden of high corporate tax rates. According to the CBO, workers bear about 70 percent of the burden of high corporate tax rates, principally through reductions in corporate investment, which lowers productivity and wages.[56] Other research has also found that high corporate tax rates contribute to lower wages by raising the cost of investment capital.[57] Additional research has concluded that high corporate tax rates have a "large adverse impact on aggregate investment, foreign direct investment, and entrepreneurial activity."[58] President Obama's Jobs Council has called the U.S. corporate tax system "an outdated and extremely inefficient system that creates economic distortions and puts U.S. businesses and workers at a disadvantage."[59]

One particularly bizarre and counterproductive aspect of the current corporate tax code is that it powerfully incentivizes U.S. businesses to keep foreign profits overseas. The United States is the only major industrial nation that applies income tax to the worldwide earnings of U.S.-based corporations. Most other nations maintain a "territorial" framework whereby taxes are paid only to the government of the country in which the profits are earned. Indeed, 27 of the 34 OECD countries have territorial tax systems. Moreover, of the seven nations that still maintain a worldwide tax system, the United States maintains the highest corporate tax rate by far.

The U.S. government does provide a foreign tax credit up to the amount of taxes U.S. companies pay to foreign governments. Most importantly, income earned overseas is taxed only if it is transferred back to the United States. As long as foreign-earned profits remain abroad, taxes are indefinitely deferred. The U.S. system of assessing taxes on income earned anywhere in the world, together with the deferral of taxation until earnings are repatriated, creates a powerful incentive for U.S.-based corporations to keep their foreign earnings overseas and reinvest them anywhere but back in the United States.

It has been estimated that U.S. corporations currently hold as much as $1.7 trillion overseas and could add as much as $300 billion annually in coming years.[60] Moody's has noted that the practice is particularly common in the technology sector. Recent research indicates that industry sectors that depend on high rates of innovation and, therefore, continuous research and development are particularly sensitive to repatriation taxes.[61] The tech sector doubled its overseas holdings between 2006 and 2011 and, according to Moody's, could double it again by 2014. If that happened, technology companies would hold nearly 80 percent of their cash overseas.[62] Microsoft reportedly holds almost 90 percent of its cash and short-term investment overseas.[63]

Current tax treatment, therefore, encourages many of America's high growth companies to invest outside the United States. Even worse, a recent survey of senior tax officers at more than 400 U.S. corporations found that 20 percent have invested foreign earnings in assets with a lower rate of return than U.S.-based options, while 44 percent reported that they had actually borrowed money to finance dividend payments, share repurchases, debt payments, and pension contributions while keeping tens of billions of dollars parked unproductively overseas.[64]

It should be emphasized that overseas investment by U.S. corporations should not be discouraged or penalized. U.S. companies earn a large and growing share of their total earnings overseas as foreign markets continue to grow, particularly in rapidly growing emerging market nations. Overseas operations generate higher earnings, create additional value for shareholders, and promote economic growth and job creation back home (see trade-related recommendation later in the chapter). But the global allocation of companies' resources should not be artificially driven by powerful and illogical tax-related incentives.

The current worldwide taxation framework misallocates resources, distorts companies' balance sheets and financing practices, undermines shareholders' access to significant value, and creates opportunities for earnings management and other accounting abuses.[65] More fundamentally, large foreign earnings held abroad represent an enormous loss for the U.S. economy. Economist Douglas Holtz-Eakin has estimated that the repatriation of overseas corporate profits would increase GDP by approximately $360 billion annually and help create nearly 3 million new jobs.[66]

With all this in mind, we join many others in urging comprehensive competitiveness-enhancing tax reform. As in 1986, the goal should be a simpler and more fair tax code, with lower rates and a broader base achieved by eliminating as many loopholes and expenditures as possible. According to the Joint Committee on Taxation, there were nearly 200 individual income tax expenditures in 2010 totaling nearly $1 trillion in lost revenue—an astonishing number, especially considering that $2.2 trillion in individual income tax revenue was collected that year. If the number of expenditures was reduced or even significantly curtailed—especially by limiting the top few—statutory rates could be dramatically reduced without a reduction in net revenue.

"Tax reform right now has one fundamental thing in common with 1986," Ed Kleinbard, former chief of staff of the Joint Committee on Taxation, told *Politico* recently. "That is the country is drowning in tax expenditures."[67]

In our view, tax reform should also include a shift to a territorial framework, whereby the foreign earnings of U.S.-based companies would not be subject to U.S. taxation. Such a provision, as part of a simpler, flatter, and lower-rate tax structure would dramatically enhance U.S. international competiveness, promote investment in America by U.S. corporations, attract greater foreign investment, and, thereby, promote economic growth and job creation.

Increase the Research and Development Tax Credit— and Make It Permanent

It has long been understood that innovation is the force principally responsible for driving economic progress. Austrian-American economist Joseph Schumpeter pioneered the connection between innovation and economic development, defining innovation as "doing things differently in the realm of economic life"[68] and characterizing innovation's role in driving economic progress as "a perennial gale of creative destruction."[69] Later, economist Robert Solow demonstrated that more than half of economic growth cannot be attributed to increases in capital and labor, as most economists had previously theorized, but only to technological innovation.[70] For his work, Solow won the Nobel Prize in 1987.

Innovation propels economic progress by raising productivity—the average value of output produced by each worker. As workers become more productive, salaries and living standards rise, demand increases, the economy expands, and more jobs are created to meet the appetite of a wealthier population.[71] As 2008 Nobel Laureate economist Paul Krugman has observed:

> Productivity isn't everything, but in the long run it is almost everything. A country's ability to improve its standard of living over time depends almost entirely on its ability to raise its output per worker. . . Compared with the problem of slow productivity growth, all our other long-term economic concerns—foreign competition, the industrial base, lagging technology, deteriorating infrastructure, and so on—are minor issues.[72]

Economic progress depends on productivity growth, which in turn depends on innovation. For these reasons, the economic growth and job creation prospects of any nation are dramatically enhanced by research and development.

In the previous chapter we mentioned that the Research and Experimentation Tax Credit—commonly known as the research and development (R&D) tax credit—was created as part of the Economic Recovery and Tax Act of 1981 to incentivize technological progress and innovation by allowing businesses to deduct a portion of the cost of research and product development from their taxable earnings. The United States was one of the first countries to incentivize R&D by way of the tax code and claimed the world's most generous tax treatment of R&D into the early 1990s.

Since its introduction, the R&D tax credit has been shown to be a powerful driver of innovation and economic growth.[73] A large and growing body of research indicates that R&D investment is associated with future gains in profitability and market value at the firm level, and with increased productivity at the firm, industry, and broader economy levels.[74] R&D also has significant "spill over" benefits, as research conducted by one firm can lead to progress that increases the productivity, profitability, and market value of other firms in related fields.[75] A 2001 study of 16 OECD nations over the period 1980 to 1998 found that every $100 in additional R&D spending boosted GDP by $113.[76] As a recent Congressional Budget Office analysis observed:

> A consensus has formed around the view that R&D spending has a significantly positive effect on productivity

growth, with a rate of return that is about the same size as (or perhaps slightly larger than) the rate of return on conventional investments.[77]

This compelling evidence notwithstanding, implementation of the R&D tax credit in the United States has been far from ideal. First, the original credit was temporary, with an expiration date of year-end 1985. Over the years, the credit has expired eight times and has been extended 14 times, most recently as part of The American Taxpayer Relief Act of 2012, signed by President Obama on January 3, 2013, to avoid the "fiscal cliff." Failure to make the credit permanent has created year-to-year uncertainty, undermining businesses' ability to plan their R&D investment coherently. This uncertainty and inability to confidently plan has likely undermined the incentive power of the tax credit. Further exacerbating this uncertainty is the fact that, even when renewed, the formula for calculating the credit has changed many times.

Importantly, the United States can no longer boast the most generous R&D tax credit in the world. Today, 26 of the 34 OECD nations offer R&D tax incentives, and other non–OECD nations such as Brazil, China, India, Russia, Singapore, and South Africa do as well.[78] Not only have other nations caught up, they've left the United States in the dust. As Figure 9.3 shows, as of 2009 the United States ranked 18th in encouraging private sector R&D. A 2012 analysis found that the United States now ranks 27th of 42 nations studied in terms of R&D tax treatment.[79]

More favorable tax treatment of R&D means that foreign companies are able to invest more heavily in relative terms, with potentially profound implications for innovative advantage over the longer term. Moreover, as global companies look for places to invest in R&D, many other countries are now substantially more attractive than the United States.

This is a crucial point, as R&D investment has become increasingly mobile. Multinational corporations headquartered in the United States, Europe, and Asia account for more than 90 percent of business-funded R&D and are locating more of their investment outside their home countries. Investment location decisions are determined by many factors, including the growth of foreign markets, production costs, talent and skills availability, as well as tax and other incentives offered by governments.[80] Between 2004 and 2009, U.S. multinationals almost

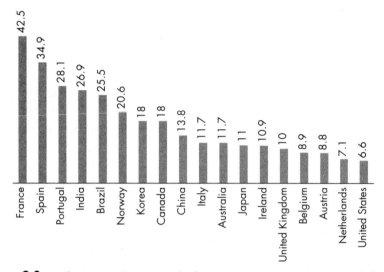

Figure 9.3   Effective R&D Tax Credit for Large Companies (cents per dollar of R&D expenditure. 2008-2009)
SOURCE: Organisation for Economic Co-operation and Development.

doubled their overseas R&D employment, from 138,000 to 267,000, while creating only 22,300 domestic R&D positions.[81] In an increasingly competitive global economy in which innovation is the key to economic success, the United States' dismal ranking with regard to R&D tax treatment represents an enormous policy failure.

Global statistics show that while the United States still leads the world in business sector R&D expenditures—investing $270 billion in 2007, more than twice the next largest expenditure of $115 billion invested by Japanese businesses—its relative position has been eroding for years as businesses in other nations increase R&D expenditures at a faster rate. As of 2007, R&D spending by U.S. businesses as a share of GDP ranked sixth (1.96 percent)—behind Israel (3.84 percent), Japan (2.68 percent), Sweden (2.66 percent), Finland (2.51 percent), and South Korea (2.45 percent).

Even more alarming, over the prior decade business R&D as a percentage of GDP grew by just 4 percent in the United States. By stark contrast, business R&D as a percentage of GDP grew by 30 percent in Japan, 36 percent in South Korea, 41 percent in Finland, 101 percent in Israel—and by 251 percent in China.[82] China's performance is particularly remarkable given that its GDP (the denominator) grew at an annual rate of nearly 10 percent over the period.

We, therefore, propose two fundamental enhancements to the R&D tax credit. First, the credit should be made permanent. For U.S. businesses to invest effectively and consistently, they must be able to plan with confidence. Indeed, removing the perennial uncertainty surrounding the credit would likely increase the economic power of its incentive, generating higher R&D expenditures per dollar lost in tax revenue.[83] Moreover, as mentioned above, the credit has been repeatedly extended or renewed for more than three decades. Making the credit permanent will codify in advance what is likely to occur anyway. Finally and most fundamentally, the global economy is increasingly technology-based and ever more competitive. America's economic progress and leadership depends on a permanent commitment to innovation.

We also propose that policymakers restore the United States R&D tax credit to its former status as the most favorable in the world. Businesses currently have two choices for calculating the credit—a very complex and even archaic formula, or the alternative simplified credit (ASC).[84] Making the credit the most favorable in the world would require raising the ASC from the current 14 percent to about 45 percent, according to a recent analysis.[85] In September of 2010, President Obama proposed increasing the ASC to 17 percent.[86] But even increasing the credit to 20 percent would only improve the relative ranking of America's tax treatment of R&D to 10th in the world. In an ever more competitive global economy in which innovation is the key to success and R&D investment is increasingly mobile, nothing less than being the world's most attractive R&D investment location is acceptable if America intends to remain the world's most innovative and productive nation.

Restoring America's preeminence in incentivizing R&D will not be cheap. But losing the innovation advantage our nation has enjoyed for decades would be much more costly. To argue that we can't afford to meet the competition is to argue that we can't afford to own the future. It's that simple. Moreover, academic research regarding the stimulative effect of R&D investment on the rate of economic growth and job creation, as well as the significant "spillover" impact of such investment, strongly suggest that any short-term loss in tax revenue will be substantially or even entirely recovered through faster economic growth and job creation over the longer run. A recent analysis by the Information Technology & Innovation Foundation determined that increasing the ASC from the current 14 percent to 20 percent would increase GDP by $90 billion annually, create 162,000 new jobs, and generate $17 billion in new tax revenues.[87]

Return Federal Funding of R&D to 2 Percent of GDP

In addition to significantly enhancing the tax treatment of private R&D, the United States must also renew its commitment to government-funded R&D. The federal government accounts for about 30 percent of all R&D investment. Most critically, whereas businesses fund and conduct the vast majority of applied R&D, 70 percent of basic research is funded by the government and conducted primarily at universities and colleges.[88]

Basic or pure research is conducted to gather general information and to build on existing knowledge and understanding. Applied research is conducted for more targeted purposes—to resolve a particular question or to achieve a specific commercial objective. For example, a neurologist who studies the human brain to understand its structure and general workings is conducting basic research. A neurologist who studies the brain to determine the causes of Alzheimer's disease is conducting applied research.

While businesses conduct some basic research—about 20 percent of total basic research in 2009[89]—they are not well suited for such research. First, individual businesses are generally unable to take on the scale and risk that basic research entails. Moreover, firms are highly unlikely to invest in research that has an unknown outcome or that is unlikely to produce an immediate practical application. Basic research results are also not patentable. Finally, because businesses naturally hope to capture the full economic payoff of any R&D expenditure, they are less inclined to share any spillover benefits, limiting the broader societal value of such research.

And yet basic research—in addition to expanding human understanding of science and technology—is also the basis for applied research, establishing the context of knowledge and understanding within which additional progress can be made regarding specific inquiries. In this sense, applied research by businesses depends on basic research funded by government. Indeed, government funding of basic research has played a critical role in driving many technological breakthroughs that have helped U.S. industry become a global technology leader. Google, Sun Microsystems, Pfizer, Genentech, and Cisco are examples of companies whose origins can be traced back to basic research funded by the government.

Unfortunately, the U.S. government's commitment to R&D has waned dramatically in recent years. After growing at an inflation-adjusted average annual rate of 7 percent between 1950 and 1990, growth in government outlays for R&D fell to an annual average of just 1.4 percent between 1990 and 2012. Meanwhile, other nations have dramatically expanded government support of R&D. Over the period 1992 to 2009, Australia expanded government R&D spending at an average annual rate of 9 percent, South Korea by 11 percent, Singapore by 14 percent, and China by nearly 19 percent.[90]

Circumstances are even more alarming when R&D expenditures are considered as a percentage of GDP. As Figure 9.4 shows, U.S. government R&D fell steadily from a high of 2.0 percent of GDP in 1964 to a low of 0.7 percent of GDP in 2000, and has remained at or below 1 percent of GDP ever since.

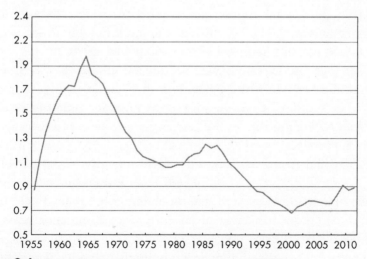

Figure 9.4 Federally Funded R&D as Percentage of GDP
SOURCE: National Science Foundation, Office of Management and Budget.

Given such trends, it is not surprising that America's R&D "intensity"—that is, total government and business R&D as a percentage of GDP—has changed very little in recent years. Between 1987 and 2008, America's R&D intensity increased by just 3 percent, while other nations' intensity increased much more substantially, including Japan (22 percent), Canada (31 percent), Sweden (34 percent), Ireland (75 percent), Korea (91 percent), Israel (110 percent), and China (110 percent).[91]

Again, China's performance is especially impressive given that its GDP grew at an annual rate of nearly 10 percent over the period. China's overall R&D—government and business—is expected to grow 12 percent to $220 billion in 2013. Given recent rates of growth, China is expected to overtake the United States in total R&D spending within 10 years.[92]

America's current R&D intensity, at about 2.8 percent of GDP, ranks eighth in the world behind Israel (4.3 percent), Finland (4.0 percent), Sweden (3.6 percent), South Korea (3.4 percent), Japan (3.3 percent), Denmark (3.0 percent), and Taiwan (2.9 percent).[93]

These troubling circumstances have been made even worse by the impact of sequestration—the significant across-the-board cuts to government spending that took effect on March 1, 2013. An analysis by the Information Technology & Innovation Foundation has determined that sequestration will cut government R&D by 8.8 percent, or $12.5 billion, in 2013, with similar cuts required each year through 2021. These reductions, the ITIF estimates, will result in GDP losses of up to $860 billion by 2021 and job losses of 450,000 by 2016.[94]

With all this in mind, we recommend restoring U.S. government funding of R&D to 2 percent of GDP. To do so, funding would need to be increased from the current $140 billion annually to about $320 billion. Adding this level of government funding to the approximately $280 billion that U.S. businesses are expected to invest in R&D in 2013 would raise America's total R&D intensity to 3.8 percent of GDP, the third highest in world behind Israel and Finland.

We understand that more than doubling government R&D funding is a significant challenge given current fiscal circumstances. But, again, for all the reasons presented above, we are strongly of the view that America's economic future depends utterly on such a commitment.

Consider this:

In November of 2011, China confirmed its rumored "Innovation 2020" strategy, by which it intends to invest $1.7 trillion over the next seven years in seven "strategic emerging sectors": alternative sources of energy, biotechnology, next-generation information technology, high-end manufacturing, advanced materials, alternative fuels, energy efficiency, and environmentally friendly technologies.[95] For the United States to match such investment on a comparable GDP basis, it would have to increase R&D investment by $800 billion—the equivalent of the American Recovery and Reinvestment (the "Stimulus") Act—every year.

Jump-Start America's Trade Agenda

America's two principal economic challenges following the Great Recession are, first, to put millions of unemployed and underemployed Americans back to work and, second, to significantly accelerate economic growth. Unfortunately, until just recently, the United States had all but abandoned one of the most powerful tools at our disposal for accomplishing both objectives—freer and more open trade.[96]

After negotiating 19 free trade agreements (FTAs) between 1994 and 2007[97]—an average of more than one each year—the United States has not negotiated a single new FTA in six years. President Obama signed FTAs with South Korea, Colombia, and Peru, but all three were negotiated during the administration of George W. Bush.[98] The United States is a participant in the Trans-Pacific Partnership, an agreement currently being negotiated between 11 Pacific nations, but the United States did not initiate the dialogue and U.S. participation was announced by the Bush Administration in September of 2008.

Meanwhile, the rest of the world has been passing us by. The European Union currently has 28 FTAs in force and has launched negotiations with India, Canada, and Ukraine. China has negotiated 10 FTAs with 20 countries and has initiated five others. India has 13 FTAs in force with a total of 25 countries and another three in negotiation.[99] Most recently, Japan, China, and South Korea launched negotiation of a three-way FTA in May of 2012.[100]

A recent Council on Foreign Relations task force comprised of 22 academic scholars and former senior policymakers of both political parties assessed America's recent trade posture in stark terms:

> Today, the United States lacks an ambitious trade policy and has not kept pace with other countries in opening new markets abroad, especially in the fast-growing economies of Asia and Latin America that are now major engines of global growth. If the United States is to prosper in today's global economy, it must enhance its ability to attract the investment and jobs linked to producing goods and services for these large and prospering markets. In short, the United States must become a great trading nation.[101]

America's inactive trade agenda is both ironic and unfortunate. Ironic, because the United States has been the principal advocate of global trade liberalization since the negotiation of the General Agreement on Tariffs and Trade (GATT) in Geneva, Switzerland, in 1947. Unfortunate, because the United States has benefited enormously from freer and more open trade—and stands to benefit even more from further liberalization.

The GATT was created as part of the world's response to the devastation of World War II and the policy failures and Great Depression that led in part to that historic calamity. The organizing principal was simple yet inspired—to promote global stability and security by expanding economic opportunity and raising living standards around the world. The great significance of the GATT was that it marked the first time the world had enshrined these principles in a multinational framework aimed at promoting global economic growth and development through, as the Agreement's preamble states, the "substantial reduction of tariffs and other trade barriers and the elimination of preferences, on a reciprocal and mutually advantageous basis."

The connection between trade and economic growth was first made by Adam Smith in his classic work *The Wealth of Nations*. Trade, Smith explained, provides access to the resources, goods, and services that nations lack or can only produce with great difficulty or at high cost. Trade also increases the size of markets, thereby promoting competition and all the associated benefits, such as greater efficiency, lower prices, and innovation. Trade, therefore, promotes the creation of wealth, as well as peace between nations by substituting internal development for territorial enlargement through conquest. To these seminal observations, British economist David Ricardo added his notion of comparative advantage, whereby countries with very different capacities and levels of productivity can still trade to mutual benefit.

In the 70 years since GATT, global trade and prosperity have flourished well beyond the hopes of the 23 nations who negotiated the agreement. Since 1948, the average tariff rate of industrialized countries has been reduced from 40 percent to less than 4 percent, and world economic output has expanded by more than 700 percent as annual global exports of goods have exploded from just $60 billion to more than $18 *trillion*.[102] Perhaps most importantly, more than 500 million people in the developing world have been lifted out of poverty, creating new markets and new avenues for additional prosperity.

Academic research has confirmed that countries that have more open economies and that engage in international trade enjoy higher growth rates and faster reductions in poverty than more closed economies.[103] The World Bank has also determined that developing countries that engage in trade enjoy the fastest growth in wages.[104]

Nobel Laureate economist Robert Solow and Martin Baily, former chairman of President Clinton's Council of Economic Advisors, have argued that free trade and increased global engagement also promote economic growth by exposing nations to global best practices, which leads to higher productivity:

> . . . when an industry is exposed to the world's best practice, it is forced to increase its own productivity. This finding emerged from a study that compared nine manufacturing industries in the United States, Germany, and Japan . . . the more a given industry is exposed to the world's best practice high productivity industry, the higher is its relative productivity (the closer it is to the leader). Competition with the productivity leader encourages higher productivity.[105]

In what has been the most dynamic era of economic development in human history, trade has become the basis for a prosperous world economy. By capitalizing on what different countries do best, trade lowers costs, frees up capital and other resources to be used more productively, raises living standards, and promotes growth and development—all of which promote faster job creation.

The United States—representing about 20 percent of global trade and as the world's third largest exporter—has benefited enormously from freer and more open trade. In 1994, the GATT was replaced by the creation of the World Trade Organization (WTO).[106] Since then, U.S. exports have quadrupled to more that $2 trillion. Since the North American Free Trade Agreement (NAFTA) became law in 1994, U.S. exports to Canada have tripled and U.S. exports to Mexico have quintupled. In 2012, U.S. trade with Mexico and Canada surpassed $1 trillion for the first time. And since China joined the WTO in 2001, U.S. exports to China have increased 600 percent—seven times faster than U.S. exports to the rest of the world.[107]

The relative importance of trade to the U.S. economy has also increased. Twenty-five years ago, the total value of U.S. exports and imports amounted to 15 percent of America's GDP. In recent years, nearly a third of GDP and as much as a quarter of economic growth have been trade related.[108] In 2010 and 2011, expanding exports accounted for about half of total U.S. economic growth.

The net result of the substantial trade liberalization achieved in recent decades is that America's national income is at least $1 trillion higher *each year*.[109] Moreover, further liberalization focused on cross-border investment and trade in services could raise national income by an additional $500 billion annually.[110] Such sizeable additional gains are possible because barriers to trade in services remain comparatively high, about 80 percent of U.S. economic output and a comparable share of U.S. employment is services-related, and because the United States maintains a strong comparative advantage in many service activities.

Perhaps most importantly, trade creates jobs. According to the Commerce Department, each additional $1 billion in exports of American-made goods creates approximately 5,000 new jobs, while each additional $1 billion in exports of American-provided services creates about 4,000 new jobs. At present, nearly 10 million American jobs are tied directly to exports—including a fifth of all manufacturing jobs—and those jobs pay salaries 13 to 18 percent more than the national average.[111] Add to that the more than 6 million American workers employed by foreign firms who outsource jobs to the United States.[112] Research has indicated that growth in exports produces twice as many jobs as an equivalent expansion of domestic output.[113] And exporting companies, when compared to nonexporters, tend to generate about twice as many sales, be about 10 to 15 percent more productive per worker, and, therefore, pay about 10 to 15 percent more in salaries.[114]

In his 2010 State of the Union Address, President Obama announced the National Export Initiative (NEI), with the goal of doubling exports to more than $3 trillion within five years and creating 2 million new American jobs.[115] The goal was enormously ambitious. To double within five years, exports would need to grow by 15 percent each year. The fastest five-year growth in exports occurred between 1986 and 1991, when exports rose 85 percent. Exports rose 78 percent in the last five years of George W. Bush's administration.

"If we're going to grow," President Obama said in November of 2011, "it's going to be because of exports."[116]

The initiative got off to a promising start, with exports expanding by 14.5 percent in 2010 and nearly 10 percent in 2011. In 2011, U.S. exports topped $2 trillion for the first time, accounting for nearly 14 percent of GDP.[117] But export growth plunged to just 2.9 percent in 2012, as emerging market economies slowed and as Europe teetered on the edge of recession, dimming chances of achieving the President's goal.

Then, in his 2013 State of the Union Address, President Obama announced the beginning of negotiations toward a U.S.–EU Transatlantic Trade and Investment Partnership (TTIP).[118] If achieved, the agreement would be the most ambitious since the founding of the WTO—encompassing 28 nations, half of global economic output, and a third of all trade.

Existing tariffs on goods traded between Europe and the United States are already low, averaging less than 3 percent. But the lowering or removal of remaining tariffs, along with the harmonization of regulations, product standards, and other non-tariff "behind-the-border" barriers to trade could yield enormous gains, given the size of the two economies.[119] Economists estimate that the TTIP could boost transatlantic trade by $120 billion per year,[120] and could add 1.6 percentage points to U.S. economic growth and 1.2 percent to Europe's—sizable gains for two economies currently struggling with below-trend growth.[121]

The TTIP is an excellent first step toward a more robust U.S. trade agenda. But America should not be satisfied with a trade agenda comprised of a single set of negotiations, no matter how significant. We propose that the United States build on that impressive start by initiating free trade talks with a number of nations—in particular, large trading partners like Japan and Taiwan, and large emerging market countries like Brazil, India, and China. With the exception of South Korea, the FTAs negotiated over the past 20 years have been with small countries. The combined GDP of the 20 nations with whom the United States has active FTAs is about $7 trillion—less than China's GDP. It's time for America to focus on the big prizes. Between 2005 and 2010, economic output from emerging market economies rose by 41 percent—including 70 percent in China and 55 percent in India—while output in advanced economies expanded by just 5 percent.[122]

A very positive development in this regard is that Japan has expressed interest in joining the Trans-Pacific Partnership trade negotiations among 11 Pacific nations including the United States. Japan's participation is expected by mid-summer 2013.

Future trade negotiations should also focus on industry sectors offering the greatest market-expanding and job-creating opportunities. Freer trade in services should be a particular focus. As mentioned above, expanded trade in services—software, telecommunications, finance, consulting, accounting, and engineering—offers enormous potential gains because barriers to trade in services remain comparatively high, about 80 percent of U.S. economic output and a comparable share of U.S. employment is services-related, and the United States maintains a strong comparative advantage in many service activities.[123] In 2012, the United States posted a services trade surplus of $196 billion, compared to a deficit of $540 billion in merchandise trade.[124]

Freer global trade has been an unqualified economic, political, international, and human success story since Word War II, fueling the most dramatic expansion of global economic output, wealth and job creation, and poverty alleviation in history. By offering prosperity in return for peaceful exchange and market-led cooperation, trade has become a critical cornerstone for progress and peace around the world. Trade has also been, and remains, a major strategic element of U.S. foreign policy.

Given the importance of faster economic growth to new business formation and survival, job creation, and debt and deficit reduction, the critical task before us now is to build on the achievements of the past 70 years by capturing the gains offered by further trade liberalization. With 95 percent of the world's consumers living beyond our borders, trade is an essential tool for promoting economic growth and job creation, and advancing U.S. global interests more broadly.

Negotiate a U.S–China Free Trade Agreement

One FTA opportunity deserves special focus. Within the context of what a more robust trade agenda would mean for U.S. economic growth and job creation, the United States should capitalize on one of the most significant events in human history—the continuing economic emergence of China—by negotiating a U.S.–China free trade agreement. Though daunting with regard to its scale, complexity, and cultural challenges, successful negotiation of a U.S.–China FTA would yield enormous gains for the world's two largest economies—and, therefore, the global economy—and would serve as a solid foundation for greater economic, political, and strategic cooperation between the world's two most powerful nations.

China's economy has grown at an annual rate of nearly 10 percent for three decades. The world's seventh largest economy as recently as 1999, China has now surpassed Japan to become the world's second largest economy. The rate of China's economic growth and the ongoing integration of its 1.3 billion people—a fifth of the world's population—into the global economy are unprecedented in human history, with profound implications for U.S. economic growth and job creation.

As Figure 9.5 shows, U.S. exports to China have increased more than sixfold since China joined the WTO in December of 2001. China is now America's third largest export market, and the largest market for U.S. goods and services outside North America. Top American exports to China include agricultural products, computers and electronics, chemicals, and transportation equipment, especially aerospace and autos.[125]

As Figure 9.6 shows, China is also America's fastest growing export market *by far*—growing at seven times the rate of U.S. exports to the rest of the world. Since 2001, 48 states have experienced at least triple-digit

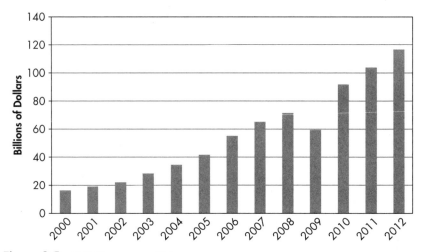

Figure 9.5   U.S. Exports to China
SOURCE: Department of Commerce.

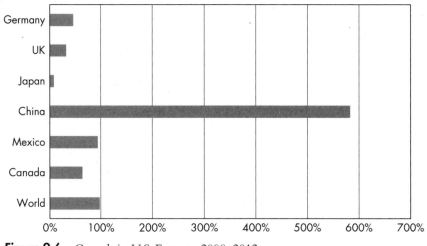

Figure 9.6   Growth in U.S. Exports, 2000–2012
SOURCE: Department of Commerce.

growth in their exports to China, far outpacing growth in their exports to the rest of the world. Twenty states have recorded quadruple-digit growth. Indeed, virtually every Congressional district in the United States has experienced dramatic growth in exports to China.[126]

Of course, as the U.S.–China economic relationship has grown in magnitude and complexity, frictions have emerged. Issues complicating the relationship include the large trade imbalance, product safety concerns, intellectual property infringements, China's foreign exchange rate policies, and, most recently, alleged cyber-espionage.[127] While not surprising, and perhaps even inevitable, such festering problems have caused some U.S. policymakers, and many Americans, to question the benefits of maintaining an open and expanding economic relationship with China.

China's membership in the WTO beginning in December of 2001 was the culmination of nearly 15 years of negotiations with the WTO, and 25 years of political and economic engagement by the United States.[128] To achieve membership, China implemented thousands of reforms in hundreds of aspects of its economy and legal and regulatory system.[129] But the work to fully integrate China into the global economy is not finished. Indeed, in a very real sense, only the easy part is over.

In our view, U.S. policy with regard to China should move beyond the monitoring of China's compliance with a discrete set of specific WTO-related obligations to a broader and more sophisticated policy that seeks more proactive cooperation in an increasingly dynamic relationship. The aim of such policy should be to ensure that China participates fully and constructively as a mature and responsible stakeholder in the global economy from which it has benefited so profoundly. Negotiation of a U.S.–China FTA can cement progress achieved to date and ensure a more balanced, equitable, and durable bilateral relationship.

Such an agreement should focus on further opening China's economy to U.S. exports; lowering or even eliminating import tariffs and other legal and regulatory barriers in both countries to expanded trade; ensuring robust protection of intellectual property; ensuring non-discriminatory national treatment of U.S. and Chinese businesses with regard to licensing, corporate form, and permitted products and services; greater regulatory and judicial transparency in China; and greater foreign participation in China's financial sector.

Initial discussion of an FTA can occur as part of the ongoing U.S.–China Strategic and Economic Dialogue (S&ED).[130] Established in September of 2006 by President George W. Bush and President Hu Jintao to enhance the management of the growing bilateral relationship, the S&ED created an unprecedented channel of communication between Cabinet-level U.S. and Chinese policymakers, and provided an overarching framework for the examination of long-term strategic issues, as well as coordination of ongoing bilateral policy discussions.

Negotiating a U.S.–China FTA will not be easy. All FTA negotiations are complex, painstaking, arduous work. Moreover, having been to China several times ourselves and sat in many meetings with senior government officials, regulators, and business people, we understand that the United States and China are very different countries, with very different cultures, values, priorities, and even ways of thinking.[131] Negotiation of an FTA with China would surely take years. There will be quarrels and setbacks. At times, success might seem unachievable.

But, in our view, the logic and even necessity of a U.S.–China FTA is undeniable. The United States and China are the world's largest economies and will be for decades to come, although their positions are likely to switch.[132] Together the two economies currently account for a third of global economic output and half of global economic growth.

Moreover, the two economies are already integrated to the point of mutual dependence. Like it or not, healthy economic growth and job creation in America depends in large part on continued growth in China, and vice versa. Former Treasury Secretary Henry M. "Hank" Paulson has called the U.S.–China economic relationship "the most important bilateral economic relationship in the world today."[133] Without question, how this critical relationship develops, evolves, and is managed will be among the most important factors determining the growth and stability of the global economy in the twenty-first century.

For China, the value of an FTA with the United States might well be nothing less than economic survival. After nearly three decades of astonishing growth and development, China now faces daunting challenges that threaten the success achieved to date and its economic future. Such challenges include an economic model too dependent on physical investment and exports, domination of the economy by state-owned enterprises, environmental degradation, high social and economic inequality, and a comparatively primitive financial sector that remains largely closed to foreign participation.[134] According to the World Bank, unless China meaningfully addresses these and other structural problems, it runs the risk of significant and sudden deceleration of economic growth.[135] Greater participation in China's economy by American companies, consumers, and investors under the terms of an FTA would help accelerate the structural and macroeconomic reforms necessary for China to ensure sustained growth and stability over the long term.

For the Unites States, the FTA will ensure that American manufacturers, service providers, farmers—and entrepreneurs—can participate in, contribute to, and benefit from the continuing emergence of the greatest commercial market in history. A quick back-of-the-napkin calculation reveals what an expanding Chinese economy can mean for U.S. economic growth and job creation.

Last year, U.S. exports to Japan totaled $70 billion, while U.S. exports to China totaled $110.5 billion. But China's population is *10 times* that of Japan. If China's citizens eventually consume American-made goods and services at the same rate as the Japanese currently do, U.S. exports to China would grow to more than $700 billion annually. That's seven times what America exported to China last year, an amount equivalent to nearly 5 percent of U.S. GDP, and nearly twice what we imported from China last year—turning a $315 billion trade deficit into a $275 billion surplus.

Using the Commerce Department's export and jobs metrics discussed above, increasing U.S. exports to China to $700 billion a year would create more than 3 million new American jobs.

Combine and Modernize Unemployment Insurance and Trade Adjustment Assistance

While liberalized global trade has been an unqualified boon to the U.S. economy—increasing national income by at least $1 trillion each year and promising an additional $500 billion per year if further liberalization focused on cross-border investment and services is achieved—such gains are not distributed evenly. Many Americans have prospered in the age of globalization, others have not. As resources, capital, and production are reallocated to reflect the comparative economic advantages of trading partners, painful adjustments can and do occur. Certain industries and businesses might be disrupted or forced to downsize, employee salaries might be reduced by employers to remain competitive, and certain jobs might be relocated or even eliminated.

And such trade-related pressures are not limited to those directly affected. Due to the pronounced dynamism and competition in U.S.

labor markets described in Chapter 2, the impact of trade and global engagement inevitably spreads throughout the economy, affecting, both positively and negatively, the employment prospects, earnings, and living standards of every American.

Such changes, and especially the accelerating rate of change, have become cause for anxiety and even fear for many Americans.[136] This reality is reflected in public polling on the subject of trade. For example, two NBC/*Wall Street Journal* polls, the first conducted in December of 1999 and the second in September of 2010, found that the percentage of people who think that free trade agreements "have hurt the United States" increased from 30 percent in 1999 to 53 percent in 2010, while the percentage of those polled who think that FTAs "have helped the United States" fell from 39 percent in 1999 to just 17 percent in 2010.[137]

It should be pointed out that the aggregate gains associated with freer trade have been shown to far exceed the associated costs. In fact, academic research has concluded that trade-related economic gains outstrip aggregate costs by a factor of 20 and even 100.[138] Moreover, the U.S. economy is in a constant state of change, impacted by many forces other than trade pressures. Technological advancement, innovation of various kinds, demographic changes, economic cycles, changing consumer tastes, and governmental policies continuously impact and determine the job security, economic prospects, earnings, and living standards of American workers in much more powerful ways than trade.

Finally, and perhaps most fundamentally, change and adjustment is essential to the health of the U.S. economy. Without the constant reallocation of capital, labor, and other resources from less productive sectors to more productive sectors, economic growth, job creation, and living standards would be harmed, not improved.

Nevertheless, the concerns and anxieties felt by many Americans with regard to freer trade are genuine, powerful, and understandable. Trade can and does impose real and often persistent costs on some American industries, firms, communities, and workers.

Making the case for freer trade, therefore, and strengthening the political consensus for freer trade, requires a meaningful and specific policy response to this reality.[139] The aim of that policy response should be to expand the numbers of those who benefit directly and significantly from freer trade and global engagement, and to provide effective transition assistance to those adversely affected by evolving trade patterns and globalization.

Specifically, we propose combining the current Unemployment Insurance (UI) and Trade Adjustment Assistance (TAA) programs into a new integrated and significantly expanded Economic Adjustment Assistance (EAA) program. The new EAA program would offer American workers who have been displaced for *any* reason—trade-related or otherwise—a flexible twenty-first century menu of short-term assistance options. This idea was originally proposed in 2007 by Matthew Slaughter of the Tuck School of Business at Dartmouth, Robert Lawrence of Harvard's Kennedy School of Government, and Grant Aldonis, former Under Secretary of Commerce for International Trade.[140]

UI was created as part of the Social Security Act of 1935 and has not changed fundamentally since then. UI benefits are intended to reduce the hardship of involuntary unemployment, help maintain the purchasing power of the unemployed, and preserve the local workforce so that workers are available when employers are ready to rehire. In effect, UI was designed to support an unemployed worker until he or she is rehired by the previous employer or a similar employer. But the challenges that confront unemployed workers today are much more complex, and can include finding a new employer, often in a new field or industry; upgrading or adding to existing skills; learning altogether new skills; and coping with lost earnings and benefits, especially healthcare.

TAA, created as part of the Trade Expansion Act of 1962 and further defined under the Trade Act of 1974, was designed to supplement UI by providing assistance to workers displaced specifically by competition from imports. But, again, rather than facing one-time adjustments to isolated increases in import competition, firms and workers today face continuous adjustment challenges due to an ever-changing competitive landscape driven by technological advancement, competition from overseas, changing consumer tastes, business cycles, and governmental policy. In fact, data collected by the Bureau of Labor Statistics show that only about 1 percent of employer layoffs of 50 or more people in recent years have been due to competition from imports.[141]

And yet, TAA offers assistance only to workers who have been displaced due to trade. Moreover, the principal assistance provided through TAA is training within the affected worker's current field, rather than a broad array of more tailored options responding to the specific challenges confronting a particular displaced worker.[142] For these reasons, as well as reportedly daunting administrative complexities, less than a quarter of eligible workers have taken advantage of TAA benefits in recent years. Indeed, just 196,000 workers participated in some aspect of the TAA program in fiscal year 2011—fewer than the number of jobs lost on an average day.[143]

UI and TAA are well-intentioned government programs designed to soften the blow of economic displacement. But as currently structured and administered, both programs are relics of an economy that no longer exists and, therefore, are insufficient to meet the varied adjustment needs of a twenty-first century, globally engaged American workforce. Given the array of forces that affect their jobs, economic prospects, earnings, and living standards, American workers need and deserve a broader and more flexible framework of adjustment assistance comprised of options tailored to address their specific needs.

Some displaced workers need to upgrade or add to skills within their current fields. Others need new skills to leave a shrinking field and jump to an expanding field. Some need help with relocation expenses in order to take a new job in a different city. Still others might decide to start their own businesses and need access to start-up capital. A modern and effective EAA program should offer an array of a la carte options designed to provide the flexibility and optionality necessary to meet the varied needs of displaced workers in twenty-first century America.

Other key aspects of the EAA program would likely include a wage-loss insurance feature to ease the transition for older workers forced to take lower-paying jobs, continued health insurance coverage while workers remain eligible for EAA, and, potentially, allowing workers in transition to access tax-advantaged savings and investment accounts, like IRAs and 401(k)s, without incurring standard penalties.

Combining the UI and TAA programs into a single, expanded, and integrated new Economic Adjustment Assistance program would entail two principal advantages. First, significant cost savings would be achieved by eliminating separate and often inconsistent qualification regimes, as well as duplicative administration. Most importantly, two uncoordinated programs that offer displaced workers only limited assistance would be replaced by a broader and more modern assistance program designed to serve as a one-stop source for displaced workers—regardless of the source of their displacement—to access the specific assistance that they as individuals need to return to the active workforce.

Adjustment assistance that works, that meets the specific needs of displaced workers, and provides a pathway back to gainful employment in a growing economy will help preserve the national consensus for global engagement policies like freer trade that offer such significant additional gains, and that, therefore, must be part of America's strategy to accelerate economic growth and job creation.

Conclusion

This project was launched in response to the greatest sudden loss of employment in America in nearly 80 years. Between February of 2008 and February of 2010, nearly 9 million jobs were eliminated—wiping out all employment growth over the previous decade. The project was also launched because by the spring of 2011, two years into the weakest post-recession recovery since World War II, it was apparent that conventional policy responses, despite being implemented on an unprecedented scale—an $800 billion fiscal stimulus and 28 months of short-term interest rates near zero—had not produced the desired acceleration of economic growth and job creation.

Regrettably, two years later, the economic circumstances that gave rise to this project have only persisted. In 2012, the U.S. economy expanded at a lackluster 2.2 percent, with economic growth slowing to just 0.4 percent in the fourth quarter. And as of the spring of 2013, nearly 12 million Americans remain without work, another eight million are underemployed, and an estimated 4 million have simply given up looking for work. More than four years into the economic recovery, 15 percent of the American workforce—a fifth of American households—continue to suffer the worst effects of the Great Recession and its immediate aftermath. Moreover, at the current pace of job creation—a monthly average of just 180,000 new jobs—America will likely not return to pre-recession levels of employment until 2023.[1]

That's the bad news. But there is good news.

Thanks to research first conducted by Census Bureau economists and further analyzed by researchers at the Ewing Marion Kauffman Foundation, we now understand that new businesses—start-ups—are the engine of job creation in America, creating an average of about 3 million new jobs each year and accounting for virtually all net new job creation. By contrast, existing firms, of any age or size, shed a combined average of about 1 million jobs each year as some businesses fail, as others become more efficient and reduce head count, and as separations outpace new hires.

This is not to argue that existing small businesses or larger firms are unimportant. On the contrary, small businesses account for 99 percent of U.S. businesses and more than half of total employment. U.S. multinational companies employ tens of millions of Americans, account for outsized proportions of U.S. exports, R&D spending, and productivity growth, and provide much of the demand for the goods and services produced by smaller firms, including new firms. But if the policy target is job creation, new business formation is the bull's-eye.

We also now know, with unprecedented clarity, what obstacles are currently in the way of American entrepreneurs. As we discussed in Chapter 3, one of the major take-aways from our series of roundtables—and enormously significant from the standpoint of potential policy solutions—is that the problems and obstacles encountered by entrepreneurs across the country are remarkably consistent. Notwithstanding differences in local economic conditions and regulatory environments from region to region—and acknowledging differences in emphasis from one city to the next—entrepreneurs from Austin to Boston and from Seattle to Orlando identified the same burdens, frustrations, and difficulties that are undermining their efforts to start new businesses, expand young firms, and hire. Over the course of this book we have reported those obstacles through the words and experiences of our participating entrepreneurs, and presented 30 specific policy proposals based on what America's entrepreneurs told us they need.

Our summer on the road made several critical realities vividly clear to us.

First, young businesses are extremely fragile—a third fail by their second year, half by their fifth. And yet, those new businesses that survive tend to grow and create jobs at very rapid rates.

Second, the policy needs and priorities of new businesses are unique. Start-ups are different from existing businesses. The challenges they confront are different and their ability to successfully navigate those challenges is more limited. Policies intended to enhance the circumstances of large corporations or even existing small businesses—however well intended or legitimate—often miss the needs of new businesses and can even undermine their prospects.

Third, policy help for America's job creators is urgently needed. After remaining remarkably consistent for decades, the number of new firms launched each year—and the number of new jobs created by those new firms—has declined precipitously in recent years. Given the critical role they play in our nation's economy as the principal source of innovation, growth, and job creation, America's young businesses need and deserve a comprehensive and *preferential* policy framework designed to cultivate and nurture start-ups.

It's important to emphasize that the urgency of significantly accelerating job creation here in the United States stems not just from the fact that 24 million Americans remain out of work or are underemployed, as serious and unacceptable as those circumstances are. As Jim Clifton, chairman and chief executive officer of Gallup points out in his recent book *The Coming Jobs War*, in our ever-more integrated, competitive, and mobile world, the capacity to produce gainful employment for their citizens has emerged as an essential national imperative:

The coming world war is an all-out global war for good jobs . . . [O]f the 7 billion people on Earth, there are 5 billion adults aged 15 and older. Of these 5 billion, 3 billion tell Gallup they work or want to work . . . The problem is that there are currently only 1.2 billion full-time, formal jobs in the world . . .

[T]he lack of good jobs will become the root cause of almost all world problems that America and other countries will attempt to deal with through humanitarian aid, military force, and politics. The lack of good jobs will become the cause of hunger, extremism, out-of-control migration patterns, reckless environmental trends, widening trade imbalances, and on and on . . .

[T]he next 30 years won't be led by U.S. political or military force. Instead, the world will be led with economic force—a force that is primarily driven by job creation and quality GDP growth . . .

The demands of leadership have changed. The highest levels of leadership require mastery of a new task: job creation . . . The war for global jobs is like World War II: a war for all the marbles. The global war for jobs determines the leader of the free world. If the United States allows China or any other country or region to out-enterprise it, out-job-create it, out-grow its GDP, everything changes. This is America's next war for everything.

In the Introduction to this book, we stated that in highlighting the critical role of new businesses and focusing on their unique policy needs, our intent is neither to glamorize entrepreneurs nor to exaggerate the job-creating capacity of the businesses they launch. Not all new companies create jobs, or even survive. Public policy shouldn't promote or protect poor business ideas simply because they are new, nor should government pick winners and losers.

But if new businesses account for virtually all net new job creation, and if some fraction of the new firms launched each year go on to create hundreds or even thousands of new jobs, then America needs to get serious about enhancing the circumstances for new business formation, survival, and growth—particularly given the alarming reality that the number of new firms launched each year, and the number of new jobs created by those firms, has declined significantly in recent years.

In 2001, a group of New Orleans technology professionals met at Loa Bar, just off Canal Street, to swap stories and commiserate about the long, slow decline of the Big Easy.[2] Among other topics, they discussed the highly implausible: how to make New Orleans a destination for entrepreneurs. The meeting led to the creation of a nonprofit organization called The Idea Village, which provides educational and consulting services that support and facilitate entrepreneurship, and lobbies city officials to support the needs and priorities of start-ups.[3]

But in August of 2005, Hurricane Katrina hit. Within days, 80 percent of the city was under water, more than 1,200 people were dead, and the city's storefronts, infrastructure, and school system were destroyed. Within a year, the city lost more than 90,000 jobs, taking $3 billion in wages.

But Katrina also swept away much of the entrenched interests and political inertia that had frustrated previous renewal efforts.

In the years since, New Orleans has not only made remarkable progress, but has established itself as an emerging innovation hub. Successful start-ups like iSeatz and Solomon Group have located in the Big Easy, taking advantage of the low cost of living and super-cheap office space. Tax incentives that cover 25 percent of new companies' production costs and 35 percent of payroll expenses have been credited with expanding the city's tech base by 19 percent since Katrina, six times the national rate. New Orleans is now the only city in America where a majority of public school students are in charter schools.

After losing 10 percent of its population following Katrina, the city is not only growing again, but at the third fastest pace in the nation, just behind Austin, Texas, and suburban Washington, DC. In 2011, the *Wall Street Journal* named New Orleans the nation's most improved metro area. Forbes has named it America's top city for IT job growth, and CareerBuilder has said the city has the nation's third fastest wage growth.

The innovation-led renaissance underway in New Orleans is a vivid example of the creative and transformational power of the American entrepreneurial economy. We came away from our summer on the road struck most of all by our nation's stunning entrepreneurial dynamism. Despite the downward trend in the rate of new business formation in recent years, and despite very challenging economic circumstances, entrepreneurs all across America—driven by a desire to create and build, and enabled by the development of new technologies—continue to launch new companies, build those businesses, and pursue their dreams of independence and wealth. Having witnessed such dynamism and commitment first hand, we are more optimistic about the future of the U.S. economy—and its job creating capacity—than ever.

But for that tremendous potential to be fully unleashed, America's entrepreneurs need help. Fortunately, our journey also provided a road map for success. The 30 specific policy proposals presented over the course of this book amount to an altogether new, uniquely credible, and vitally important game plan for unleashing the job-creating capacity of America's entrepreneurial economy, and putting our beleaguered nation back to work.

Our sincere hope—not only for the nation's entrepreneurs, but especially for the nearly 24 million unemployed or underemployed Americans and their families—is that policymakers in Washington will hear the urgent message sent by job creators, and give serious consideration to the policy proposals we have recommended in response. The details of what we have proposed can and should be debated, and no doubt we have overlooked important issues or underestimated certain political realities. But given that our recommendations respond directly and specifically to what our participating entrepreneurs told us—indeed, a number of the recommendations were offered by the entrepreneurs themselves—there can be no doubt that the policy ideas offered, if implemented, would dramatically enhance the circumstances for new business formation, survival, and growth, and, therefore, significantly accelerate economic growth and job creation.

As we said in the Introduction, America's job creators have told us what they need. There's no time to waste.

Let's put America back to work!

Afterword

I n the fall of 2011, after 30 straight months of unemployment above 8 percent and no signs of improvement, we began looking for new ways to spur growth in the American economy. We were both relatively new to the Senate and belonged to different political parties, but found we had a common goal: to grow our economy and help Americans find work. So we decided on a new approach, one that is based on a proven track record of success—the success of the American entrepreneur.

Research conducted by the Kauffman Foundation in Kansas City has shown that between 1980 and 2005, companies less than five years old accounted for nearly all the new job growth in the United States. In fact, new firms have been consistently creating about 3 million jobs each year since the 1970s. However, while the United States once ranked among the top five countries in the world for "start-up friendliness," in recent years, the United States has dropped out of the top 10, landing at 13th in 2012 according to analysis conducted by the World Bank.

The numbers are staggering. In 2010, more than 394,000 new businesses were created in the United States; however, this was the smallest number created in a single year since data collection began in 1977. Though these new companies created more than 2.3 million jobs, that figure is well below the historical average and represents the third smallest number of jobs created by new businesses in more than 30 years. Entrepreneurs, who have more choices than ever before about where to start a business, are beginning to look elsewhere for opportunities. Other countries, including Canada, Chile, and the United Kingdom, have begun to aggressively court entrepreneurs, offering incentives such as immediate permanent residency and government investment to attract more job creators.

The United States cannot afford to turn a blind eye to our competitors on an issue so critical to our economic future. The analysis presented in *Where the Jobs Are* builds a strong case for how essential entrepreneurs are to our country's overall economic success. To get the U.S. economic engine roaring once again, we must free up entrepreneurs to do what they do best—pursue big dreams. But how do we do that?

To begin, policymakers must listen to entrepreneurs and identify the challenges standing in their way. By meeting with more than 200 entrepreneurs, the authors of this book gained valuable insight into how lawmakers can increase the likelihood that entrepreneurs will not only be successful, but also get our economy growing again. Many of the recommendations that stemmed from these conversations are included in a bill that we introduced in 2011—the Startup Act. We have since strengthened the bill and introduced a new version called Startup Act 3.0 with bipartisan support from colleagues in both chambers of Congress.

One of the greatest challenges facing start-ups is acquiring enough capital to get off the ground, so our plan includes tax incentives to encourage investment in start-up companies. Startup Act 3.0 also makes changes to the federal regulatory process so the costs of new regulation do not outweigh the benefits, and the bill encourages federal agencies to consider the impact of proposed regulation on start-ups.

Our plan also seeks to improve the process of commercializing federally funded research, so good ideas get out of the lab and into the marketplace more quickly where they can spur economic growth.

Startup Act 3.0 will also help identify which states are more start-up friendly, by directing the Commerce Department to publish reports on new business formation and the entrepreneurial environment in each state. And finally, our plan will provide new opportunities for highly educated and entrepreneurial immigrants to stay in the United States, where their talents and ideas can fuel economic growth and create American jobs.

The role of policymakers in Washington is to work for the good of all Americans. What better way to do that than by growing our economy and creating jobs? Entrepreneurs need a voice in Washington, and we intend to be that voice.

The United States has long been known as the land of opportunity where individuals risk it all to live out their dreams. Individual tenacity is rewarded and appreciated here. Many Fortune 500 companies like Apple and General Electric got their start with a handful of folks, a great idea, and a lot of hard work. We believe entrepreneurs hold the key to our future economic success, and we are committed to helping the spirit of entrepreneurship flourish across our country.

Senator Jerry Moran
Senator Mark Warner*

---

*Republican Senator Moran is from Kansas; Democratic Senator Warner is from Virginia.

Appendix: Summary of Recommendations

Establish a Preferential Tax and Regulatory Framework to Cultivate New Business Formation and Growth

- The Internal Revenue Service (IRS) should be directed to establish a new entrepreneur—or "e-corp"—tax status, whereby newly launched businesses would be subject to a flat 5 percent income tax for the critical first five years after formation. Such favorable and predictable tax treatment will help cultivate new business formation, survival, and growth by allowing new businesses to retain and reinvest most of what they earn, preserving critical cash flow, and eliminating the distraction and burden of tax complexity and uncertainty.
- The Congressional Budget Office (CBO) and the Office of Management and Budget (OMB) should be directed to co-develop a preferential regulatory framework to which fragile new businesses would be subject for their first five years. The framework should be comprised of only the most essential product

safety, environmental, and worker protection regulations. To minimize regulatory uncertainty, the new-business framework should
also protect new businesses from new regulations for the first five
years. Co-development of the preferential framework by CBO
and OMB is important since regulation is the implementation of
Congressional intent by executive branch agencies.

- To avoid abuse of the preferential tax and regulatory framework—
  such as business owners simply renaming or reconstituting existing companies every five years—the IRS, working with CBO and
  OMB, should develop appropriate definitions, characteristics, and
  limitations regarding the meaning of "new business."

- New businesses should be permitted to use the cash method of
  accounting during the critical first five years of their operation.
  The cash method is simpler, less costly, and easier for new businesses to understand than accrual accounting or other more complex accounting methods to which some businesses are subject.

- New businesses should be permitted 100 percent first-year expensing of business-related capital, equipment, off-the-shelf software,
  and real estate investment costs for the first five years after formation. New businesses with no taxable earnings in particular years
  during their initial five years should be permitted to carry forward
  the deduction of such expenses for 15 years beyond the year in
  which the capital expenses were incurred.

- Because new businesses often have no earnings in their initial years of operation, new firms should be permitted to deduct
  R&D spending up to $250,000 from the payroll taxes they pay on
  employee wages in the following year, rather than against income
  taxes, for the first five years after formation.

Enhance the Quality, Technical Capacity, and Flexibility of the American Workforce

- Students who complete an undergraduate or post-graduate degree
  in science, technology, engineering, or mathematics should be
  provided a $50,000 federal tax credit that can be deducted from

taxable income up to $10,000 per year over the initial five years of their post-graduate employment.

- High quality and experienced talent needed to successfully scale new businesses should be incentivized to consider joining rapidly growing start-ups by meaningfully offsetting the "life risk" often associated with new businesses. In particular, the proceeds of all exercised stock options issued to employees of new businesses less than five years old should be taxed at the reduced long-term capital gain rate. In addition, the $100,000 per employee annual vesting limit on incentive stock options (ISOs) and the requirement to pay the ISO strike price at the time of exercise should be eliminated.

- The Department of Education, in partnership with nationwide business groups, should launch an ongoing dialogue between business and education leaders to regularly examine kindergarten through grade 12, college, and university curricula to ensure that the nation's education system serves the broader educational needs of students, as well as the skill requirements of twenty-first century businesses. A major focus of the dialogue should be to facilitate business community input into curricula determinations, aptitude standards, and work-study programs, as well as to increase opportunities for active business professionals and other practitioners to participate in and outside the classroom as instructors, assistants, advisors, and mentors.

- The Department of Education, in partnership with national education groups, should launch an ongoing dialogue among educators at all levels regarding how to make American education—both at the systemic level and with regard to classroom techniques and methodologies—more flexible, creative, and innovative. Specifically, core skills such as reading, writing, math, and science should be augmented by personal motivation, creative problem-solving, communication, and collaboration skills.

- The Unemployment Insurance (UI) and Trade Adjustment Assistance (TAA) programs should be combined and modernized to create a world-class, twenty-first century framework of economic adjustment assistance for displaced American workers.

Modernize Immigration Laws to Attract and Retain the World's Best Talent

- Eliminate the cap on H1-B visas.
- A permanent residency card—"graduation green card"—should be automatically awarded to any foreign-born student meeting national security requirements who graduates from an American college or university with an undergraduate or post-graduate degree in science, technology, engineering, or mathematics.
- A high-skill immigrant green card category of at least 50,000 annually should be established to attract top international graduates in STEM fields who meet national security requirements. These preferential green cards should be awarded based on a points system that rewards skills, level of education and training, entrepreneurship, English proficiency, and other key metrics in order to attract applicants with desired economic backgrounds.
- A special "start-up visa" should be created for foreign-born entrepreneurs meeting national security requirements who want to start a business in the United States and who have secured at least $100,000 in initial funding. Foreign-born entrepreneurs would be admitted on a temporary two-year basis. If by the end of that two-year period their business has been successfully launched, is producing verifiable revenue, and has produced jobs for at least two nonfamily members, the temporary visa would be extended by an additional three years. If the new business continues to be successful and produce verifiable revenue, and has created jobs for at least five nonfamily members by the end of the five-year period, the foreign-born entrepreneur would be granted permanent residency.
- A new service-toward-citizenship program—"CitizenCorps"—should be established whereby undocumented workers could earn U.S. citizenship over a period of years through extended service to their communities. The program should be modeled on AmeriCorps, the federal program created by the National and Community Service Trust Act of 1993, in which participants serve their communities through a network of partnerships with local and national nonprofit groups.

Enhance Access to Capital for New Businesses

- The Small Business Administration (SBA) should be directed to initiate a dialogue with lending banks and entrepreneurs with the aim of making SBA lending more available, less complex and cumbersome, less physical asset–based, and less restrictive of new businesses' tactical and strategic decision making.
- The formation and commitment of angel capital should be incentivized by enacting a federal tax credit for those who invest in start-ups equal to 25 percent of the investment, and relieving from federal income tax any capital gains on investments in start-ups held for at least three years.
- Companies with annual gross revenue of less than $500 million should be exempt from compliance with section 404 of the Sarbanes-Oxley Act. In addition, companies with annual gross revenue of between $500 million and $5 billion should be permitted to opt out of compliance with section 404 during the first five years of operation, based on a majority vote of the company's shareholders.
- In order to restore the economics necessary to support a robust market for small IPOs, the SEC should create an optional pricing regime for the shares of public companies with a market capitalization of less than $700 million (borrowing from the definition of "emerging growth company" established by the JOBS Act). The new pricing regime would establish fixed minimum tick sizes—say, 10 cents for stocks under $5 per share, 20 cents for stocks valued at $5 or higher. Participation in the alternative pricing regime would be optional—small issuers could choose to list under the alternative regime or under the current regime. Companies already public with a market capitalization of less than $700 million could also choose to move into the alternative pricing regime. The two parallel regimes, operating side-by-side, would preserve the pricing and other benefits to investors of one-penny spreads in the market for larger company stocks, while also preserving the economics necessary to support the research, underwriting, and liquidity upon which a thriving market for smaller IPOs depends.

Reduce Regulatory Burden, Complexity, and Uncertainty

- CBO and OMB should be directed to co-conduct third-party analysis of the economic costs and benefits of all proposed new regulations. The third-party review should include analysis of the costs of the proposed regulation in relation to other federal regulations, as well as in relation to existing state and local regulations. In particular, the third-party review should focus on the impact of the proposed new regulation on new and small businesses.
- Proposed regulations determined to have economic costs, or costs to new and small businesses, that exceed identifiable benefits should require Congressional approval for enactment.
- Congress and the President should create through signed legislation a federal Regulatory Improvement Commission (RIC), modeled on the Base Closure and Realignment Commission (BRAC). The RIC's purpose would be to serve as a procedural mechanism for the regular evaluation, simplification, streamlining, consolidation, and elimination of selected existing regulations.
- The Commerce Department should be directed to launch a nationwide initiative, in partnership with entrepreneurship organizations and facilities around the country, to develop a research framework by which all 50 states will be ranked as to their regulatory friendliness to new business formation, survival, and growth. Metrics and rankings should be published online for easy and widespread use by entrepreneurs. To further incentivize a "race to the top" among states, the federal government might consider allocating economic development block grants to states based on their annual ranking for the purpose of funding enhancements of their entrepreneurship ecosystem.

Accelerate Scientific and Commercial Innovation

- Federal funding of research and development should be restored to its historical high of 2 percent of GDP annually.
- The research and development tax credit should be restored to its former status as the most favorable in the world—and should be made permanent.

Accelerate Economic Growth by Reducing Fiscal and Economic Uncertainty

- Gradual but significant long-term deficit and debt reduction should be enacted, including meaningful changes to federal entitlement programs, with an emphasis on spending reduction.
- Comprehensive, competitiveness-enhancing reform of the U.S. tax code should be enacted to simplify individual and corporate tax frameworks, significantly lower rates, incentivize work and investment, and permit the repatriation of overseas corporate profits.
- President Obama's initiative to double exports within five years should be accelerated by jump-starting the U.S. trade agenda. Specifically, the United States should launch additional market-opening freer trade initiatives around the world, focusing on large trading partners like Japan and Taiwan, as well as rapidly growing emerging markets like Brazil, India, and China. Negotiations should emphasize industry sectors (manufacturing, software, telecommunications, finance, consulting, accounting, engineering) with the greatest potential market—and job creating—opportunities.

Notes

Introduction

1. See Motoko Rich, "Job Growth Falters Badly, Clouding Hope for Recovery," *New York Times*, July 8, 2011.

2. Scott A. Shane, *The Illusions of Entrepreneurship: The Costly Myths that Entrepreneurs, Investors, and Policymakers Live By* (New Haven, CT: Yale University Press, 2008).

3. "The Importance of Jobs," *Wall Street Journal*, August 26, 2011, Review & Outlook.

Chapter 1: America's Jobs Emergency

1. See The Hamilton Project, "Closing the Jobs Gap," The Brookings Institution, 2013.

2. Neil Irwin, "Aughts Were a Lost Decade for U.S. Economy, Workers," *Washington Post*, January 2, 2010.

3. The federal funds rate is the interest rate at which depository institutions lend balances at the Federal Reserve to other depository institutions overnight. By altering the desired quantity of banks' reserves by way of open market operations—purchases and sales of U.S. Treasury and federal agency securities—the Fed is able to target the price of such interbank borrowing.

4. Over the next two years, the Fed extended and expanded its efforts to revive the floundering economy. In September of 2011, citing "continuing weakness in overall labor market conditions," the Federal Open Market Committee (FOMC) announced that it would buy $400 billion of longer-term Treasury securities and sell an equal amount of short-term Treasuries—a maneuver referred to by market participants as "Operation Twist," the intention of which was to support business and consumer borrowing by reducing longer-term interest rates. In June of 2012, the FOMC announced that it would extend the "twist" through the end of the year. On September 13, 2012, the FOMC, stating that "without further policy accommodation, economic growth might not be strong enough to generate sustained improvement in labor market conditions," announced a third and highly controversial round of quantitative easing ("QEIII"). The FOMC said that the Fed would purchase $40 billion worth of additional agency mortgage-backed securities every month until labor market conditions improved "substantially." The Committee also reiterated that it would continue through year-end 2012 its program announced in June to extend the average maturity of its securities holdings ("Operation Twist"), and that it would maintain its existing policy of reinvesting principal payments from its holdings of agency debt and agency mortgage-backed securities. Additionally, the FOMC said that the federal funds rate would remain at 0 to ¼ percent, at least until mid-2015. Then, on December 12, 2012, the FOMC announced that it would continue purchasing additional agency mortgage-backed securities at a pace of $40 billion per month, as well as longer-term Treasury securities at a pace of $45 billion per month. Most significantly, the FOMC, rather than specifying a particular date through which its highly accommodative policy would continue, for the first time specified that policy would continue until the unemployment rate fell to 6.5 percent. See Jon Hilsenrath, "How Bernanke Pulled the Fed His Way," *Wall Street Journal*, September 27, 2012, and Binyamin Applebaum, "Fed Ties Rates to Joblessness, With Target of 6.5 Percent," *New York Times*, December 12, 2012.

5. *The Budget and Economic Outlook: Fiscal Years 2012 to 2022* (Washington, DC: Congressional Budget Office, January 2012).

6. Edward C. Prescott and Lee E. Ohanian, "Taxes Are Much Higher Than You Think," *Wall Street Journal*, December 11, 2012.

7. *The Good Jobs Deficit*, July 2011, and *The Low-Wage Recovery and Growing Inequality*, August 2012, both by National Employment Law Project, New York. See also Catherine Rampell, "Majority of New Jobs Pay Low Wages, Study Finds," *New York Times*, August 30, 2012, and Joseph Brusuelas, "Labor Market Gains Increasingly Driven by Low-Wage Jobs," *Bloomberg*, April 5, 2012.

8. Sarah Bloom Raskin, "Focusing on Low- and Moderate-Income Working Americans," Federal Reserve Board of Governors, March 22, 2013.

9. Paul Wiseman, "Economic Recovery Is Weakest Since World War II," Associated Press, August 15, 2012. Also see Kevin Hassett, "Stimulus Optimists vs. Economic Reality," *Wall Street Journal*, August 3, 2011.

10. Phil Gramm and Mike Solon, *U.S. Policy Metrics*, February 2, 2012. See also "The 1.7 Percent Year," *Wall Street Journal*, January 30, 2012.

11. Paul Krugman, "The Obama Gap," *New York Times*, January 9, 2009. Also see Paul Krugman, *End This Depression Now!* (New York: W.W. Norton & Company, 2012).

12. Christina D. Romer, "The Fiscal Stimulus, Flawed But Valuable," *New York Times*, October 20, 2012.

13. See John B. Taylor, "Government Is More to Blame for Weak Recovery than Fading Stimulus," *Bloomberg*, June 9, 2011; Alfred Laffer, "The Real Stimulus Record," *Wall Street Journal*, August 5, 2012; Senator Bob Corker, "Bernanke Should Show Some Humility," *Financial Times*, August 28, 2012; Edward Lazear, "There Is No Structural Unemployment Problem," *Wall Street Journal*, September 3, 2012; and Robert J. Samuelson, "Bernanke on the Brink," *Washington Post*, September 17, 2012.

14. Neil Irwin, "Why a Bull Run for Business Investment May Be Over," *Washington Post*, September 27, 2012. Also see Timothy Aeppel, "Man vs. Machine, a Jobless Recovery," *Wall Street Journal*, January 17, 2012.

15. John W. Schoen, "Are Employers to Blame for Skills Gap?" *NBC News*, December 6, 2012.

16. Peter Cappelli, *Why Good People Can't Get Jobs: The Skills Gap and What Companies Can Do About It* (Philadelphia: Wharton Digital Press, 2012). Also see David Wessell, "Software Screening Raises Bar for Hiring," *Wall Street Journal*, May 30, 2012.

17. Catherine Rampell, "With Positions to Fill, Employers Wait for Perfection," *New York Times*, March 6, 2013.

18. Rakesh Kochhar, Richard Fry, and Paul Taylor, "Wealth Gaps Rise to Record Highs Between Whites, Blacks, and Hispanics," Pew Research Center, July 26, 2011.

19. Ylan Q. Mui, "For Black Americans, Financial Damage from Subprime Implosion Is Likely to Last," *Washington Post*, July 8, 2012.

20. "Tight Lending Is Choking Nascent Housing Recovery," *NBC News*, November 20, 2012.

21. Jon Hilsenrath, "Fed Wrestles with How Best to Bridge the Credit Divide," *Wall Street Journal*, June 10, 2012.

22. Carmen M. Reinhart and Kenneth S. Rogoff, *This Time Is Different: Eight Centuries of Financial Folly*, (Princeton, NJ: Princeton University Press, 2009). Also see Carmen M. Reinhart and Kenneth S. Rogoff, "What Other Financial Crises Tell Us," *Wall Street Journal*, February 3, 2009.

23. It is worth noting that Rogoff and Reinhart reject the term "Great Recession." In their view the moniker implies that the recent recession was merely a more severe but otherwise conventional recession. They prefer the term "Second Great Contraction," the first being the Great Depression.

24. Carmen M. Reinhart and Vincent R. Reinhart, "After the Fall," Federal Reserve Bank of Kansas City Jackson Hole Symposium, August 27, 2010.

25. More than half of New York City's working-age African-American population is unemployed. See Patrick McGeehan, "Blacks Miss Out as Jobs Rebound in New York City," *New York Times*, June 20, 2012.

26. Pew Research Center, "Young, Underemployed, and Optimistic: Coming of Age, Slowly, in a Tough Economy," February 9, 2012. Also see Hope Yen, "U.S. Jobs Gap Between Young and Old Is Widest Ever," Associated Press, February 9, 2012; and, Shannon Bond, "Jobless Generation Puts Brakes on U.S.," *Financial Times*, July 30, 2012.

27. Catherine Rampell, "More Young Americans Out of High School Are Also Out of Work," *New York Times*, June 6, 2012. Also see Daniel Lippman, "About 2.7 Million Jobs for Youth Are Missing," *Wall Street Journal*, July 12, 2012.

28. Clive R. Belfield, Henry M. Levin, and Rachel Rosen, "The Economic Value of Opportunity Youth," The Corporation for National and Community Service and the White House Council for Community Solutions, January 2012.

29. Susan Saulny, "After Recession, More Young Adults Are Living on the Street," *New York Times*, December 18, 2012.

30. Eric Risberg, "Half of New Graduates Are Jobless or Underemployed," Associated Press, April 22, 2012. Also see Catherine Rampell, "Many with New College Degree Find the Job Market Humbling," *New York Times*, May 18, 2011.

31. Charley Stone, Carl Van Horn, and Cliff Zukin, *Chasing the American Dream: Recent College Graduates and the Great Recession* (New Brunswick, NJ: Heldrich Center for Workplace Development, Rutgers University, 2012). Also see Catherine Rampell, "It Takes a B.A. to Find a Job as a File Clerk," *New York Times*, February 19, 2013; and Questin Fottrell, "Trading Caps and Gowns for Mops," *MarketWatch*, August 23, 2012.

32. Steven Greenhouse, "Jobs Few, Grads Flock to Unpaid Internships," *New York Times*, May 5, 2012.

33. Sarah Ayres, "The High Cost of Youth Unemployment," Center for American Progress, April 5, 2013. Also see Elliott Blair Smith, "American Dream Fades for Generation Y Professionals," *Bloomberg*, December 21, 2012.

34. Christopher S. Rugaber and Paul Wiseman, "Rate of Discouraged Workers Reaches Highest Level in Decades," Associated Press, April 5, 2013.

35. Peter Whoriskey, "Job Recovery Is Scant for Americans in Prime Working Years," *Washington Post*, May 29, 2012.

36. Motoko Rich, "For the Unemployed Over 50, Fears of Never Working Again," *New York Times*, September 19, 2010.

37. "A Year or More: The High Cost of Long-Term Unemployment," The Pew Charitable Trust, May 2012. Also see Ben Casselman, "For Middle-Aged Job Seekers, a Long Road Back," *Wall Street Journal*, June 22, 2012; and Catherine Rampell, "Older Workers without Jobs Face Toughest Time Out of Work," *New York Times*, May 6, 2011.

38. Binjamin Applebaum, "The Enduring Consequences of Unemployment," *New York Times*, March 28, 2012. Also see David Wessel, "Job Market's Vanishing Act," *Wall Street Journal*, May 16, 2012; and Annie Lowrey and Catherine Rampell, "Little Federal Help for the Long-Term Unemployed," *New York Times*, November 1, 2012.

39. Rich Morin and Rakesh Kochhar, "Lost Income, Lost Friends, and Loss of Self-Respect—The Impact of Long-Term Unemployment," Pew Research Center, July 22, 2010. Also see Daniel Lippman, "Long-Term Unemployment Wreaks Mental Toll on Jobless," *McClatchy Newspapers*, August 15, 2011.

40. Don Peck, "How a New Jobless Era Will Transform America," *The Atlantic*, March 2010.

41. Dan Sullivan and Till von Wachter, "Job Displacement and Mortality: An Analysis Using Administrative Data," *The Quarterly Journal of Economics* 124, no. 3 (2009): 1265–1306.

42. Jessica Godofsky, Carl Van Horn, and Cliff Zukin, "The Shattered American Dream: Unemployed Workers Lose Ground, Hope, and Faith in their Futures," (New Brunswick, NJ: Heldrich Center for Workforce Development, Rutgers University, 2010).

43. Michelle Hirsch and Eric Pianin, "The Recession's Silent Mental Health Epidemic," *Fiscal Times*, October 2, 2011.

44. Speech before the National Association of Business Economics Annual Conference, March 26, 2012. See Motoko Rich, "For Jobless, Little Hope of Restoring Better Days," *New York Times*, December 1, 2011; and Peter S. Goodman, "Despite Signs of Recovery, Chronic Joblessness Rises," *New York Times*, February 10, 2010.

45. BLS data. Also see Christopher Leonard, "Unemployed Face Tough Competition: Underemployed," Associated Press, September 4, 2011.

46. Erin Hatton, "The Rise of the Permanent Temp Economy," *New York Times*, January 26, 2013.

47. Lawrence Mishel, Josh Bivens, Elise Gould, and Heidi Shierholz, *The State of Working America*, 12th ed., An Economic Policy Institute Book (Ithaca, NY: Cornell University Press, 2012).

48. Michael Cooper, "Lost in Recession, Toll on Underemployed and Underpaid," *New York Times*, June 18, 2012. Also see John W. Schoen, "Discouraged Workers Face Tough Road Back to Employment," NBC News, October 4, 2012.

49. Heidi Shierholz, "The Unemployment Rate Is Hugely Understating Slack in the Labor Market," Economic Policy Institute, April 5, 2013.

50. Lucia Mutikani, "America's Hidden Unemployed: Too Discouraged to Count," Reuters, September 23, 2012.

51. See Sara Murray, "Labor Force Participation Hits New Low," *Wall Street Journal*, August 5, 2011.

52. Anastasia Christman and Christine Riordan, "Filling the Good Jobs Deficit," National Employment Law Project, October, 2011.

53. Gordon Green and John Coder, "Changes in Household Income During the Economic Recovery: June 2009 to June 2012," Sentier Research, LLC, August 23, 2012.

54. Jeff Kearns, "U.S. Incomes Fell More in Recovery, Sentier Says," *Bloomberg*, August 23, 2012.

55. Chana Joffe-Walt, "The Startling Rise of Disability in America," *National Public Radio*, March 2013. Also see Mort Zuckerman, "By Any Measure, the Jobs Disaster Continues," *Wall Street Journal*, February 15, 2013.

56. Damian Paletta and Caroline Porter, "Use of Food Stamps Swells Even as Economy Improves," *Wall Street Journal*, March 27, 2013.

57. U.S. Census Bureau, "Income, Poverty and Health Insurance Coverage in the United States: 2011," September 12, 2012. Also see Steven R. Hurst, "Help Shrinks as Poverty Spikes in the U.S.," Associated Press, April 2, 2013; and Alison Linn, "Sprawling and Struggling: Poverty Hits America's Suburbs," NBC News, March 22, 2013.

Chapter 2: Not Just Small Businesses . . . *New*

1. Statistics of U.S. Businesses, U.S. Census Bureau.

2. John Haltiwanger, Ron Jarmin, and Javier Miranda, "Business Dynamics Statistics Briefing: Jobs Created from Business Start-Ups in the United States," Ewing Marion Kauffman Foundation, January 2009.

3. Tim Kane, "The Importance of Start-Ups in Job Creation and Job Destruction," Ewing Marion Kauffman Foundation, July 2010.

4. Mark deWolf and Katherine Klemmer, Bureau of Labor Statistics, "Job Openings, Hires, and Separations Fall During the Recession," *Monthly Review*, May 2010.

5. Job Openings and Labor Turnover Survey, Bureau of Labor Statistics.

6. Edward P. Lazear, "Why the Job Market Feels So Dismal," *Wall Street Journal*, May 16, 2011.

7. Since August 6, 2012, Bob Litan has been Director of Research at Bloomberg Government.

8. Mike Horrell is currently pursuing a PhD at the University of Chicago.

9. Robert E. Litan and Michael Horrell, "After Inception: How Enduring Is Job Creation by Start-Ups?," Ewing Marion Kauffman Foundation, July 2010. Also see Dane Stangler and Robert E. Litan, "Where Will the Jobs Come From?," Ewing Marion Kauffman Foundation, November 2009.

10. John C. Haltiwanger, Ron S. Jarmin, and Javier Miranda, "Who Creates Jobs? Small vs. Large vs. Young," NBER Working Paper Series, Working Paper 16300; August 2010.

11. Jonathan Cummings et al., "Growth and Competitiveness in the United States: The Role of Its Multinational Companies," McKinsey Global Institute, July 2010. See also Martin Baily, Matthew Slaughter, and Laura D'Andrea Tyson, "The Global Jobs Competition Heats Up," *Wall Street Journal*, July 1, 2010.

12. Anthony Breitzman and Diana Hicks, "An Analysis of Small Business Patents by Industry and Firm Size," Small Business Administration, Office of Advocacy, November 2008.

13. Robert Litan and Carl Schramm, *Better Capitalism* (New Haven, CT: Yale University Press, 2012).

14. Dane Stangler and Paul Kedrosky, "Exploring Firm Formation: Why Is the Number of New Firms Constant?," Ewing Marion Kauffman Foundation, January 2010.

15. See Scott Shane, "The Great Recession's Effect on Entrepreneurship," Federal Reserve Bank of Cleveland, March 24, 2011. Also see John Bussey, "Shrinking in a Bad Economy: America's Entrepreneur Class," *Wall Street Journal*, August 12, 2011.

16. Carol Leming, "Entrepreneurship and the U.S. Economy," Business Employment Dynamics, Bureau of Labor Statistics.

17. Catherine Rampell, "When Job-Creation Engines Stop at Just One," *New York Times*, October 4, 2012.

18. BLS data. See Eleanor J. Choi and James R. Spletzer, Bureau of Labor Statistics, "The Declining Average Size of Establishments: Evidence and Explanations," *Monthly Labor Review*, March 2012.

19. BLS data. Also see Jeremy Greenfield, "Job Growth Stalls as New Businesses Fail to Take Off," *Wall Street Journal*, August 14, 2011.

20. See Carl Schramm and Bob Litan, Start-Up Act Whiteboard (Kansas City, MO: Ewing Marion Kauffman Foundation, www.youtube.com/watch?v=Z rwl5yO3vC4&feature=related.

Chapter 4: "Not Enough People with the Skills We Need"

1. Our focus on the shortage of skilled talent in STEM fields should not be interpreted to mean that education in the humanities is unimportant or without value. On the contrary, humanities graduates can and do offer unique and essential value to the modern economy, even in technology-based fields. See Michael S. Malone, "How to Avoid a Bonfire of the Humanities," *Wall Street Journal*, October 24, 2012; and Norm Augustine, "The Education Our Economy Needs," *Wall Street Journal*, September 21, 2011.

2. Our entrepreneurs aren't alone in questioning the value of a four-year college degree. See Megan McArdle, "Is College a Lousy Investment?" *Newsweek*, September 9, 2012; Louis Menand, "Live and Learn," *The New Yorker*, June 6, 2011; and Gary Gutting, "What Is College For?" *New York Times*, December 14, 2011.

3. See *60 Minutes* segment on Mr. Thiel and his "20 Under 20" initiative at www.cbsnews.com/8301-18560_162-57436775/dropping-out-is-college-worth-the-cost/. Also see William J. Bennett, "Are Colleges Afraid of Peter Thiel?," *CNN.com*, April 18, 2012.

4. ManpowerGroup, "2013 Talent Shortage Survey," May 28, 2013.

5. Deloitte LLP and The Manufacturing Institute, "Boiling Point: The Skills Gap in U.S. Manufacturing," October 17, 2011. Also see "Challenges Facing America's Workplaces and Classrooms," testimony of Jay Timmons, President and CEO, The National Association of Manufacturers, before the House Committee on Education and the Workforce, February 5, 2013; and Peter Whoriskey, "U.S. Manufacturing Sees Shortage of Skilled Factory Workers," *Washington Post*, February 19, 2012.

6. Brad Smith, "How to Reduce America's Talent Deficit," *Wall Street Journal*, October 18, 2012.

7. Margo D. Beller, "Need a Job? Siemens Still Seeking 3,000 U.S. Workers," CNBC, October 7, 2011.

8. Timothy Aeppel, "Man vs. Machine, a Jobless Recovery," *Wall Street Journal*, January 17, 2012. Circumstances are particularly grim for the 25 million Americans over the age of 25 who lack a high-school diploma, less than 40 percent of whom are currently employed. See Clare Ansberry, "As Job Market Mends, Drop-Outs Fall Behind," *Wall Street Journal*, February 21, 2012.

9. A possible shift in the Beveridge Curve was among the topics discussed at our roundtable of noted economists on July 20, 2011 in Kansas City, Missouri.

10. Job Openings and Labor Turnover Survey (JOLTS), Bureau of Labor Statistics.

11. Emily Maltby and Sarah E. Needleman, "Small Firms Seek Skilled Workers, But Can't Find Any," *Wall Street Journal*, July 26, 2012.

12. Consumer Financial Protection Bureau and The Department of Education, "Private Student Loans," July 20, 2012. Also see Blake Ellis, "Class of 2013 Grads Average $35, 200 in Total Debt," CNN Money, May 17, 2013.

13. "Raising the Bar: Employers' Views on College Learning in the Wake of the Economic Downturn," survey conducted among employers on behalf of the Association of American Colleges and Universities, Hart Research Associates, January 20, 2010.

14. Aysegul Sahin, Joseph Song, Giorgio Topa, and Giovannie L. Violante, "Measuring Mismatch in the U.S. Labor Market." Federal Reserve Bank of New York, November 2010. Also see Justin Lahart and Ben Casselman, "Seeking to Match Skills and Jobs," *Wall Street Journal*, October 3, 2011.

15. "Young, Underemployed, and Optimistic."

16. National Commission on Excellence in Education, "A Nation at Risk: The Imperative for Educational Reform," April 1983.

17. Diane Ravitch, "The Test of Time," *Education Next*, Spring 2003.

18. "How Shanghai's Students Stunned the World," *NBC News*, November 2, 2011.

19. Sam Dillon, "Top Test Scores from Shanghai Stun Educators," *New York Times*, December 7, 2010.

20. Eric A Hanushek, Paul E. Peterson, and Ludger Woessmann, "Achievement Growth: International and U.S. State Trends in Student Performance," Taubman Center for State and Local Government, John. F. Kennedy School of Government, Harvard University, July 2012.

21. See Joel Klein, "The Failure of American Schools," *The Atlantic*, June 2011.

22. Joel I. Klein and Condoleezza Rice (chairs), "U.S. Education Reform and National Security," Independent Task Force Report No. 68, March 2012. For a spirited critique of the task force report, see Diane Ravitch, "Do Our Public Schools Threaten National Security?," *New York Review of Books*, June 7, 2012.

23. Paul E. Peterson, Ludger Woessmann, Eric A. Hanushek, and Carlos X. Lastra-Anadon, "Globally Challenged: Are U.S. Students Ready to Compete?," Taubman Center for State and Local Government, John F. Kennedy School of Government, Harvard University, August 2011. Also see George P. Shultz and Eric A. Hanushek, "Education Is the Key to a Healthy Economy," *Wall Street Journal*, April 30, 2012.

24. Joe Nocera, "Filling the Skills Gap," *New York Times*, July 2, 2012.

25. Anthony P. Carnevale, Stephen J. Rose, and Andrew R. Hanson, "Certificates: Gateway to Gainful Employment and College Degrees," Center on Education and the Workforce, Georgetown University, June 2012.

26. Testimony of Robert G. Templin, Jr., President, Northern Virginia Community College, before the Senate Committee on Health, Education, Labor and Pensions, February 24, 2010.

27. "Challenges Facing America's Workplaces and Classrooms," testimony of Jay Timmons, President and CEO, The National Association of Manufacturers, before the House Committee on Education and the Workforce, February 5, 2013.

28. "Pathways to Prosperity: Meeting the Challenges of Preparing Young Americans for the 21st Century," Harvard University, Graduate School of Education, February 2011.

29. Tony Wagner, *Creating Innovators: The Making of Young People Who Will Change the World* (New York: Scribner, 2012).

30. Thomas L. Friedman, "Need a Job? Invent It," *New York Times*, March 30, 2013.

31. Nick Shultz, "The Most Important Start-Up," *The American*, March 21, 2012.

32. David Rowan, "Reid Hoffman: The Network Philosopher," *Wired*, March 1, 2012.

33. Tamar Lewin, "Universities Reshaping Education on the Web," *New York Times*, July 17, 2012. Also see Douglas Belkin and Melissa Korn, "Web Courses Woo Professors, *Wall Street Journal*, May 30, 2013.

34. Andy Kessler, "Professors Are About to Get an Online Education," *Wall Street Journal*, June 2, 2013.

35. Martha C. White, "The $7,000 Computer Science Degree—And the Future of Higher Education," *Time*, May 21, 2013.

Chapter 5: "Our Immigration Policies Are Insane"

1. Matthew Herper, "Gene Machine," *Forbes*, January 17, 2011.

2. See John M. MacDonald and Robert J. Sampson, "Don't Shut the Golden Door," *Wall Street Journal*, June 19, 2012.

3. Institute of International Education, "Open Doors 2012: International Student Enrollment Increased by 6 Percent," press release, November 12, 2012.

4. U.S. Department of Commerce.

5. September 13, 2012, letter to President Barack Obama and Congressional leadership from the presidents of more than 150 U.S. universities, www.renewoureconomy.org/sites/all/themes/pnae/university-letter.pdf.

6. On April 8, 2008, DHS announced an extension of Optional Practical Training for qualified students. U.S. State Department, http://travel.state.gov/visa/temp/types/types_1268.html. Also see Grant Gross, "DHS Extends Time Foreign Students Can Stay in U.S.," *Computerworld*, April 7, 2008.

7. Three other lesser known and small-number options are the O-1, EB-1, and EB-5 visas. O-1 visas permit foreign nationals of "extraordinary ability" to work in the United States for three years. The EB-1 visa is similar, but leads to permanent residency. The EB-5 visa permits entry for foreign

nationals willing to invest at least $500,000 and willing to create at least 10 full-time jobs for U.S. workers. 12,200 O-1s were issued in 2011, along with about 25,000 EB-1s, according to the U.S. Citizenship and Immigration Service. See Sarah McBride, "U.S. 'Genius' Visa Attracts Entrepreneurs and Playmates," Reuters, June 29, 2012.

8. In addition to these requirements, the sponsoring employer must also obtain a labor condition attestation (LCA) from the Department of Labor prior to filing the H-1B petition with the Immigration & Naturalization Service. A LCA is required to ensure that foreign workers are not exploited by U.S. employers and are paid the same salaries and obtain the same benefits as their American counterparts.

9. Department of Homeland Security.

10. See www.uscis.gov, H-1B Fiscal Year (FY) 2013 Cap Season. Allen Smith, "H-1B Visa Cap Reached Much Sooner Than in 2011," Society for Human Resource Management, June 14, 2012.

11. Miriam Jordan, "Employer Demand Soars for Skilled-Worker Visas," *Wall Street Journal*, April 5, 2013. Also see Miriam Jordan, "Visa Demand Jumps," *Wall Street Journal*, April 1, 2013.

12. The Brookings Institution, "The Search for Skills: Demand for H-1B Immigrant Workers in U.S. Metropolitan Areas," July 18, 2012.

13. See www.us-immigration.com/index.html?referrer=adwords&gclid=CLLLn e6eg7MCFcid4Aod-QQAqQ.

14. National Foundation for American Policy, "Still Waiting: Green Card Problems Persist for High-Skill Immigrants," June 2012.

15. Vivek Wadhwa, *The Immigrant Exodus: Why America Is Losing the Global Race to Capture Entrepreneurial Talent*, (Philadelphia: Wharton Digital Press, 2012). Also see Edward Luce, "U.S. Immigration Policy Is Killing Innovation," *Financial Times*, October 21, 2012.

16. Visa Bulletin for September 2012, State Department, www.travel.state.gov/ visa/bulletin/bulletin_5759.html.

17. L. Gordon Crovitz, "The Economics of Immigration," *Wall Street Journal*, February 3, 2013. Also see David Skorton, "Congress Must Reform Immigration Laws that Send Top Stem Graduates to China," *Christian Science Monitor*, August 22, 2012.

18. www.renewoureconomy.org/sites/all/themes/pnae/university-letter.pdf.

19. The Defense Advanced Research Projects Agency (DARPA), the primary engine of innovation for the Department of Defense, was established in 1958 to maintain the technological superiority of the U.S. military. To fulfill its mission, the Agency relies on diverse performers to apply multi-disciplinary approaches to both advance knowledge through basic research and to create

innovative technologies that address current practical problems through applied research. DARPA's scientific investigations range from laboratory efforts to the creation of full-scale technology demonstrations in the fields of biology, medicine, computer science, chemistry, physics, engineering, mathematics, material sciences, social sciences, neurosciences and more. For more information, see www.darpa.mil/.

20. Vivek Wadhwa, AnnaLee Saxenian, Richard Freeman, and Alex Salkever, "Losing the World's Best and Brightest," Ewing Marion Kauffman Foundation, March 2009.

21. Chris Morris, "The Immigrant Exodus: Will the U.S. Run Out of Entrepreneurs?" *CNBC*, October 23, 2012. Also see Wadhwa, *The Immigrant Exodus.*

22. Bettina Hein, "An Entrepreneur at Heart," *New York Times*, May 19, 2012.

23. Robert W. Fairlie, "Kauffman Index of Entrepreneurial Activity, 1996–2010," Ewing Marion Kauffman Foundation, March 2011. Also see Peter H. Schuck and John Tyler, "Give Us Your Huddled Masses of Engineers," *Wall Street Journal*, May 13, 2011.

24. David Dyssegaard Kallick, "Immigrant Small Business Owners: A Significant and Growing Part of the Economy," Fiscal Policy Institute, June 2012. Also see Robert W. Fairlie, "Estimating the Contribution of Immigrant Business Owners to the U.S. Economy," Small Business Administration, Office of Advocacy, November 2008; and Miriam Jordan, "Migrants Keep Small-Business Faith," *Wall Street Journal*, June 13, 2012.

25. Partnership for a New American Economy, "The 'New American' Fortune 500," June 2011. Also see remarks by Michael R. Bloomberg, mayor of New York City, before the Council on Foreign Relations, June 5, 2011.

26. Stuart Anderson, "Immigrant Founders and Key Personnel in America's 50 Top Venture-Funded Companies," National Foundation for American Policy, December 2011.

27. Editorial Board, "STEMming the Decline of Foreign-Born Tech Graduates," *Washington Post*, September 19, 2012.

28. The Partnership for a New American Economy, "Patent Pending: How Immigrants Are Reinventing the American Economy," June 2012. Also see Jennifer Hunt and Marjolaine Gauthier-Loiselle, "How Much Does Immigration Boost Innovation?" *American Economic Journal: Macroeconomics* 2, no. 2 (2010): 31–56; and Andrew Martin, "Immigrants Are Crucial to Innovation, Study Says," *New York Times*, June 25, 2012.

29. Madeline Zavodny, "Immigration and American Jobs," American Enterprise Institute and the Partnership for a New American Economy, December 2011. Also see "Visa Protectionism," Review & Outlook, *Wall Street Journal*, April 12, 2012.

30. Address at the Immigration and American Competitiveness Conference, U.S. Chamber of Commerce and the Partnership for a New American Economy, September 28, 2011.

31. President's State of the Union Address, January 24, 2012.

32. See http://judiciary.house.gov/issues/issues_STEM%20Jobs%20Act.html. See also Lamar Smith, "Foreign Graduates in STEM Fields Can Boost U.S.," *Politico*, September 18, 2012.

33. Jennifer Martinez, "President Opposes GOP Visa Bill," *The Hill*, November 28, 2012.

34. Fawn Johnson, "First Business after Inauguration: Immigration," *National Journal*, November 15, 2012.

35. Mark Landler, "Obama Urges Speed on Immigration Plan, but Exposes Conflicts," *New York Times*, January 29, 2013.

36. Sara Murray and Janet Hook, "Senate Approves Overhaul of Immigration Laws," *Wall Street Journal*, June 27, 2013.

37. Neil G. Ruiz and Jill H. Wilson, "A Balancing Act for H-1B Visas," The Brookings Institution, April 18, 2013.

38. David A. Vise, "Gates Cites Hiring Woes, Criticizes Visa Restrictions," *Washington Post*, April 28, 2005.

39. Arlene Holen, "The Budgetary Effects of High-Skilled Immigration Reform," Technology Policy Institute, March 2009.

40. National Science Foundation.

41. Vauhini Vara, "Start-Up Visas Get New Push," *Wall Street Journal*, November 22, 2012.

42. See "The Start-Up Act," www.kauffman.org/uploadedFiles/startup_act.pdf.

43. Dane Stangler and Jared Konczal, "Give Me Your Entrepreneurs, Your Innovators: Estimating the Employment Impact of a Start-Up Visa," Ewing Marion Kauffman Foundation, February 2013.

44. Emily Maltby, "A New Push for Entrepreneur Visas," *Wall Street Journal*, February 12, 2013.

45. See Yuri Ammosov, "Start-Up Act 2.0: Great for Foreign Graduate Students, but Not Foreign Tech Entrepreneurs," *TechCrunch*, June 10, 2012.

46. For a terrific defense of the humanities in the technology age, see "The Triumph of the Humanities," speech by Michael S. Malone before the Rothermere American Institute, Oxford University, October 18, 2012.

47. See Julia Preston, "Obama Will Seek Citizenship Path in One Fast Push," *New York Times*, January 12, 2013.

48. www.americorps.gov.

49. Major Garrett, "Fixing the Immigration Problem," *National Journal*, November 13, 2012.

50. Brooke Donald, "Blueseed Start-Up Sees Entrepreneur-Ship as Visa Solution for Silicon Valley," Associated Press, December 16, 2011.

51. Kai Ryssdal, "Don't Have a Visa to Work Here? I Have Some Office Space to Rent You in the Ocean," *Marketplace*, March 14, 2013.

Chapter 6: "Not All Good Ideas Get Funded Anymore"

1. Survey of Small Business Finances, Federal Reserve Board. Also see Scott A. Shane, *The Illusions of Entrepreneurship: The Costly Myths That Entrepreneurs, Investors, and Policy Makers Live By*, (New Haven, CT: Yale University Press, 2008), 79–80. 1996 dollar figure converted to 2012 dollars by way of CPI Inflation Calculator, Bureau of Labor Statistics: www.bls.gov/data/inflation_calculator.htm.

2. Survey of Consumer Finances, Federal Reserve Board. See Elizabeth Duke, Governor, Federal Reserve Board, "Small Business Credit Availability," April 14, 2011.

3. Walter Isaacson, *Steve Jobs*, (New York: Simon & Schuster, 2011), 62–67.

4. Mark E. Schweitzer and Scott A. Shane, "The Effect of Falling Home Prices on Small Business Borrowing," *Economic Commentary*, December 20, 2010.

5. Robert H. Scott III, "The Use of Credit Card Debt by New Firms," Ewing Marion Kauffman Foundation, August 2009.

6. Ibid.

7. Survey of Consumer Finances, Federal Reserve Board. See Duke, "Small Business Credit Availability."

8. Sarah E. Needleman, "Angels Can Fund Your Next Step," *Wall Street Journal*, August 25, 2012.

9. Federal Reserve Board, "Changes in U.S. Family Finances from 2007 to 2010: Evidence from the Survey of Consumer Finances," *Federal Reserve Bulletin*, June 2012. Also see Ylan Q. Mui, "Americans Saw Wealth Plummet 40 Percent from 2007 to 2010, Federal Reserve Says," *Washington Post*, June 11, 2012.

10. Lisa Scherzer, "Credit Card Issuers Cut Off Consumers," *Wall Street Journal*, May 9, 2008, and Beth Healy, "Lenders Abruptly Cut Lines of Credit," *Boston Globe*, January 31, 2009.

11. Federal Reserve statistical release: Consumer Credit-G.19.

12. Ilyce Glink, "Nearly Half of Younger Homeowners Are Underwater," *CBS MoneyWatch*, August 23, 2012.

13. "Housing Still Drowning in Underwater Mortgages," *Wall Street Journal*, March 2, 2012.

14. Robbie Whelan, "When the Home Bank Closes," *Wall Street Journal*, February 1, 2012. Also see Ian Mount, "Why It's Getting Harder, and Riskier, to Bet the House," *New York Times*, November 30, 2011.

15. Dennis P. Lockhart, President and Chief Executive Officer, Federal Reserve Bank of Atlanta, "Start-Ups, Job Creation, and Bank Financing," Conference on Small Business and Entrepreneurship During an Economic Recovery, Washington, DC, November 10, 2011.

16. Pui-Wing Tam, "Venture Capital to Suppress Its Appetite for Risk in 2013," *Wall Street Journal*, December 25, 2012.

17. For a terrific overview of the venture capital industry, see Paul A. Gompers and Josh Lerner, *The Money of Invention: How Venture Capital Creates New Wealth*, (Boston: Harvard Business School Publishing, 2001).

18. Paul Kedrosky, "Right-Sizing the Venture Capital Industry," Ewing Marion Kauffman Foundation, June 10, 2009.

19. Deborah Gage, "The Venture Capital Secret: 3 or 4 Start-Ups Fail," *Wall Street Journal*, September 19, 2012.

20. Doriot founded ARDC along with Ralph Flanders, an industrialist and former President of the Federal Reserve Bank of Boston (who later served as a Republican Senator from Vermont), and Karl Compton, former president of MIT. See Spencer E. Ante, *Creative Capital: Georges Doriot and the Birth of Venture Capital*, (Boston: Harvard Business School Press, 2008).

21. Paul A. Gompers, "The Rise and Fall of Venture Capital," *Business and Economic History* 23 (Winter 1994): 1–26.

22. For a terrific history of the origins of the west coast venture capital industry, see William H. Draper III, *The Start-Up Game*, (New York: St. Martin's Press, 2011).

23. Steve Kaplan and Antoinette Schoar, "Private Equity Performance: Returns, Persistence, and Capital Flows," *Journal of Finance* 60: 1791–1824. Also see "The VC Shakeout," Joseph Ghalbouni and Dominique Rouzies, *Harvard Business Review*, July 2010.

24. Josh Lerner, *Private Equity Returns: Myth and Reality*, (Boston: Harvard Business School, 2009).

25. Sean Carr, Malgorzata Glinska, and Andrew King, "What Ever Happened to Venture Capital?" *Batten Briefing* 1, no. 1, Batten Institute, Darden School of Business, University of Virginia, February 2011.

26. Some funds charge as much as 2.5 percent of assets under management and 30 percent of any profits. See Rebecca Buckman, "Venture Firms Are Doling Out Large Pay Deals," *Wall Street Journal*, September 14, 2006, and Rebecca Buckman, "Venture Capital's Coming Collapse," *Forbes*, January 12, 2009.

27. National Venture Capital Association statistics. Also see Bryan Pearce and Martin Haemming, "Back to Basics: Global Venture Capital Insights and Trends," Ernst & Young, 2010.

28. *Sarbanes-Oxley Section 404 Costs and Implementation Issues: Spring 2006 Survey Update* (Washington, DC: CRA International, April 17, 2006).

29. Interview with *BloombergBusinessweek*, March 13, 2012.

30. "Sustaining New York's and the US' Global Financial Services Leadership," January 22, 2007.

31. For an explanation of the history of, and reasoning for, decimalization, see "Report to Congress on Decimalization," Staff of the Securities and Exchange Commission, July 2012. Other market structure–related contributing factors include SEC order-handling rules in 1997, Regulation ATS in 1998, and the emergence and growing popularity of ETFs.

32. See David Weild and Edward Kim, "Market Structure Is Causing the IPO Crisis—And More," Grant Thornton, June 2010.

33. For a discussion of how the IPO Task Force was formed and its deliberations, see James Freeman, "Kate Mitchell: How Silicon Valley Won in Washington," The Weekend Interview, *Wall Street Journal*, April 6, 2012.

34. IPO Task Force, "Re-Building the IPO On-Ramp: Putting Emerging Companies and the Job Market Back on the Road to Growth," October 20, 2011.

35. The Global Analyst Research Settlement was a settlement of enforcement actions against 12 investment banking firms arising from an investigation of research analyst conflicts of interest. The firms reached the settlement with the Commission, NASD Inc. (now FINRA), the New York Stock Exchange, Inc., the Attorney General of the State of New York, and other state regulators. The U.S. District Court for the Southern District of New York approved the settlement on October 31, 2003. The Global Analyst Research Settlement requires firms subject to the terms of the settlement to adhere to certain rules designed to address conflicts of interest abuses in research analyst activities. The Global Analyst Research Settlement has subsequently been amended by the parties and such amendments have been approved by the court.

36. Testimony of David Weild, Senior Advisor, Grant Thornton LLP, before the Subcommittee on Capital Markets and Government Sponsored Entities of the House Financial Services Committee, June 20, 2012.

37. Polachi, Inc. Also see Scott Austin, "Majority of VCs in Survey Call Industry 'Broken,'" Scott Austin, *Wall Street Journal*, June 29, 2009.

38. Matt Richtel, "Venture Investors Wrap Up an Unusually Bleak Quarter," *New York Times*, June 28, 2008.

39. Cambridge Associates, press release, November 1, 2010. Also see Diane Mulcahy, Bill Weeks, and Harold S. Bradley, "We Have Met the Enemy . . . And

He Is Us: Lessons from Twenty Years of the Kauffman Foundation's Investments in Venture Capital Funds and the Triumph of Hope Over Experience," Ewing Marion Kauffman Foundation, May 2012.

40. Kim Hart, "Venture-Backed IPO Tally: Zero," *Washington Post*, July 1, 2008.

41. Claire Cain Miller, "After a Dreary 2008, Venture Capitalists Are Cautious," *New York Times*, January 5, 2009. Also see John Jannarone, "Facing Up to Venture Capital's Slow Future," *Wall Street Journal*, January 28, 2012.

42. Convertible notes are an example of such innovation. In contrast to standard Series A Preferred Stock financing by which angel investors or venture firms take an equity stake in the new business, in a convertible debt financing the investment is made without establishing an explicit valuation of the new business. Instead, the investor extends the company a loan, which converts to equity as part of the next priced equity round.

43. Evelyn M. Rusli and Peter Eavis, "Facebook Raises $16 Billion in IPO," *New York Times*, May 17, 2012.

44. National Venture Capital Association, news release, January 2, 2013, p. 3. Also see Sarah McBride, "Venture Capital Feels the Heat From Ongoing DotCom Turmoil," *Reuters*, August 15, 2012, and Shira Ovide, "For IPOs, the Comeback Never Came," *Wall Street Journal*, December 28, 2011.

45. For a discussion on economic incentives for young companies to sell to large companies, see Xiaohui Goa, University of Maryland and University of Hong Kong; Jay R. Ritter, University of Florida; and Zhongyan Zhu, Chinese University of Hong Kong, "Where Have All the IPOs Gone?" December 17, 2012.

46. David Weild and Edward Kim, "Why Are IPOs in the ICU?" Grant Thornton, November 2008.

47. *Global Insight and Survey of Top 136 VC-Based Companies that Went Public 1970–2005*, National Venture Capital Association.

48. Testimony of David Weild, Senior Advisor, Grant Thornton LLP, before the Subcommittee on Capital Markets and Government Sponsored Entities of the House Financial Services Committee, June 20, 2012.

49. "Why IPOs Look to Be Entering a Slow Deep Freeze for Now," Associated Press, November 25, 2012.

50. Telis Demos and Matt Jarzemsky, "IPOs Set to Raise Most Cash Since Crisis," *Wall Street Journal*, May 12, 2013.

51. "The decline in funding for seed/early stage companies is firmly in place—we've seen a drop in dollars and deals both quarter-over-quarter and year-over-year," said Tracy T. Lefteroff, global managing partner of the venture capital practice at PricewaterhouseCoopers, commenting on third quarter of 2012 industry figures. "We're seeing fewer new venture funds being raised,

which means less capital is available for new investments. And, we're seeing venture capitalists be very cautious with the capital that is available due to the lack of a significant number of liquidity events." NVCA news release, October 19, 2012. Also see Pui-Wing Tam, "Venture Firms Narrow Sights in Tough Times," *Wall Street Journal*, February 3, 2013.

52. Matt McCall, "VC's Mathematical Challenge," *VC Confidential*, www.vcconfidential.com/2009/06/vcs-mathematical-challenge.html.

53. See Fred Wilson, "The Venture Capital Math Problem," www.avc.com/a_vc/2009/04/the-venture-capital-math-problem.html.

54. Needleman, "Angels Can Fund Your Next Step."

55. Pui-Wing Tam and Spencer E. Ante, "Super Angels Alight," *Wall Street Journal*, August 16, 2010.

56. Robert Wiltbank and Warren Boeker, "Returns to Angel Investors in Groups," Ewing Marion Kauffman Foundation and the Angel Capital Association, November 2007.

57. See "Financing High-Growth Firms: The Role of Angel Investors," Directorate for Science, Technology, and Industry, OECD, January 2012. Also see Angus Loten, "Angel Investors Play Big Role for Start-Ups, Think Tank Says," *Wall Street Journal*, January 24, 2012.

58. Data from the Angel Capital Association and National Venture Capital Association.

59. "Seed Investing Report—Start-Up Orphans and the Series A Crunch," *CB Insights*, December 19, 2012. Also see Nicole Perlroth, "After Rocky Year for Start-Ups, Investors Are Pickier," *New York Times*, January 13, 2013.

60. According to the wealth research firm Spectrum Group, the number of U.S. households with a net worth of at least $1 million (not including primary residences) fell 27 percent to 6.7 million in 2009 from 9.2 million in 2007. The number of households with investible assets of at least $1 million fell 26 percent to 4.4 million.

61. Jeffrey Sohl, "The Angel Investor Market in Q1Q2 2010: Where Have All the Seed Investors Gone?," Center for Venture Research, University of New Hampshire, October 26, 2010. Also see Wendy Lee, "Number of Angel Investors Declining," *Minneapolis Star Tribune*, April 17, 2011.

62. Jeffrey Sohl, "The Angel Investor Market in 2012: A Moderating Recovery Continues," Center for Venture Research, April 25, 2013.

63. Angus Loten, "Chasing the New Angel Investor," *Wall Street Journal*, December 15, 2011.

64. Andrew Ackerman and Jared A. Favole, "Obama Signs Bill Easing IPO Rules," *Wall Street Journal*, April 5, 2012.

65. For companies wishing to remain private for longer, the Act also increases from 500 to 2,000 the number of private shareholders a young company can have before having to register with the SEC, and raises the cap on private offerings from $5 million to $50 million. For an excellent summary of the JOBS Act and its provisions, see "An Overview of the JOBS Act," McGladrey LLP, May 1, 2012.

66. "What A Difference a Year Can Make," Kate Mitchell, March 27, 2012. www .scalevp.com/the-difference-a-year-can-make.

67. Accredited investors legally approved to make private investments in young companies must earn more than $200,000 in income annually, or have more than $1 million in liquid net worth, not counting the value of any owned real estate.

68. See testimony of Lynn E. Turner before the Senate Committee on Banking, Housing, and Urban Affairs, "Spurring Job Growth Through Capital Formation While Protecting Investors," March 6, 2012. Also see Steven Rattner, "A Sneaky Way to Deregulate," *New York Times*, March 3, 2013.

69. "Investor Protection Is Needed for True Capital Formation: Views on the JOBS Act," public statement by SEC Commissioner Luis Aguilar, March 16, 2012.

70. Jean Eaglesham and Telis Demos, "SEC Chief Delayed Rule Over Legacy Concerns," *Wall Street Journal*, December 2, 2012.

71. "Remarks at the 2012 SEC Government-Business Forum on Small Business Capital Formation," Commissioner Elisse B. Walter, U.S. Securities and Exchange Commission, November 15, 2012.

72. Michael Rapoport, "In Wake of Groupon Issues, Critics Wary of JOBS Act," *Wall Street Journal*, April 2, 2012.

73. www.whitehouse.gov/the-press-office/2012/04/05/remarks-president-jobs -act-bill-signing.

74. Robb Mandelbaum, "Crowdfunding Rules Are Unlikely to Meet Deadline," *New York Times*, December 26, 2012. Also see Angus Loten, "Stalled Crowdfunding Rules Leave Business Plans on Ice," *Wall Street Journal*, December 12, 2012.

75. www.sba.gov/about-sba-services/7367/329571.

76. Equity acquired on convertible notes and warrants is increasingly common and should also qualify. In contrast to standard Series A Preferred Stock financing by which angel investors or venture firms take an equity stake in the new business, in a convertible debt financing the investment is made without establishing an explicit valuation of the new business. Instead, the investor extends the company a loan, which converts to equity as part of the next priced equity round.

77. Thomas L. Hungerford, "The Economic Effects of Capital Gains on Taxation," Congressional Research Service, June 18, 2010.

78. Testimony of David Verrill, Chairman, Angel Capital Association, before the House Committee on Ways and Means and the Senate Committee on Finance, September 20, 2012.

79. For information about existing state tax credit programs, see www.angelcapitalassociation.org/public-policy/existing-state-policy/.

80. Carrie Ghose, "Ohio Technology Investment Tax Credit Dries Up, Surprising Entrepreneurs," *Columbus Business First*, November 9, 2012.

81. Rich Kirchen, "Angel Investors Tap Unheralded Tax Credits," *The Business Journal*, March 23, 2012.

82. "Study of the Sarbanes-Oxley Act of 2002 Section 404 Internal Control over Financial Reporting Requirements," Securities and Exchange Commission, Office of Economic Analysis, September 2009. Also see "What Ever Happened to IPOs?" Review & Outlook, *Wall Street Journal*, March 22, 2011.

83. An "emerging growth company" is no longer considered an EGC and, therefore, its period of compliance exemption ends, when the earliest of the following occurs: the last day of the fiscal year during which the issuer has total gross revenues of $1 billion or more; the date on which the issuer has issued more than $1 billion in non-convertible debt over the previous three-year period; the date on which the issuer achieves a market capitalization greater than $700 million; or the last day of the fiscal year following the fifth anniversary of the issuer's IPO.

84. "Report to Congress on Decimalization," Staff of the Securities and Exchange Commission, July 2012.

85. Our proposal is based on a similar proposal by David Weild and Edward Kim of Grant Thornton; see "A Wake-Up Call for America," November 2009, 29–30. Also see David Weild, "How to Revive Small-Cap IPOs," *Wall Street Journal*, October 27, 2011.

Chapter 7: "Regulations Are Killing Us"

1. "Clearing the Way for Jobs and Growth: Retrospective Review to Reduce Red Tape and Regulations," statement of Michael Mandel, PhD, before the Subcommittee on Courts, Commercial and Administrative Law of the U.S. House Committee on the Judiciary, July 12, 2012.

2. Federal labor law imposes strict standards for unpaid internships. See Steven Greenhouse, "The Unpaid Intern, Legal or Not," *New York Times*, April 2, 2010, and Josh Sanburn, "The Beginning of the End of the Unpaid Internship," *Time*, May 2, 2012.

3. See Hannah Seligson, "Hatching Ideas, and Companies, by the Dozens, at MIT," *New York Times*, November 24, 2012.

4. Andrew Von Eschenbach and Ralph Hall, "FDA Approvals Are a Matter of Life and Death," *Wall Street Journal*, June 17, 2012.

5. Testimony of Jonathan H. Adler, Director of the Center for Business Law and Regulation, Case Western Reserve School of Law, before the Subcommittee on Courts, Commercial, and Administrative Law of the House Judiciary Committee, January 24, 2011.

6. James L. Gattuso and Dianne Katz, "Red Tape Rising: A 2011 Mid-Year Report on Regulation," The Heritage Foundation, July 25, 2011. Also see James L. Gattuso and Dianne Katz, "Red Tape Rising: Obama-Era Regulation at the Three Year Mark," The Heritage Foundation, March 13, 2012.

7. Statistics in this paragraph are taken from Clyde Wayne Crews, "Ten Thousand Commandments: An Annual Snapshot of the Federal Regulatory State," Competitive Enterprise Institute, 2013. Also see "Red Tape Record Breakers," Review & Outlook, *Wall Street Journal*, May 19, 2013.

8. Susan Dudley and Melinda Warren, "Growth in Regulators' Budget Slowed by Fiscal Stalemate: An Analysis of the U.S. Budget for Fiscal Years 2012 and 2013," Regulatory Studies Center at George Washington University and the Weidenbaum Center on the Economy, Government, and Public Policy at Washington University, St. Louis, July 2012.

9. John Merline, "Regulation Business, Jobs Booming Under Obama," *Investor's Business Daily*, August 15, 2011.

10. President Barack Obama, "Toward a 21st-Century Regulatory System," *Wall Street Journal*, January 18, 2011.

11. John McArdle and Emily Yehle, "Obama Administration Outlines 500 Reforms to Save Businesses Billions," *The New York Times*, August 23, 2011.

12. Nicole V. Crain and W. Mark Crain, *The Impact of Regulatory Costs on Small Firms* (Washington, DC: Small Business Administration, Office of Advocacy, September 2010).

13. For a similar discussion on how regulations create powerful incentives not to hire, see Jay Goltz, "Why I'm (Still) Reluctant to Hire," from "You're the Boss: The Art of Running a Small Business," *New York Times*, September 7, 2011.

14. See Michael Mandel and Diana G. Carew, "Regulatory Improvement Commission: A Politically Viable Approach to U.S. Regulatory Reform," Progressive Policy Institute, May 2013,

Chapter 8: "Tax Payments Can Be the Difference Between Survival and Failure"

1. Robert Carroll, Douglas Holtz-Eakin, Mark Rider, and Harvey Rosen, "Entrepreneurs, Income Taxes, and Investment," in *Does Atlas Shrug? The Economic Consequences of Taxing the Rich*, ed. Joel Slemrod (New York: Russell Sage Foundation and Harvard University Press, 2002), 427–455; and William M. Gentry and R. Glenn Hubbard, "Success Taxes, Entrepreneurial Entry,

and Innovation," National Bureau of Economic Research, Working Paper No. 10551, June 2004. Also see Robert Carroll, Douglas Holtz-Eakin, Mark Rider, and Harvey Rosen, "Income Taxes and Entrepreneurs' Use of Labor," *Journal of Labor Economics* 18, no. 2 (April 2000): 324–351.

2. Emily Maltby and Angus Loten, "Cliff Fix Hits Small Business," *Wall Street Journal*, January 3, 2013.

3. The term refers to Chapter 1, Subchapter S of the Internal Revenue Code. For definition, requirements, restrictions and other details, see www.irs.gov/Businesses/Small-Businesses-&-Self-Employed/S-Corporations.

4. Robert Carroll and Gerald Prante, "Long-Run Macroeconomic Impact of Increasing Tax Rates on High-Income Taxpayers in 2013," Ernst & Young, July 2012. Also see J. D. Harrison, "Obama Plan to Lift Top Tax Rate Would Plague Millions of Small Businesses, Study Warns," *Washington Post*, July 17, 2012.

5. John D. McKinnon, "More Firms Enjoy Tax-Free Status," *Wall Street Journal*, January 10, 2012.

6. *Taxing Businesses Through the Individual Income Tax* (Washington, DC: Congressional Budget Office, December 2012.

7. National Federation of Independent Business.

8. Robert Carroll and Gerald Prante, "The Flow-Through Business Sector and Tax Reform," Ernst & Young, April 2011. Also see Trip Gabriel, "A Fuller Picture in the Small-Business Tug of War," *New York Times*, July 13, 2012.

9. Scott Shane, "The Politics and Economics of Taxing Small Business Owners," *Business Insider*, July 16, 2012.

10. See Emily Maltby, "Small Firms Fret Over Higher Taxes," *Wall Street Journal*, December 5, 2012.

11. The term "fiscal cliff," first used by Federal Reserve Chairman Ben Bernanke in testimony before the House Financial Services Committee on February 29, 2012, referred to unique and highly adverse fiscal policy circumstances facing Washington policymakers as of January 1, 2013. Those circumstances included tax increases associated with the expiration of The Tax Relief, Unemployment Insurance Reauthorization, and Job Creation Act of 2010, and major defense and non-defense spending reductions mandated under The Budget Control Act of 2011.

12. See "Tax Revenues to More Than Double by 2023, While Top Tax Rates Hit Highest Level Since 1986," Chairman David Camp, House Committee on Ways and Means, press release, February 13, 2013. Also see Emily Maltby and Angus Loten, "Small Firms Scramble to Redraw Plans," *Wall Street Journal*, January 2, 2013.

13. Director Elmendorf discussed the impact of higher rates on jobs beginning in minute 29:30 of a press briefing on February 5, 2013: www.c-span.org/Events/

CBO-Report-Deficit-Will-Fall-to-Less-Than-1-Trillion-in-2013/10737 437810.

14. Crain and Crain, *Impact of Regulatory Costs on Small Firms.*

15. *Taxes and Spending: Small Business Owner Opinions* (Washington, DC: National Federation of Independent Business, March 7, 2013).

16. The original credit's expiration date was December 31, 1985. The credit has expired eight times and has been extended 14 times.

17. "Startups Advise Obama: Focus on Taxes and Talent As Second Term Begins," Silicon Valley Bank, January 18, 2013.

18. Gary Guenther, *Section 179 and Bonus Depreciation Expensing Allowances: Current Law, Legislative Proposals in the 112th Congress, and Economic Effects* (Washington, DC: Congressional Research Service, August 2, 2012).

19. Kevin A. Hassett and Glenn Hubbard, "Obama Discovers Incentives," *Wall Street Journal,* September 10, 2010.

20. *The Case for Temporary 100 Percent Expensing: Encouraging Business to Expand Now by Lowering the Cost of Investment* (Washington, DC: Office of Tax Policy, U.S. Department of the Treasury, October 29, 2010).

21. The bill was originally introduced on July 31, 2012.

22. See Karen E. Klein, "The R&D Tax Credit Explained for Small Business," *BloombergBusinessweek,* August 16, 2011.

23. For more information on the Start-Up Innovation Credit Act, see www .coons.senate.gov/newsroom/releases/release/senators-coons-enzi-introduce -randd-tax-credit-for-startup-companies. Also see Jennifer Martinez, "Bipartisan Group of Senators Re-Introduce Start-Up Tax Credit Bill," *The Hill,* January 31, 2013.

24. Also see Senator Chris Coons and Senator Mike Enzi, "R&D Tax Credit Spurs Innovation," *Politico,* March 7, 2013.

25. Anthony Breitzman and Diana Hicks, *An Analysis of Small Business Patents by Industry and Firm Size* (Washington, DC: Small Business Administration, Office of Advocacy, November 2008).

26. Laura Tyson and Greg Linden, *The Corporate R&D Tax Credit and U.S. Innovation and Competitiveness: Gauging the Economic and Fiscal Effectiveness of the Credit* (Washington, DC: Center for American Progress, January 2012), 15–16.

Chapter 9: "There's Too Much Uncertainty—and It's Washington's Fault"

1. Jan Bouten, "Memphis' Start-Up Niche: Bio-Engineering and Logistics," *Wall Street Journal,* January 29, 2013.

2. Paul Wiseman, "U.S. Economic Recovery Is Weakest Since World War II," Associated Press, August 15, 2012.

3. Edward P. Lazear, "The Worst Economic Recovery in History," *Wall Street Journal*, April 2, 2012.

4. Catherine Rampell, "Hiring Picks Up in July, But Data Gives No Clear Signal," *New York Times*, August 3, 2012.

5. Nelson D. Schwartz, "Recovery in U.S. Is Lifting Profits, But Not Jobs," *New York Times*, March 3, 2013.

6. For a similar presentation of the kinds of comments and sentiments we heard from our participants, see the following segment from the *PBS Newshour*: "Why Are Small Businesses Reluctant to Hire?" December 5, 2011; www.pbs.org/ newshour/extra/video/blog/2011/12/why_are_small_businesses_reluc.html.

7. The debt ceiling is a legislative restriction on the amount of national debt that can be issued by the Treasury Department. Because actual government expenditures are authorized by Congress through legislation, the debt ceiling does not limit or reduce government deficits. Rather, it can only restrain the Treasury from paying for expenditures that have already been incurred.

8. The Tax Relief, Unemployment Insurance Reauthorization, and Job Creation Act of 2010. Without passage of the 2010 law, income taxes would have returned to Clinton Administration–era rates in January 2011. The Act also extended some provisions from the American Recovery and Reinvestment Act of 2009, commonly known as "the Stimulus Act," and included several other measures as part of a compromise agreement between President Obama and Congressional Republicans, mostly notably an extension of unemployment benefits and a one-year reduction in the FICA payroll tax.

9. The Economic Growth and Tax Relief Reconciliation Act of 2001 and the Jobs and Growth Tax Relief Reconciliation Act of 2003.

10. Rates affected included income taxes, the Earned Income Tax Credit, capital gains and dividend taxes, payroll taxes, and the estate tax.

11. In testimony before the House Financial Services Committee on February 29, 2012, Bernanke stated, "Under current law, on January 1, 2013, there's going to be a massive fiscal cliff of large spending cuts and tax increases. I hope that Congress will look at that and figure out ways to achieve the same long-run fiscal improvement without having it all happen at one date."

12. Rebecca Berg, "Fear of Year-End Fiscal Stalemate May Be Having Effect Now," *New York Times*, July 11, 2012.

13. Jeff Werling, "Fiscal Shock—America's Economic Crisis: The Impact of the Pending Fiscal Crisis on Jobs and Economic Growth," University of Maryland, October 2012. Also see Lori Montgomery, "One Million Jobs Already Lost Due to Fiscal Cliff," *Washington Post*, October 26, 2012.

14. Emily Maltby and Angus Loten, "Cliff Fix Hits Small Business," *Wall Street Journal*, January 3, 2013. Also see Sudeep Reddy and Scott Thurm, "Investment Falls Off a Cliff," *Wall Street Journal*, November 19, 2012.

15. "Consumer Sentiment Plunges in December," *Reuters*, December 7, 2012; Catherine Rampell, "Small-Business Optimism Plunges," *New York Times*, December 11, 2012. Also see Catherine Rampell, "Forecast Is Sunnier, But Washington Casts a Big Shadow," *New York Times*, December 16, 2012.

16. Lori Montgomery and Paul Kane, "Obama, Senate Republicans Reach Agreement on Fiscal Cliff," *Washington Post*, December 31, 2012.

17. Director Elmendorf discussed the impact of higher rates on jobs beginning in minute 29:30 of a press briefing on February 5, 2013: www.c-span.org/Events/CBO-Report-Deficit-Will-Fall-to-Less-Than-1-Trillion-in-2013/10737437810/

18. David Rogers, "Sequestration: Senate Fails in Last-Chance Bid to Avoid Sequester," *Politico*, February 28, 2013; see also Devin Dwyer and Mary Bruce, "Obama Signs Order to Begin Sequester Cuts after President, Congress Can't Reach Deal," *ABC News*, March 1, 2013.

19. "We think that would reduce the level of employment by the end of the year about 750,000 jobs," Elmendorf told a House Budget Committee Hearing on February 13, 2013. Also see David Wessel, "Biggest Drag on Economy? Washington," *Wall Street Journal*, March 20, 2013.

20. David Brown, "Cheating the Future: The Price of Not Fixing Entitlements," *Third Way*, February 2013. Also see Robin Harding, "Jobs Start to Go as U.S. Sequestration Cuts In," *Financial Times*, March 6, 2013.

21. Alan Blinder, "The Debt Ceiling Is Scarier Than the Fiscal Cliff," *Wall Street Journal*, January 14, 2013.

22. NFIB press release, February 12, 2013. Also see Catherine Rampell, "Small Businesses Still Struggle, and That's Impeding the Recovery," *New York Times*, February 13, 2013.

23. Scott R. Baker, Nicholas Bloom, and Steven J. Davis, "Measuring Economic Policy Uncertainty," June 4, 2012.

24. David Wessel, "Trying to Calculate the Cost of Uncertainty," *Wall Street Journal*, December 5, 2012.

25. See Scott R. Baker, Nicholas Bloom, and Steven J. Davis, "Policy Uncertainty Is Choking Recovery," *Bloomberg*, October 5, 2011. Also see "Measuring Economic Policy Uncertainty," October 10, 2011.

26. Bill McNabb, "Uncertainty Is the Enemy of Recovery," *Wall Street Journal*, April 28, 2013.

27. David Wessel, "CEOs Call for Deficit Action," *Wall Street Journal*, October 25, 2012.

28. Allan Murray, "CEOs to Washington: Strike a Deal—and Do It Now," *Wall Street Journal*, November 19, 2012."

29. Kim Dixon, "CEOs Step Up Push for Compromise of Fiscal Cliff," *Reuters*, December 11, 2012.

30. Scott Malone, "CEO Confidence Drops to Three-Year Low: Roundtable," *Reuters*, September 26, 2012.

31. James Politi and Ed Crooks, "Fiscal Cliff Dims Business Mood," *Financial Times*, September 26, 2012.

32. Michael J. De La Merced, "Einhorn Sues Apple Over Plan to Discard Preferred Stock," *New York Times*, February 7, 2013.

33. Bruce Bartlett, "The Growing Corporate Cash Hoard," *New York Times*, February 12, 2013; and "Corporations Sitting On Piles Of Cash? Not Really," *USA Today*, November 26, 2011.

34. Robert Pollin, James Heintz, Heidi Garrett-Peltier, and Jeannette Wicks-Lim, "19 Million Jobs for U.S. Workers: The Impact of Channeling $1.4 Trillion in Excess Liquid Asset Holdings Into Productive Investments," Political Economy Research Institute, University of Massachusetts, December 2011.

35. *The Budget and Economic Outlook: Fiscal Years 2013 to 2023, Alternative Fiscal Scenario* (Washington, DC: Congressional Budget Office, February 5, 2013).

36. See Carmen M. Reinhart and Kenneth S. Rogoff, "Growth in a Time of Debt," NBER Working Paper No. 15639, January 2010; and Carmen M. Reinhart and Kenneth S. Rogoff, "A Decade of Debt," NBER Working Paper No. 16827, February 2011.

37. Carmen M. Reinhart and Kenneth S. Rogoff, "Too Much Debt Means the Economy Can't Grow," *Bloomberg*, July 14, 2011.

38. See Stephen G. Cecchetti, M.S. Mohantly, and Fabrizio Zampolli, "The Real Effects of Debt," The Bank for International Settlements, September 2011; and Manmohan S. Kumar and Jaejoon Woo, "Public Debt and Growth," Working Paper No. 10/174, International Monetary Fund, July 1, 2010.

39. Thomas Herndon, Michael Ash, Robert Pollin, "Does High Public Debt Consistently Stifle Economic Growth? A Critique of Reinhart and Rogoff," Political Economy Research Institute, University of Massachusetts—Amherst, April 15, 2013.

40. Carmen M. Reinhart and Kenneth S. Rogoff, "Debt, Growth, and the Austerity Debate," *New York Times*, April 25, 2013.

41. Office of Management and Budget, Historical Tables, Table 1.1

42. Alison Acosta Fraser, "Federal Spending by the Numbers 2012," The Heritage Foundation, October 16, 2012.

43. Data in this paragraph from "Budget of the U.S. Government: FY 2013," Office of Management and Budget, February 2012, Historical Tables, Table 8.7.

44. Mort Zuckerman, "Brace for an Avalanche of Unfunded Debt," *US News & World Report*, December 28, 2012.

45. Chris Cox and Bill Archer, "Why $16 Trillion Only Hints at the True U.S. Debt," *Wall Street Journal*, November 26, 2012.

46. "Mullin: Debt Is Top National Security Threat," *CNN*, August 27, 2010.

47. Kate Brannen, "Mike Mullin Focuses on Debt as Security Threat," *Politico*, December 6, 2012.

48. John F. Cogan, John B. Taylor, Volker Wieland, and Maik Wolters, "Fiscal Consolidation Strategy," abstract, June 14, 2012. Also see Michael J. Boskin, "Larger Spending Cuts Would Help the Economy," *Wall Street Journal*, March 4, 2013.

49. Floyd Norris, "Tax Reform Might Start with a Look Back to '86," *New York Times*, November 22, 2012. Also see Elaine Kamarck and James P. Pinkerton, "Tax Reform Lessons From 1986," *The Hill*, August 27, 2012.

50. See "Background Information on Expenditure Analysis and Historical Survey of Tax Expenditure Estimates," Joint Committee on Taxation, February 28, 2011.

51. "Estimates of Federal Tax Expenditures for Fiscal Years 2010–2014," Joint Committee on Taxation, Table 1, December 21, 2010.

52. See testimony of Robert A. McDonald, chairman, Fiscal Policy Initiative, Business Roundtable, before the House Committee on Ways and Means, Hearing on Tax Reform, January 20, 2011.

53. Katarzyna Bilicka, Machael Devereux, and Clemens Fuest, G-20 Corporate Tax Ranking 2011 (Oxford, UK: Oxford University Center for Business Taxation, 2011).

54. "Global Effective Tax Rates," PriceWaterhouseCoopers, April 14, 2011.

55. McDonald testimony, January 20, 2011.

56. William C. Randolph, "International Burdens of the Corporate Income Tax," Congressional Budget Office, Working Paper 2006-09, August 1, 2006.

57. See Rosanne Altshuler, Benjamin H. Harris, and Eric Toder, "Capital Income Taxation and Progressivity in a Global Economy," Urban Institute, November 30, 2011; Kevin Hassett and Apurna Mathur, "Taxes and Wages," AEI Working Paper, July 6, 2006; Apurna Mathur and Matthew Jensen, "Corporate Tax Burden on Labor: Theory and Evidence," AEI Tax Notes, June 6, 2011.

58. Simeon Djankov, Tim Ganser, Caralee McLiesh, Rita Ramalho, and Andrei Shleifer, "The Effect of Corporate Taxes on Investment and Entrepreneurship," *American Economic Journal: Macroeconomics* 2, no. 3 (July 2010): 31–64.

59. "Reform the Outdated Tax System to Enhance American Competitiveness," President's Council on Jobs and Competitiveness.

60. Kate Limbaugh, "Firms Keep Stockpiles of 'Foreign' Cash in U.S.," *Wall Street Journal*, January 22, 2013.

61. C. Fritz Foley, Jay Hartzell, Sheridan Titman, and Garry Twite, "Why Do Firms Hold So Much Cash? A Tax-Based Explanation," *Journal of Financial Economics* 86, no. 3 (December 2007): 579–607.

62. Zachary Tracer, "U.S. Technology Companies May Double Overseas Cash, Moody's Says," *Bloomberg*, June 27, 2011.

63. Limbaugh, "Firms Keep Stockpiles."

64. John R. Graham, Michelle Hanlon, and Terry Shevlin, "Barriers to Mobility: The Lock-Out Effect of U.S. Taxation of Worldwide Corporate Profits," *National Tax Journal* 63, no. 4, part 2 (December 2010): 1111–1144. Also see Kate Limbaugh, "Top U.S. Firms Are Cash-Rich Abroad, Cash-Poor at Home," *Wall Street Journal*, December 4, 2012.

65. David Reilly, "Foreign Profits Can Create Earnings Illusion," *Wall Street Journal*, October 7, 2012.

66. "The Need for Pro-Growth Corporate Tax Reform: Repatriation and Other Steps to Enhance Short- and Long-Term Economic Growth," Douglas Holtz-Eakin, prepared for the U.S. Chamber of Commerce, August 2011.

67. Lauren French, "1986 Redux on Tax Reform? Maybe," *Politico*, October 15, 2012.

68. Joseph Schumpeter, *Business Cycles: A Theoretical, Historical and Statistical Analysis of the Capitalist Process* (New York: McGraw-Hill, 1939).

69. Joseph Schumpeter, *Capitalism, Socialism, and Democracy* (New York: McGraw-Hill, 1942).

70. Robert M. Solow, "Technical Change and the Aggregate Production Function," *Review of Economics and Statistics* (The MIT Press) 39, no. 3 (1957): 312–320.

71. Michael Greenstone and Adam Looney, *A Dozen Economic Facts About Innovation* (Washington, DC: The Hamilton Project, Brookings Institution, August 2011).

72. Paul Krugman, *The Age of Diminished Expectations* (Washington, DC: The Washington Post Company, 1990), 9–13.

73. Bronwyn Hall, "The Private and Social Returns to Research and Development," in *Technology, R&D, and the Economy*, eds. Bruce L.R. Smith and Claude E. Barfield (Washington, DC: The Brookings Institution and the American Enterprise Institute, 1996), 146–148, 159.

74. Bronwyn H. Hall, Jacques Mairesse, and Pierre Mohhnen, "Measuring the Returns to R&D," NBER Working Paper 15622, December, 2009. For an excellent review of the research into the effectiveness of the R&D credit, see Laura Tyson and Greg Linden, "The Corporate R&D Tax Credit and U.S. Innovation and Competitiveness: Gauging the Economic and Fiscal Effectiveness of the Credit," Center for American Progress, January 2012.

75. Nicholas Bloom, Mark Schankerman, and John Van Reenen, "Identifying Technology Spillovers and Product Market Rivalry," NBER Working Paper No. 13060, April 17, 2012.

76. Dominique Guellec and Bruno van Pottelsberghe De La Potterie, "R&D and Productivity Growth: Panel Data Analysis of 16 OECD Countries," *OECD Economic Studies* 33 (2001): 103–126.

77. "R&D and Productivity Growth," Background Paper, Congressional Budget Office, June 2005.

78. "The International Experience with R&D Tax Incentives," testimony by the OECD before the Senate Finance Committee, September 20, 2011.

79. Luke A. Stewart, Jacek Warda, and Robert D. Atkinson, "We're #27!: The United States Lags Far Behind in R&D Tax Incentive Generosity," The Information Technology & Innovation Foundation, July 2012.

80. Tyson and Linden, "The Corporate R&D Tax Credit."

81. Steven J. Markovich, "Promoting Innovation Through R&D," Council on Foreign Relations, November 5, 2012.

82. Tyson and Linden, "The Corporate R&D Tax Credit," 16–18.

83. Testimony of Kevin Hassett, American Enterprise Institute, before the House Science Committee's Subcommittee on Technology, July 1, 1999.

84. The alternative simplified credit is currently set at 14 percent of R&D expenses in excess of 50 percent of a firm's average R&D expenditures over the preceding three tax years.

85. Robert D. Atkinson, "Create Jobs by Expanding the R&D Tax Credit," The Information Technology & Innovation Foundation, January 26, 2010.

86. Julie Pace, "Obama to Push for Research and Development Tax Credits," *Associated Press*, September 5, 2010.

87. Atkinson, "Create Jobs by Expanding the R&D Tax Credit."

88. *Science and Engineering Indicators 2012*, National Science Foundation, Chapter 4, Research and Development: National Trends and International Comparisons, Table 4-3.

89. Ibid.

90. OECD data.

91. Patrick J. Clemins, "Historical Trends in Federal R&D," Chapter 2 in *Research and Development FY 2012*, American Association for the Advancement of Science, 2011.

92. "2013 Global R&D Funding Forecast," *Battelle and R&D Magazine*, December 2012, 29. Also see Patrick Thibodeau, "China Set to Surpass U.S. in R&D Spending in 10 Years," *ComputerWorld*, December 24, 2012.

93. *Science and Engineering Indicators 2012*, National Science Foundation. Chapter 4, "Research and Development: National Trends and International Comparisons," Table 4-19.

94. Justin Hicks and Robert D. Atkinson, "Eroding Our Foundation: Sequestration, R&D, Innovation and U.S. Economic Growth," The Information Technology & Innovation Foundation, September 2012. Also see Rafael Reif and Craig Barrett, "Science Must Be Spared Washington's Axe," *Financial Times*, February 25, 2013.

95. Chris Buckley, "China Confirms $1.7 Trillion Spending Plan," *Reuters*, November 21, 2011.

96. C. Fred Bergsten, "An Overlooked Way to Create Jobs," *New York Times*, September 28, 2011.

97. The U.S. has active free-trade agreements with Australia, Bahrain, Canada, Chile, Colombia, Costa Rica, the Dominican Republic, El Salvador, Guatemala, Honduras, Israel, Jordan, South Korea, Mexico, Morocco, Nicaragua, Oman, Panama, Peru, and Singapore.

98. Binyamin Appelbaum and Jennifer Steinhauer, "Congress Ends Five-Year Stand-Off on Trade Deals in Rare Accord," *New York Times*, October 12, 2011.

99. "The Future of U.S. Trade Negotiations," prepared Statement of Intel Corporation for the House Ways and Means Committee, February 29, 2012.

100. Chris Buckley and Terril Yue Jones, "East Asian Powers Set to Push Trade Pact Talks," *Reuters*, May 12, 2012.

101. Andrew H. Card, Thomas A. Daschle, Edward Allen, and Matthew J. Slaughter, "U.S. Trade and Investment Policy," Council on Foreign Relations, Independent Task Force Report No. 67, September 19, 2011.

102. World Trade Organization.

103. David Dollar and Aart Kraay, "Trade, Growth, and Poverty," Development Research Group, World Bank, June 2001; Jeffery Frankel and David Romer, "Does Trade Cause Growth?," World Bank, 1999; and Francisco Alcala and Antonio Ciccone, "Trade and Productivity," World Bank, October 2001.

104. *World Development Report* (Washington, DC: World Bank, 1995), 55.

105. Martin Neil Baily and Robert M. Solow, "International Productivity Comparisons Built from the Firm Level," *Journal of Economic Perspectives* 15, no. 3 (Summer, 2001): 151–172. Also see Robert Z. Lawrence, "Does a Kick in the Pants Get You Going or Does It Just Hurt? The Impact of International Competition on Technological Change in U.S. Manufacturing," in *The Impact of International Trade on Wages*, ed. Robert C. Feenstra (Chicago: University of Chicago Press, 2000), 197–224.

106. The WTO was established in 1994 during the Uruguay round of trade negotiations—the eighth round of multinational negotiations held under the General Agreement on Tariffs and Trade (GATT). The purpose of the WTO is to administer GATT agreements and to settle disputes among WTO members. WTO membership now includes 159 nations.

107. Data in this paragraph from the Commerce Department.

108. U.S. Commerce Department, Bureau of Economic Analysis.

109. See C. Fred Bergsten, "The United States in the World Economy," Peterson Institute for International Economics, Chautauqua Lecture Series, August 12, 2011.

110. Scott C. Bradford, Paul L.E. Grieco, and Gary Clyde Hufbauer, "The Pay-Off to America from Global Integration," in *The United States and the World Economy: Foreign Economic Policy for the Next Decade*, ed. C. Fred Bergsten (Washington, DC: Institute for International Economics, 2005).

111. Martin Johnson and Chris Rasmussen, "Jobs Supported by Exports 2012: An Update," Office of Competition and Economic Analysis, Department of Commerce, February 26, 2013. Salary data from the Office of the United States Trade Representative.

112. James K. Jackson, "Outsourcing and Insourcing Jobs in the U.S. Economy: Evidence Based on Foreign Investment Data," Congressional Research Service, May 10, 2012.

113. Lori G. Kletzer, "Imports, Exports, and Jobs: What Does Trade Mean for Employment and Job Loss?" W.E. Upjohn Institute for Employment Research, 2002.

114. Matthew J. Slaughter, "Exports Sagging? Try Some Free Trade," *Wall Street Journal*, January 22, 2013.

115. Helene Cooper, "Obama Sets Ambitious Export Goal," *New York Times*, January 29, 2010.

116. Comments at Asia-Pacific Economic Cooperation Summit, Honolulu, Hawaii, November 12, 2011.

117. Binyamin Appelbaum, "The Quiet Driver of Economic Growth: Exports," *New York Times*, January 27, 2012.

118. Philip Blenkinsop and Ethan Bilby, "EU, US to Start Free Trade Talks," *Reuters*, February 13, 2013.

119. Jack Ewing, "Trade Deal Between U.S. and Europe May Come to the Forefront," *New York Times*, November 25, 2012.

120. U.S. Chamber of Commerce estimate.

121. Stormy-Annika Mildner and Claudia Schmucker, "A Trade Deal Worth Making," *Wall Street Journal*, February 13, 2013. Also see David Cameron, "A British-American Tax and Trade Agenda," *Wall Street Journal*, May 12, 2013.

122. Martin Wolf, "In the Grip of a Great Convergence," *Financial Times*, January 4, 2011.

123. Andrew H. Card, Thomas A. Daschle, Edward Allen, and Matthew J. Slaughter, "A Pro-Trade Agenda for U.S. Jobs," *Wall Street Journal*, September 17, 2011.

124. U.S. Department of Commerce data.

125. U.S.-China Business Council.

126. For information on exports to China from all 50 states and all 435 Congressional districts, including links to local news stories on U.S. companies doing business with China, see https://www.uschina.org/public/exports/2000_2011/state-alphabetical-list.html. Also see Keith B. Richburg, "U.S. Exports to China Boom, Despite Trade Tensions," *Washington Post*, March 11, 2012.

127. David E. Sanger, "In Cyberspace, New Cold War," *New York Times*, February 24, 2013.

128. See "WTO Successfully Concludes Negotiations on China's Entry," press release, WTO, September 17, 2001.

129. See Nicholas R. Lardy, "Issues in China's WTO Accession," testimony before the U.S.-China Security Review Commission, May 9, 2001.

130. Originally called the U.S-China Strategic Economic Dialogue (SED), and led initially by Treasury Secretary Henry M. "Hank" Paulson and Chinese Vice Premier Wang Qishan. A central focus of the SED was accelerating financial reform in China. Upon taking office, the Obama Administration renamed the Dialogue as the "Strategic and Economic Dialogue," broadening the talks to include other issues such as human rights, environmental issues, security issues, and diplomatic cooperation.

131. Our work and background with regard to China stems from our participation in Engage China, a coalition that the Financial Services Forum has chaired since 2006. Engage China is a coalition of 12 financial services trade associations united in support of high-level engagement between the United States and China, with a particular emphasis on accelerated financial reform and modernization in China.

132. Simon Rabinovitch, "China Forecast to Overtake US by 2016," *Financial Times*, March 22, 2013.

133. Statement of Henry M. Paulson, Secretary of the Treasury, press briefing following the announcement of the U.S.–China Strategic Economic Dialogue, Beijing, China, September 21, 2006.

134. See John R. Dearie, "China's Financial Conditions and Their Impact on U.S. Interests," testimony before the U.S.–China Economic and Security Review Commission, March 7, 2013.

135. "China 2030: Building a Modern, Harmonious, and Creative High-Income Society," World Bank, February 27, 2012. Also see Bob Davis, "New Push for Reform in China," *Wall Street Journal*, February 23, 2012.

136. For an insightful analysis of the reasons for declining public support for freer trade policies, see Andrew H. Card, Thomas A. Daschle, Edward Allen, and

Matthew J. Slaughter, "U.S. Trade and Investment Policy," Council on Foreign Relations, Independent Task Force Report No. 67, September 19, 2011, 22–29.

137. Ronald G. Shafer, the *Wall Street Journal/NBC News* Poll: A Special Weekly Report from the *Wall Street Journal's* Capital Bureau, *Wall Street Journal*, December 17, 1999; and Janet Hook, "Senate Outsourcing Bill Stalls," *Wall Street Journal*, September 29, 2010.

138. Robert E. Baldwin, John H. Mutti, and J. David Richardson, "Welfare Effects on the United States of a Significant Multilateral Tariff Reduction," *Journal of International Economics* 10, no. 3 (1980): 405–423; and Stephen P. Magee, "The Welfare Effects of Restrictions on U.S. Trade," *Brookings Papers on Economic Activity* 3 (1971): 645–701.

139. See Kenneth F. Scheve and Matthew J. Slaughter, "A New Deal for Globalization," *Foreign Affairs*, July/August 2007, 34–47.

140. Grant D. Aldonis, Robert Z. Lawrence, and Matthew J. Slaughter, "Succeeding in the Global Economy: A New Policy Agenda for the American Worker," Policy Research Paper, The Financial Services Forum, June 26, 2007. Also see Matthew J. Slaughter and Robert Z. Lawrence, "More Trade More Aid," *New York Times*, June 8, 2011.

141. "Extended Mass Lay-Offs," Tables 2 and 10, Bureau of Labor Statistics. Also see "Few Mass Lay-Offs Are Due to Overseas Competition," The Heritage Foundation, February 4, 2011.

142. "Trade Adjustment Assistance: Changes to the Workers Program Benefited Participants, but Little Is Known about Outcomes," Government Accountability Office, September 2012.

143. "Trade Adjustment Assistance for Workers," Fiscal Year 2011 Report to the Senate Finance Committee and House Ways and Means Committee.

Conclusion

1. See The Hamilton Project, "Closing the Jobs Gap," The Brookings Institution.

2. Derek Thompson, "The Big Comeback: Is New Orleans America's Next Great Innovation Hub?" *The Atlantic*, April 8, 2013.

3. See http://ideavillage.org.

Acknowledgments

This project began as a very simple if admittedly ambitious idea: contribute something new and significant to the increasingly urgent effort to put tens of millions of Americans left unemployed by the Great Recession back to work. Between original conception of the project and the completion of this book, we relied on the interest, guidance, and contributions of literally hundreds of people.

For their intellectual assistance and generosity, critical guidance, and hospitality we are enormously grateful to Carl Schramm, former President and CEO of the Ewing Marion Kauffman Foundation, now a professor at Syracuse University and the Carlyse Ciocca Professor of Innovation and Entrepreneurship at the University of California at Davis; Bob Litan, previously Vice President for Research and Policy at Kauffman and now Director of Research at Bloomberg Government; and Cameron Cushman, who remains at the Kauffman Foundation as Senior Advisor. We are also grateful to Bob for his contribution to our poll of more than 800 entrepreneurs, as well as his review of Chapter 2 of this book.

From our first conversations about our hope to develop new policy alternatives to accelerate job creation, Rob Nichols, President and CEO of the Financial Services Forum, understood the importance of what we had proposed. He was enthusiastic and generous in his encouragement throughout our summer project, and enormously accommodating of our ambition to write a book about what we had heard and learned from the nation's entrepreneurs.

Special thanks to John F.W. Rogers for his vision and trust as we pursued this project.

Our deepest debt, of course, is to the more than 200 entrepreneurs who participated in our 12 roundtables. We thank them all for responding to our invitation to participate, for their time, their observations and insights, their candor and generosity, and, most especially, for what they do every day—taking the risks, both economic and personal, necessary to launch new businesses, expand those businesses, and create jobs, careers, and wealth for thousands of their fellow Americans. They, and millions of other entrepreneurs across the nation, are the true heroes of this book. Without them, there would be no net new job creation in the United States. This is their story, as told by them. We were privileged to meet them, to learn about their businesses, and to hear their observations and insights regarding the many challenges they confront on a daily basis. Most of all, we are honored to have the opportunity to bring their stories to the nation by way of our book. We are particularly grateful to those who have allowed us to use their comments and observations with attribution. Their remarkable and vividly personal expression of their ambitions, hopes, frustrations, and challenges not only adds remarkable clarity and credibility to the issues considered, but reminds us that business formation and job creation are about people and families, not just economic trends and statistics.

A number of people played a critical role in helping us identify and make contact with the entrepreneurs we invited to our roundtables, including Maria Gotch, President and CEO of the New York City Investment Fund; Tom Moebus and Helene Rude of the Levin Institute at the State University of New York; Kim Scheeler, President and CEO of the Greater Richmond Chamber of Commerce; Michael

Rollins, President of the Greater Austin Chamber of Commerce; the Washington, DC, and Columbus, Ohio, offices of Congressman Pat Tiberi; Jerry Ross, Executive Director of the National Entrepreneur Center in Orlando, Florida; Bobbie Kilberg, President and CEO of the Northern Virginia Technology Council; Tim Rowe, founder and CEO of the Cambridge Innovation Center; Nancy Saucier, Director of New Venture Development at the University of Massachusetts, Lowell; David Verrill, Executive Director of the Center for Digital Business at MIT's Sloan School of Management; Ted Ford, President and CEO of TechColumbus; Beth Flanagan, Director of the Memphis Medical Center; Kevin Roper of the University of Memphis; Nick Kistenmacher in the office of Senator Bob Corker; Jeff Marcell, President and CEO of enterpriseSeattle; Margo Shiroyama, Executive Director of Northwest Energy Angels; Sue Hesse, founder and CEO of Hesse Partners; and Alana Muller, President of Kauffman FastTrac.

Greg Hitt, Senior Vice President at Hill+Knowlton Strategies in Washington, DC, served as the moderator of our 12 roundtables, traveling with us across the country (including sitting in 100-degree heat on the tarmac in Kansas City, Missouri, for more than an hour in a plane with no air-conditioning) and presiding over our discussions with professionalism, consistency, patience, and humor. Along the way, he helped us focus our inquiry, process what we were hearing from our participating entrepreneurs, and formulate a number of our policy recommendations.

Very special thanks to John Duncan, our friend and mentor, who contributed in innumerable ways to the formulation, structure, and focus of our project, and also helped us formulate a number of our policy recommendations. John's vast political and policy expertise, together with his sophisticated analysis of the profound technology-driven changes impacting American society and the U.S. economy, made him an invaluable discussion partner and sounding board throughout the project.

On July 20, 2011, we convened a discussion of noted economists at the Kauffman Foundation in Kansas City, Missouri, to discuss the state of U.S. labor markets following the Great Recession, as well as challenges to recovery. We appreciate the participation of Bob Litan and Tim Kane of Kauffman; Matthew Slaughter of the Tuck School of Business at Dartmouth College; Robert Lawrence of Harvard University's John F. Kennedy School of Government; Garett Jones of George Mason University; Ike Brannon of the George W. Bush Institute; and Diana Furchtgott-Roth of the Manhattan Institute. Their insights helped provide the broader economic context within which we were able to consider and make sense of what we heard at our other roundtables.

We also very much appreciate the work of Adam Geller, founder (he's an entrepreneur!) and CEO of polling firm National Research, Inc. Adam helped us conduct a first-of-its-kind nationwide poll of more than 800 entrepreneurs, which generated results that confirmed and added additional texture to what we learned at our in-person roundtables.

Dozens of others contributed hours and even days of their time to helping us think about, devise, and structure our project, including: Mitch Jacobs, founder of On Deck Capital; Jeremy Smith and Mark Murphy at SecondMarket; David Owens, Professor for the Practice of Management and Innovation at Vanderbilt University; Jeff Cornwall, Director of the Center for Entrepreneurship at Belmont University; Robert Templin, President of Northern Virginia Community College; Jonathan Rowe, Director of the Entrepreneurship Center, University of North Carolina, Wilmington; Sid Chambless, Managing Partner and Executive Director at Nashville Capital Network; Marianne Hudson, Executive Director of the Angel Capital Association; Mark Heesen, President of the National Venture Capital Association; Gary Shapiro, President and CEO of the Consumer Electronics Association; Paul Sass, Deputy Staff Director at the House Small Business Committee; and Doug and Denise Clelan.

Special thanks to Ray Beeman, who provided expert guidance regarding the intricacies of tax reform, and to John Backus of New Atlantic Ventures for his insights regarding the venture capital industry.

Jen Scungio presided over the demanding logistical aspects of our project and was indispensible to the successful organization of round-tables in a dozen cities across the country. She also assisted with research, proofing of chapters, and the finalization of the book's charts. Emily Dagher, Charlotte Schockaert, Cameron Friday, and Kevin Love also provided critical assistance with research, data verification, chart work, and proofreading.

Our magnificent agent, the splendidly knowledgeable and ever-enthusiastic Alice Martell, grasped the importance of our project and its findings from the moment we shared them, and worked tirelessly with us for months to transform our summer road experience into a coherent and viable narrative. We are forever grateful for her vision, advocacy, and friendship. Sincere thanks also go to the wonderful Stephanie Finman.

Our editor at John Wiley & Sons, Kevin Commins, not only provided an opportunity to tell our story, but gave us enormous and much appreciated creative discretion in how to tell it. His colleague, Meg Freeborn, provided insightful and judicious editorial suggestions that improved aspects of the manuscript significantly. Melissa Lopez, Senior Production Editor, with her patience and persistence, made the exacting and potentially painful task of final editing a pleasure.

Finally, profound thanks to our families for their loving forbearance and patience over the course of this project.

About the Authors

John Dearie is Executive Vice President for Policy at the Financial Services Forum. Prior to joining the Forum in 2001, he spent nine years at the Federal Reserve Bank of New York, where he held positions in the Banking Studies, Foreign Exchange, and Policy and Analysis areas. His writing has appeared in the *The Wall Street Journal, The Financial Times, Politico, American Banker,* and China's *Caijing* Magazine. He lives with his wife and two children in Great Falls, Virginia.

Courtney Geduldig is Vice President of Global Regulatory Affairs at Standard & Poor's. Prior to joining S&P, she was Managing Director and Head of Federal Government Relations at the Financial Services Forum. From March of 2008 to November of 2011, Courtney served as Chief Financial Counsel to Senator Bob Corker (R-TN), handling a wide range of issues including financial markets, housing, banking, taxes, manufacturing, international trade finance, and playing a key role in drafting and advising Senator Corker on the "Dodd–Frank Wall Street Reform and Consumer Protection Act." She also spent two years as the Deputy Assistant Secretary for Banking and Finance at the U.S. Treasury Department. She is a member of the Maryland State Bar and lives with her husband, son, and daughter in McLean, Virginia.

Index